Sanskrit Glossary
of Yogic Terms

With kind regards, ॐ and prem

Swami Niranjan

Sanskrit Glossary of Yogic Terms

Compiled by

Swami Yogakanti

Yoga Publications Trust, Munger, Bihar, India

Published by Yoga Publications Trust
  First edition 2007
  Reprinted 2009

ISBN: 978-81-86336-31-1

Publisher and distributor: Yoga Publications Trust, Ganga Darshan, Munger, Bihar, India.

Website: www.biharyoga.net
  www.rikhiapeeth.net

Printed at Thomson Press (India) Limited, New Delhi, 110001

Dedication

In humility we offer this dedication to
Swami Sivananda Saraswati, who initiated
Swami Satyananda Saraswati into the secrets of yoga.

Contents

Phonetic Pronunciation Guide

अ	a	*as in* cup	ट्	t	ton
आ ा	aa	far	ठ्	th	anthill
इ ि	i	hill	ड्	d	dunk
इ ी	ee	fleet	ढ्	dh	redhead
उ ु	u	pull	ण्	n	gone
ऊ ू	oo	fool	त्	t	water (*dental*)
ऋ ृ	ri	clarity	थ्	th	thumb
ॠ ृ	ree	marine	द्	d	the
ऌ	lri	rivalry	ध्	dh	adhere (*more*
ॡ	lree	rivalry			*dental*)
		(*prolonged*)	न्	n	not
ए ॆ	e	grey	प्	p	pink
ऐ ै	ai	aisle	फ्	ph	photo
ओ ो	o	omnipresent	ब्	b	rub
औ ौ	au	cow	भ्	bh	abhor
ं	m/n	map/nap	म्	m	map
:	h	ah	य्	y	yoga
क्	k	king	र्	r	red
ख्	kh	inkhorn	ल्	l	love
ग्	g	go	व्	v	svelte
घ्	gh	yoghurt	श्	sh	shun
ङ्	n	sing	ष्	sh	assure
च्	ch	check	स्	s	sun
छ्	chh	churchhill	ह्	h	hut
ज्	j	joy	क्ष्	ksh	rickshaw
झ्	jh	hedgehog	त्र्	tr	track (*dental*)
ञ्	n	canyon	ज्ञ्	jn	gnu

Introduction

This Sanskrit glossary of yogic terms is designed to help yoga practitioners and students who are studying yoga, along with its allied philosophies and texts, without formal knowledge of Sanskrit. Such students may slowly acquire a functional vocabulary, but this needs to be continually expanding, not only in the number of words known, but in appreciation of the subtle ranges of meaning and interconnectedness between the words. This glossary is intended to help achieve this understanding.

How to find a word

In this edition, therefore, the alphabetical order is the one used in English (Roman script) rather than that of Sanskrit (Devanagri script), so it is easier for English speakers to find a word. However, to show connections between words, they are arranged in family groups. A parent word may have several derivatives indented (alphabetically) underneath it before the major alphabetical listing resumes. This grouping is followed except where the families are too big (the 'Pra' family, for example) or the relationship ambivalent or ambiguous; in such cases the family grouping has been dropped.

How to read the entries

The Sanskrit words, spelled as they are found in standard English books, are listed alphabetically in bold print. Where necessary, this is followed by a partial transliteration /in oblique strokes/ which distinguishes long from short vowels:

Dhyana /Dhyaana/.

If it is a complex word made by simply attaching two or more short words together, the conjunction point (*sandhi*) is shown by a hyphen:

Devanagri /Deva-naagaree/.

This clarifies the constituent parts. If the conjunctions are complex, they are deciphered (in brackets) according to the grammatical rules of conjunction:

Jyotirdhyana /Jyotirdhyaana/ (Jyotih-dhyaana).

The meaning of the word and, sometimes, its mythological, historical or philosophical context follows:

Jyotirdhyana /Jyotirdhyaana/ (Jyotih-dhyaana); meditation on light.

To enlarge the understanding of a word, references to other words contained in this glossary sometimes follow the main entry.

Jyotirdhyana /Jyotirdhyaana/ (Jyotih-dhyaana); meditation on light; see Dhyana.

Pictures have been used to illustrate the concepts.

How Devanagri is integrated

Although familiarity with the Devanagri script is not essential to use this glossary successfully, each entry ends with the word in Devanagri.

Jyotirdhyana /Jyotirdhyaana/ (Jyotih-dhyaana); meditation on light; see Dhyana. ज्योतिर्ध्यान

Also, before the listing of each English letter begins, the corresponding Devanagri letters that will start the Sanskrit words included within that section are presented, along with a guide on how to pronounce them. For example:

Pronunciation
ब् b – as in rub
भ् bh – as in abhor

How to use this glossary

In order to use this glossary effectively, please note the following points about its construction:

- The Phonetic Pronunciation Guide on page *viii* explains how the transition from Devanagri to Roman script has been managed. Distinction has been made between long and short vowels. Diacritic marks have not been used in this edition, so it is not possible to distinguish between the dental and palatal 'd/dh' or 't/th', the different types of 'n', etc. This makes things simpler for beginners and such distinctions have been ignored in the alphabetical order of the listing also.
- The words in bold type are listed in English alphabetical order, not according to the Sanskrit 'alphabetical' order. Whether the original bold entry consists of one, two or more words, it is treated as a single whole unit as far as this alphabetical order is concerned.
- The bold entry gives the spelling of the word commonly used in English texts. The /oblique strokes/ contain a pronunciation guide for vowels and reveal simple conjunctions of words i.e. simple sandhi. The (brackets) decipher more complex sandhi conjunctions.
- Generally, words clearly related to a 'parent' word are indented under it in a family group, e.g. all the words belonging to 'Jyoti' are grouped together. Each family group is itself in English alphabetical order. After each family group, the alphabetical order of the main listing resumes.

How to spell Sanskrit words that are becoming English

For words that are becoming increasingly used in their original form in English texts, the commonly used spelling of the Sanskrit terms are most often employed both in the alphabetical listing and when the meanings of the words are being explained. The following points should also be noted:

- There are words for which two spellings in English are now common, e.g. mooladhara and muladhara. Both spellings will be found in the main listing. One will give the meaning of the word:

    Muladhara /Moola-aadhaara/ base position, root foundation. मूलाधार

    The other spelling will give the alternate's reference:

    Mooladhara see Muladhara. मूलाधार

- Dual and plural forms of Sanskrit words have usually been given by simply adding 's' as though they are English words, for example, guna becomes gunas. Otherwise, they are left in their basic form.

- The English language spelling conventions have usually been followed when making an adjective from a noun, e.g. from the noun yoga comes the adjective yogic, similarly tamas gives tamasic (not tamasika), veda gives vedic (not vaidika).

The kernel of the project was given by Sri Swami Satyananda and it has been nurtured by Swami Niranjanananda. Many people have worked together to assemble this glossary and we hope it is useful to many people.

Sanskrit Glossary
of Yogic Terms

A

Abha /Aabhaa/ splendour, beauty; appearance; shadow, reflection. आभा

Abhasa /Aabhaasa/ reflection; the shining forth; immanent aspect of the ultimate reality, Brahman; in Vedanta the manifest world is said to be merely an appearance or abhasa; a glimpse; phenomenon. आभास

Abhasam /Aabhaasam/ effect. आभासम्

Abhasavada /Aabhaasa-vaada/ the view that the universe consists of appearances which are nevertheless real in the sense that they are aspects of the ultimate reality. आभासवाद

Abhasita /Aabhaasita/ to shine, glitter; to become clear and evident. आभासित

Abhavarana /Aabhaa-aavarana/ screening the outshining Brahman, one of the two veiling powers of maya which is removed by direct knowledge (aparoksha jnana); see Avarana Shakti. आभावरण

Abhanga devotional song in the Marathi language. अभंग

Abhava /Abhaava/ not being, non-existence, negation, non-entity; absence, want; failure; annihilation, end, death, destruction; final beatitude in which one's self is meditated upon as zero or as bereft of every quality or limitation whatsoever. अभाव

Abhavamatra /Abhaava-maatra/ presently not available; a mere appearance of; scarcity. अभावमात्र

Abhavarupavritti /Abhaava-roopa-vritti/ the function of thinking of a non-existent thing. अभावरूपवृत्ति

Abhaya freedom from fear or danger; secure, safe. अभय

Abhayam absence or removal of fear; security; protection from fear or danger. अभयम्

Abhaya Mudra /Abhaya Mudraa/ gesture of fearlessness; see Mudra. अभय मुद्रा

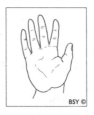

Abheda non-difference, non-distinction, undivided; identity, sameness, oneness; monism. अभेद

Abheda Ahamkara /Abheda Ahamkaara/ the pure ego that identifies itself with Brahman or the absolute. अभेद अहंकार

Abheda Bhakti highest devotion that culminates in the identity of the worshipper and the worshipped; devotion without the sense of duality. अभेद भक्ति

Abheda Bhava /Abheda Bhaava/ sense of non-separateness. अभेद भाव

Abheda Buddhi the buddhi that beholds unity. अभेद बुद्धि

Abheda Chaitanya constant thought of the identity of the inner self with Brahman; undivided consciousness. अभेद चैतन्य

Abheda Jnana /Abheda Jnaana/ knowledge of the identity of the individual (atman) with the absolute (Brahman). अभेद ज्ञान

Abhichara Mantra /Abhichaara Mantra/ formula for working out a charm; see Mantra. अभिचार मंत्र

Abhidhyanam /Abhidhyaanam/ meditation, profound thought. अभिध्यानम्

Abhijna efficient in understanding. अभिज्ञ

Abhijnanam /Abhijnaanam/ knowledge through perception. अभिज्ञानम्

Abhimana /Abhimaana/ egoism; identification with the body; conceit. अभिमान

Abhimani /Abhimaanee/ one who has egoistic feelings. अभिमानी

Abhimanyu son of Arjuna and Subhadra known for his undaunted courage and strength, husband of Uttara who gave birth to Parikshit, and the successor to the throne of Hastinapur; see Parikshit. अभिमन्यु

Abhinaya controlling, training, disciplining; expression through movement, e.g. dance. अभिनय

Abhinivesha fear of death; instinctive clinging to worldly life and bodily enjoyments and the fear that one might be cut off from them by death; indicates possessiveness and attachment to mundane things; a type of ignorance; one of the five kleshas described by Patanjali in the *Yoga Sutras*; see Klesha. अभिनिवेश

Abhisheka ceremonial bath; consecration; a most important part of diksha in Buddhist and tantric diksha. अभिषेक

Abhushana /Aabhooshana/ jewel, ornament; see Shodashopachara. आभूषण

Abhyantara /Aabhyaantara/ internal. आभ्यान्तर

Abhyasa /Abhyaasa/ constant and steady practice without any interruption; to remain established in the effort of sadhana. अभ्यास

Abhyasin /Abhyaasin/ practitioner; one who studies. अभ्यासिन्

Abuddhipurva /Abuddhi-poorva/ unintelligent, insentient. अबुद्धिपूर्व

Achala steady, immovable, fixed, permanent. अचल

Achamana /Aachamana/ water offered in worship for sipping for mental purification; see Shodashopachara. आचमन

Achara /Aachaara/ conduct; good behaviour; custom, an established rule of conduct, usual formality. आचार

Acharya /Aachaarya/ one knowing or teaching the acharas or rules; teacher, preceptor, spiritual guide. आचार्य

Acharya Upasanam /Aachaarya Upaasanam/ service to the

preceptor. आचार्य उपासनम्

Achetana unconscious. अचेतन

Achintita unexpected, sudden. अचिन्तित

Achintya incomprehensible, unthinkable. अचिन्त्य

Achintya Bhedabheda /Achintya Bheda-abheda/ one of six systems of Vedanta taught by Chaitanya Mahaprabhu; philosophy of inconceivable unity in diversity. अचिन्त्य भेदाभेद

Achintya Shakti inscrutable power. अचिन्त्य शक्ति

Achit inanimate matter; unconscious; in Sankhya philosophy it refers to the nature of prakriti, in Vedanta to universal matter. अचित्

Achit Shakti (of Brahman) tamas or great darkness; the root of matter. अचित् शक्ति

Achitta inconceivable, destitute of intellect. अचित्त

Achyuta not fallen, firm, fixed; not giving way; imperishable, permanent; name of Vishnu, the almighty being. अच्युत

Adarshana not seeing, non-vision; not being seen. अदर्शन

Adesha /Aadesha/ order, command, instruction; precept, rule; advice. आदेश

Adesha wrong place; bad country, improper place. अदेश

Adesha Kala /Adesha Kaala/ wrong place and time. अदेश काल

Adhara /Aadhaara/ basis, that which supports, foundation, substratum, receptacle; Brahman; the system composed of the five principles constituting the physical, vital, mental, intellectual and blissful sheaths (koshas); sphere of action; the 16 adharas of yoga referred to in *Yoga Chudamani Upanishad* which support the body. आधार

Adharadheyasambandha /Aadhaara-aadheya-sambandha/ relation of support and the thing supported; relation of location and the being located; relation of abode and abiding. आधाराधेयसम्बन्ध

Adhara Mudra /Aadhaara Mudraa/ perineal mudra (when the back is straight, it supports the body); see Mudra. आधार मुद्रा

Adhara lip; lower, inferior, mean, vile. अधर

Adharma disharmony; not fulfilling one's natural role in life; unrighteousness; wickedness, injustice, guilty or wicked deed, sin; all that is contrary to dharma and the law; demerit. अधर्म

Adharmika /Adhaarmika/ not fulfilling one's natural role in life; non-religious. अधार्मिक

Adharmikata /Adhaarmikataa/ unrighteousness. अधार्मिकता

Adhi /Aadhi/ disease of the mind, mental agony. आधि

Adhibhautika /Aadhibhautika/ suffering which proceeds from extrinsic causes such as other people, beasts, birds or inanimate objects; in Sankhya philosophy, one of the threefold causes of misery, viz. 1. adhyatmika, 2. adhibhautika, and 3. adhidaivika. आधिभौतिक

Adhibhautika Sharira /Aadhibhautika Shareera/ body composed of elements (bhutas). आधिभौतिक शरीर

Adhibhautika Tapa
Aadhibhautika Taapa/ pain caused by the bhutas, e.g. scorpion-sting, snake-bite etc.; extrinsic suffering caused by other beings. आधिभौतिक ताप

Adhibhuta /Adhi-bhoota/ the highest being; supreme existence (spirit) or its all-pervading influence; pertaining to the elements; in Sankhya the primordial form of matter (prakriti). अधिभूत

Adhibhuta Vidya /Aadhi-bhoota Vidyaa/ science of the physical or material world. आधिभूत विद्या

Adhidaiva ruler or governor of the subtle dimensions. अधिदैव

Adhidaivika Aadhidaivika/ pertaining to heaven or celestial beings; extrinsic sufferings due to supernatural causes; in Sankhya philosophy, one of the threefold causes of misery, viz. 1. adhyatmika, 2. adhibhautika, and 3. adhidaivika. आधिदैविक

Adhika surpassing, extraordinary, greater, better, higher, more. अधिक

Adhikarana ground, substratum; the seventh case in Sanskrit grammar (locative). अधिकरण

Adhikari /Adhikaaree/ eligible one, qualified person. अधिकारी

Adhikarika /Adhikaarika/ supreme, superior. अधिकारिक

Adhikarin /Adhikaarin/ possessed of authority, having power; qualified person. अधिकारिन्

Adhikari Vada /Adhikaaree Vaada/ doctrine upholding the necessity of prescribing a distinct course of discipline for each spiritual aspirant according to their capacity. अधिकारी वाद

Adhimatra /Adhimaatraa/ element, material world, matter. अधिमात्रा

Adhimatra Vairagya /Adhimaatraa Vairaagya/ degree of non-attachment (vairagya) when even worldly enjoyment becomes a source of pain. अधिमात्रा वैराग्य

Adhishthana /Adhishthaana/ background, support, basis, substratum, repository; underlying truth or essence (Brahman); site; authority, power of control. अधिष्ठान

Adhiyajna the supreme being; the effort one performs to realize the highest; pertaining to sacrifice (yajna). अधियज्ञ

Adhokshaja being who cannot be perceived by the outer senses; name of Bhagavan Narayana. अधोक्षज

Adhvara sacrifice, a religious ceremony. अध्वर

Adhvaryu priest who recites the *Yajurveda* in a sacrifice; any officiating priest. अध्वर्यु

Adhyaropa /Adhyaaropa/ illusory attribution, superimposition, false attribution, one thing mistaken for another, qualities of one thing transferred to another. अध्यारोप

Adhyaropa Apavada /Adhyaaropa Apavaada/ concept of superimposition and negation, used as a teaching method; see Arundhati Darshana Nyaya. अध्यारोप अपवाद

Adhyaropita /Adhyaaropita/ superimposed, fictitiously ascribed. अध्यारोपित

Adhyasa /Adhyaasa/ superimposition or reflection of the attributes

of one thing on another thing; false attribution; wrong supposition; misperception. अध्यास
Adhyasta the thing or quality superimposed; falsely cognized thing. अध्यस्त
   Adhyasta Astitva reflected existence, superimposed existence. अध्यस्त अस्तित्व
Adhyatma /Adhyaatma/ the principle of self, which makes one conscious of self apart from any definition or concept of self; belonging to oneself. अध्यात्म
Adhyatman /Adhyaatman/ supreme state of existence and consciousness; supreme spirit (manifested as the individual self) or the relation between the individual and the supreme state of existence and consciousness. अध्यात्मन्
Adhyatma Shastra /Adhyaatma Shaastra/ spiritual science; science that deals with one's identity. अध्यात्म शास्त्र
Adhyatma Vidya /Adhyaatma Vidyaa/ knowledge of the self; spiritual wisdom. अध्यात्म विद्या
Adhyatma Vit /Adhyaatma Vit/ knower of the inner self. अध्यात्म वित्
Adhyatmika /Aadhyaatmika/ pertaining to the atma (soul); relating to oneself or to the law of life; that which proceeds from intrinsic causes, such as disorders of the body and mind; in Sankhya philosophy, one of the three miseries caused by the avidya of the mind, viz. 1. adhyatmika, 2. adhibhautika, and 3. adhidaivika. आध्यात्मिक
Adhyatmika Tapa /Aadhyaatmika

Taapa/ pain caused by the mind. आध्यात्मिक ताप
Adhyatmika Vidya /Aadhyaatmika Vidyaa/ knowledge of the supreme spirit. आध्यात्मिक विद्या
Adhyavasaya /Adhyavasaaya/ perseverance, diligence; mental effort, apprehension. अध्यवसाय
Adhyayana study, especially of the Vedas; lesson or lecture; chapter or large division of a work. अध्ययन
Adi /Aadi/ beginning, commencement; first, primary; primitive; 'and so on' (of the same kind or nature etc). आदि
   Adibhuta /Aadi-bhoota/ the mahabhutas: earth, water, fire, air, space or ether; perishable objects; see Pancha Mahabhuta. आदिभूत
   Adideva /Aadi-deva/ first or supreme existence; God; Narayana or Vishnu; Shiva; the sun. आदिदेव
   Adiguru /Aadi-guru/ first guru. आदिगुरु
Adimulam /Aadi-moolam/ first foundation, primeval cause. आदिमूलम्
Adiparvam /Aadi-parvam/ name of the first book of the *Mahabharata*. आदिपर्वम्
Adishakti /Aadi-shakti/ the power of creation; that which appears to our senses; power of Maya, a name of the supreme goddess. आदिशक्ति
Adi Shankaracharya /Aadi Shankaraachaarya/ a celebrated teacher of Advaita Vedanta who wrote commentaries on the major Upanishads, the *Bhagavad Gita* and *Brahma Sutras*. The

7

founder of the Dashnami tradition of sannyasa, he established four mathas in the four quarters of India. Kanchi Matha, dedicated to Devi, and numerous smaller mathas claim him as founder. There is speculation that the Adi Shankaracharya may be a composite of two or more historical personages; see Advaita, see Shankaracharya; see Matha. आदि शंकराचार्य

Adishvara /Aadi-eeshvara/ the primeval lord, an epithet of Shiva. आदीश्वर

Aditattwa /Aadi-tattva/ moola prakriti, the first element (of matter); see Mula Prakriti. आदितत्त्व

Adivasi /Aadi-vaasee/ tribal people, original inhabitants. आदिवासी

Aditi boundlessness, immensity; mother of the gods known as Adityas; see Asura. अदिति

Aditya /Aaditya/ son of Aditi; a god; divinity; the sun as a deity; divine; a noun used for the 12 adityas, viz. Dhata, Aryama, Mitra, Varuna, Indra, Vivaswan, Tvashta, Vishnu, Anshu, Bhag, Pusha, Parjyanya. आदित्य

Adrishta unseen, invisible, unknown; that which is beyond the reach of observation or consciousness; not experienced; 'unreal' for our sense perception; the

unseen principle accepted in Nyaya Vaisheshika concerning the accumulation of unused energy of performed actions at the time of dissolution. अदृष्ट

Adrishtam the invisible one; destiny, fate, luck (good or bad). अदृष्टम्

Adrishya that which cannot be seen by the physical eye (Brahman); not seen, latent, imperceptible. अदृष्य

Advaita, Advaitam not divided into two parts, the feeling of non-duality; identity or non-difference; monistic vision of reality; non-dual experience; of one or uniform nature; that for which there is no other, especially referring to Brahman/atman; union with the universe or soul; union of soul and matter; union with the supreme existence or Brahman; see Vedanta. अद्वैत, अद्वैतम्

Advaita Avastharupa Advayam /Advaita Avasthaa-roopa Advayam/ non-duality, unity, identity; especially the identity of Brahman and the universe, or spirit and matter; the highest truth. अद्वैत अवस्थारूप अद्वयम्

Advaita Nishtha established in the state of non-duality. अद्वैत निष्ठ

Advaita Siddhi realization of the non-dual Brahman or oneness. अद्वैत सिद्धि

Advaita Vada /Advaita Vaada/ the theory that Brahman is the only existence; monism; Vedanta. अद्वैत वाद

Advaita Vedanta /Advaita Vedaanta/ non-dualistic philosophy of Adi Shankaracharya based on the experience of Brahman as the absolute reality, the union of Brahman and atma, (the universe and the soul) as expressed in the Upanishads and in the lives of saints and realized yogis; see Vedanta; see Vivarta; see Vivarta Srishti; see Gaudapada Karika. अद्वैत वेदान्त

Advayatva self-realization or non-duality (according to *Goraksha Samhita*, the aim of life). अद्वयत्व

Advitiya /Adviteeya/ one without a second, unique. अद्वितीय

    Advitiyata /Adviteeyataa/ state of being secondless. अद्वितीयता

Adwaita see Advaita. अद्वैत

Adyashakti /Aadyashakti/ primordial power; see Avyaktam; see Mula Prakriti. आद्यशक्ति

Agama /Aagama/ historical sacred literature, 'that which has come down' or literally 'to carry on' or 'to go forward'; the philosophy and scriptures of tantra where Lord Shiva teaches his consort Parvati; esoteric tradition of tantra suitable for the present age (Kali yuga); testimony or proof of an acceptable authority because the source of knowledge has been checked and found trustworthy; one of the three sources of right knowledge (pramana) enumerated by Patanjali in the description of the five modifications of mind (vrittis) in the *Yoga Sutras*; traditional doctrine or precept; secret writing or scripture. आगम

Agami Karma /Aagaamee Karma/ karma produced now to be fructified in the future; see Karma. आगामी कर्म

Agastya 'pitcher-born'; name of a celebrated rishi or sage; name of the star Canopus; see Tadaka. अगस्त्य

Agati stability. अगति

Aghamarshana vedic verses, the utterance of which while bathing purifies one; that which purifies. अघमर्षण

Aghora 'one for whom nothing is abominable'; one who is totally in tune with their nature, having mastered the elements; totally innocent. अघोर

Aghori /Aghoree/ an order of Shaiva ascetics. अघोरी

Agni fire; the god of fire; fire of the stomach, digestive faculty; metabolism; the third mahabhuta in Sankhya philosophy with the special property of form; see Pancha Mahabhuta; see Swaha. अग्नि

Agnihotra a small fire ritual, performed daily at dawn and dusk in which cow's milk is offered into the fire. अग्निहोत्र

Agni Mandala literally 'zone of fire', visualizing the entire body in the form of agni. अग्नि मण्डल

Agnimantha, Agnimathanam producing fire by friction. अग्निमन्थ, अग्निमथनम्

Agnisara Kriya /Agnisaara Kriyaa/ practice of emptying the lungs and pumping the stomach to strengthen the diaphragm and lower stomach region and awaken the digestive fire, also called vahnisara kriya. अग्निसार क्रिया

Agni Tattwa /Agni Tattva/ fire element, fire principle; see Pancha Mahabhuta. अग्नि तत्त्व

Agni Vidya /Agni Vidyaa/ process

of meditating on fire as symbolizing Brahman. अग्नि विद्या

Agochara unattainable, beyond the
range of sense organs. अगोचर

Agocharam beyond sensory perception; anything beyond the
cognizance of the senses; not being seen, observed or known;
Brahman. अगोचरम्

Agochari Mudra /Agocharee
Mudraa/ gazing at the tip of the
nose while holding the breath;
another name for nasikagra
drishti; see Mudra. अगोचरी मुद्रा

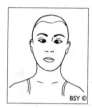

Agra tip. अग्र

Agrahya /Agraahya/ unfit to be
taken; that which cannot be
grasped (Brahman). अग्राह्य

Aguna without guna or quality; having no attribute or virtues. अगुण

Aham 'I' or ego; the personal pronoun. अहम्

Aham Brahmasmi /Aham
Brahma-asmi/ 'I am Brahman',
one of the four great vedic statements (maha vakya) used by a
meditator as an aid in reaching
the supreme state of existence.
Found in *Brihadaranyaka
Upanishad* of the *Yajurveda*, it is
also called anubhava vakya; see
Maha Vakya. अहं ब्रह्मास्मि

Aham Etat Na 'I am not this'. अहं
एतत् न

Aham Eva Sarva 'I alone am all'.
अहं एव सर्व

Ahamgraha Upasana
/Ahamgraha Upaasanaa/ kind of
meditation in vedantic worship
where one identifies oneself with
Brahman or the supreme being.
अहंग्रह उपासना

Aham Idam 'I am this'. अहं इदम्

Ahamkara /Ahamkaara/ 1. egoism or self-conceit; the self-arrogating principle 'I', 'I am-ness',
self-consciousness; 2. sattwic
ahamkara: egoism composed in
the sense of goodness and virtue; rajasic ahamkara: dynamic
egoism with passion and pride;
tamasic ahamkara: egoism as expressed in ignorance and inertia; 3. universal state of existence,
ceaselessly creating itself; universal 'I am' of which the individual
sense of 'I-ness' is a part or manifestation; 4. in Vedanta: the base
for maya's power of projection;
5. in Sankhya philosophy: the
third of the eight elements of
creation, i.e. the conception of
individuality; the principle responsible for the limitations, division and variety in the manifest world; 6. in yoga: the rajasic
state of consciousness limiting
awareness of existence. अहंकार

**Ahamkara Avachhinna
Chaitanya** /Ahamkaara
Avachchhinna Chaitanya/ intelligence associated with egoism;
the migrating soul, jivatma.
अहंकार अवच्छिन्न चैतन्य

Ahamkara Tyaga /Ahamkaara
Tyaaga/ renunciation of egoism. अहंकार त्याग

Aham Karta /Aham Kartaa/ 'I am
the doer'. अहं कर्ता

Ahamkriya /Aham-kriyaa/ selfishness. अहंक्रिया

Aham Pratyaya 'I'-feeling; self-consciousness. अहं प्रत्यय

Ahamta /Ahamtaa/ I-ness. अहंता

Aham Vritti self-arrogating thought. अहं वृत्ति

Ahankara see Ahamkara. अहंकार

Ahara /Aahaara/ third basic instinct, craving food or nourishment; food, nourishment, anything that nourishes the body/mind; see Pravritti. आहार

Ahavana /Aahaavana/ invocation; see Avahana. आहावन

Ahimsa /Ahimsaa/ absence of violence from within; non-violence; harmlessness, abstaining from killing or giving pain to others in thought, word or deed; the positive and comprehensive meaning of 'love embracing all creation'; general attitude of welfare for the entire world; one of the yamas as described in Patanjali's *Yoga Sutras*; see Yama. अहिंसा

Ahuti /Aahuti/ offering, libation. आहुति

Aihika of this world or place, temporal, secular, worldly, local. ऐहिक

Aikya, Aikyam oneness, unity, identity, sameness; especially identity of the human soul (atman) or the universe with the deity (Brahman). ऐक्य, ऐक्यम्

Aikamatya unanimity, agreement. ऐकमत्य

Aikantika /Aikaantika/ absolute; complete, perfect; assured, certain. ऐकान्तिक

Aikapadam unity of words; being formed into one word. ऐकपदम्

Aikarthya /Aikaarthya/ sameness of aim or purpose; consistency in meaning. ऐकार्थ्य

Aishan belonging to Shiva. ऐशन्

Aishvara majestic; powerful, mighty; supreme, royal; belonging to Shiva; divine. ऐश्वर

Aishvaryam material or spiritual wealth; supremacy, sovereignty, power; divine attributes like wisdom, renunciation, etc. ऐश्वर्यम्

Aistika sacrificial, ceremonial. ऐस्तिक

Aitareya name of a brahmana and an aranyaka attributed to Aitareya; an Upanishad of the *Rigveda*; originating from Aitareya; see Prajnanam Brahma. ऐतरेय

Aitihasika /Aitihaasika/ traditional; historical; one who knows or studies ancient legends. ऐतिहासिक

Aja unborn; a goat (male). अज

Ajanma /Aajanma/ from birth. आजन्म

Ajanma no birth. अजन्म

Ajata /Ajaata/ unborn; one that did not come up (as seed). अजात

Ajativada /Ajaati-vaada/ the theory of non-evolution. अजातिवाद

Ajanatam /Ajaanatam/ not knowing. अजानतम्

Ajapa /Ajapaa/ involuntary, unconscious repetition of the same thing, applied especially to the mantra or sound made in breathing, which is 'recited' 21,600 times every 24 hours. अजपा

Ajapa Japa /Ajapaa Japa/ continuous, spontaneous repetition of mantra; meditation practice in which mantra is coordinated with breath; a powerful technique for sense withdrawal which can induce concentration and deep meditation. अजपा जप

Ajapa Mantra /Ajapaa Mantra/ involuntary, unconscious repetitive sound; 'soham' and 'hamso' (I am the universal spirit); see Soham; see Hamsa Mantra. अजपा मन्त्र

Ajit /Ajita/ not conquered, invincible; a name of Lord Vishnu. अजित

Ajna /Aajnaa/ command, order. आज्ञा

Ajna Chakra /Aajnaa Chakra/ the third eye, the command or monitoring psychic/pranic centre, also known as the guru chakra. The centre of individual consciousness, it enables mind to mind communication with the external guru and one's inner self. It represents intuition or the inner pure awareness engendered by the confluence of ida, pingala and sushumna nadis. Physically, the concentration point is situated at the medulla oblongata at the top of the spinal column in the midbrain, corresponding to the pineal gland; see Chakra; see Granthi; see Aum; see Atmic Triveni. आज्ञा चक्र

Ajna Mandala /Aajnaa Mandala/ symbol of ajna chakra. आज्ञा मण्डल

Ajnana /Ajnaana/ ignorance, non-cognizance; unawareness. अज्ञान

Ajnana Avrita Ananda /Ajnaana Aavrita Aananda/ bliss enveloped by ignorance; the bliss experienced in deep sleep. अज्ञान आवृत आनन्द

Ajnanam /Ajnaanam/ ignorance; especially spiritual ignorance (avidya) which makes one consider oneself as distinct from the supreme reality or spirit; see Klesha. अज्ञानम्

Akala /Akaala/ wrong time, premature. अकाल

Akara /Aakaara/ form. आकार

Akara /Akaara/ the first, most fundamental sound represented by 'a' (अ), the first letter of the alphabet. अकार

Akarma inaction. अकर्म

Akarnya /Aakarnya/ to give ear to, to listen; see Karna. आकर्ण्य

Akarshana Shakti /Aakarshana Shakti/ power of attraction. आकर्षण शक्ति

Akarta / Akartaa/ non-doer. अकर्त्ता

Akartavya that which should not be done. अकर्त्तव्य

Akarya /Akaarya/ improper action. अकार्य

Akasha /Aakaasha/ 1. element of ether, space, sky; to shine, to appear; 2. primordial state of existence; 3. in Sankhya philosophy: the first mahabhuta, its special property is sound; that which fills all space between worlds, molecules and everything; its most subtle manifestation (tanmatra) is in the pre-nuclear state of matter; 4. the three internal spaces most often used in meditation are chidakasha, daharakasha and hridayakasha; see Pancha Mahabhuta. आकाश

Akashaja /Aakaasha-ja/ born of akasha. आकाशज
Akasha Mandala /Aakaasha Mandala/ region of ether or space. आकाश मण्डल
Akashamatra /Aakaasha-maatra/ ether only; space only. आकाशमात्र
Akasha Mudra /Aakaasha Mudraa/ a very important mudra to prepare the mind for the state of samadhi; see Mudra. आकाश मुद्रा
Akasha Nila /Aakaasha Neela/ blueness of the sky. आकाश नील
Akasha Tattwa /Aakaasha Tattva/ space element; ether principle; see Pancha Mahabhuta. आकाश तत्त्व
Akashavani /Aakaasha-vaanee/ eternal heavenly voice. आकाशवाणी
Akashi Mudra /Aakaashee Mudraa/ awareness of the inner space; practice of the external stage of dharana; gazing into space with the head tilted back; see Mudra. आकाशी मुद्रा

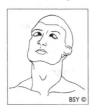

BSY ©

Akasmika /Aakasmika/ accidental, unexpected. आकस्मिक
Akhanda unbroken, indivisible, whole, entire. अखण्ड
Akhanda Ananda /Akhanda Aananda/ unbroken bliss. अखण्ड आनन्द
Akhandaikarasa /Akhanda-ekarasa/ the one undivided essence. अखण्डैकरस
Akhandaikarasa Vritti /Akhanda-ekarasa Vritti/ the pure homogeneous brahma-karavritti (flow of mind towards Brahman) that is produced by meditation on Brahman. अखण्डैकरस वृत्ति
Akhandakara /Akhandaakaara/ of the nature of indivisibility; uninterrupted. अखण्डैकार
Akhandakara Vritti /Akhandaakaara Vritti/ constant uninterrupted state of thought waves in the mind. अखण्डाकार वृत्ति
Akhanda Kirtan /Akhanda Keertan/ ongoing, unbroken kirtan. अखण्ड कीर्तन
Akhandam uninterruptedly. अखण्डम्
Akhanda Mauna unbroken silence. अखण्ड मौन
Akhara /Akhaaraa/ a place for training in arms; headquarters of the Naga sect. अखाड़ा
Akhila having no gap; entire, all. अखिल
Akritabhigama /Akrita-abhigama/ occurrence of fruits of actions that are not performed. अक्रिताभिगम
Akrodha freedom from anger, absence or suppression of anger. अक्रोध
Akrodhana freedom from anger. अक्रोधन
Aksham eye; organ of sense; object of sense. अक्षम्
Akshajam direct knowledge or cognition. अक्षजम्
Akshara letter, form; quality of a mantra; syllable; literally 'that which does not perish'; sounds which do not die; imperishable, indestructible; fixed, firm. अक्षर

Aksharabrahmayoga (Akshara-brahma-yoga); 'yoga of the imperishable Brahman', the eighth chapter of the *Bhagavad Gita* in which guidance is given on meditation, death and immortality. अक्षरब्रह्मयोग

Akshara Shuddhi clear pronunciation of the letters of the mantras. अक्षर शुद्धि

Aksharatma /Akshara-aatmaa/ imperishable self. अक्षरात्मा

Aksharavat /Aksharavat/ imperishability. अक्षरवत्

Akshata unbroken and uncooked rice used in worship as a sign of auspiciousness, well being and prosperity. अक्षत

Akshayapatra /Akshaya-paatra/ wish-yielding pot. अक्षयपात्र

Akshobha emotionless, undisturbed, absence of agitation. अक्षोभ

Akshobhya immovable, imperturbable. अक्षोभ्य

Alakha which can not be seen; flame; inner illumination. अलख

Alakh Bara /Alakha Baaraa/ 'invisible boundary'; place where paramahamsa sannyasins live in seclusion. अलख बाड़ा

Alakh Niranjan /Alakha Niranjana/ that which cannot be seen; uninvolved; untainted or stainless. अलख निरंजन

Alakshana without distinctive marks or signs; undefined, undistinguished. अलक्षण

Alambanam /Aalambanam/ support, thing depended on, that on which one rests or leans, protection; primal idea or the basic cause. आलम्बनम्

Alarkalam ashram in which Lord

Buddha received his training in the Sankhya way of practice. अलर्कलम्

Alasya /Aalasya/ idleness, sloth, lack of energy. आलस्य

Alata Chakra /Alaata Chakra/ a stick burning at one end, which when waved around quickly produces an illusion of a circle of fire. अलात चक्र

Alaya Vijnana /Alaya Vijnaana/ internal cognition, the supreme state according to the yogacharyas. अलय विज्ञान

Alinga without mark; state of undifferentiated existence. अलिङ्ग

Aloka /Aaloka/ luminous; light; investigation (in the light of). आलोक

Aloka not of this dimension; see Loka. अलोक

Alpa little. अल्प

Amala without impurity. अमल

Amalam free from the impurity of maya. अमलम्

Amalaka the tree *Emblic myrobalan*, whose fruit is good for the eyes according to folklore and is used in ayurvedic medicine. अमलक

Amanas, Amanaska without the organ of desire, thought; the mind that is free from thought and desire. अमनस्, अमनस्क

Amanoshata state of being mindless. अमनोशत

Amanitvam /Amaanitvam/ humility, absence of pride. अमानित्वम्

Amara immortal. अमर

Amaroli drinking of one's own urine in order to detoxify the body and develop immunity, stamina and vitality. अमरोली

Amartya immortal, imperishable, divine. अमर्त्य

Amarsha the emotion of anger and jealousy combined; not enduring or bearing. अमर्ष

Amatra /Amaatra/ boundless; immeasurable. अमात्र

Amba /Ambaa/ mother; Shiva's consort. अम्बा

Amma /Ammaa/ mother. अम्मा

Amrita literally 'deathless' (God); immortal, immortality; life; the nectar of immortality which descends from bindu; also called soma. अमृत

Amrita Nadi /Amrita Naadee/ a special psychic energy flow branching from the heart. अमृत नाड़ी

Amsha part; fragment. अंश

Amurta /Amoorta/ without form (amurta elements: air and ether). अमूर्त

Anadi /Anaadi/ beginningless. अनादि

Anadi Ananta /Anaadi Ananta/ without beginning and end; infinite; Brahman. अनादि अनन्त

Anadi Kala /Anaadi Kaala/ eternity; beginningless time. अनादि काल

Anadi Pravartanam /Anaadi Pravartanam/ beginningless flow; everlastingness; beginningless but terminable. अनादि प्रवर्तनम्

Anagata /Anaagata/ belonging to the future; not yet arrived. अनागत

Anagha sinless, faultless, innocent; handsome. अनघ

Anahad Nada see Anahata Nada. अनहद् नाद

Anahata /Anaahata/ 'unstruck' or 'unbeaten' sound heard by yogis; see Nada; see Nadanusandhana. अनाहत

Anahata Chakra /Anaahata Chakra/ psychic centre in the region of the heart, the vibration or 'beat' of which regulates life from birth to death; corresponds to the cardiac plexus in the physical body; corresponds to hridayakasha in meditative practice; centre of emotions which, when developed, gives the psychic force to materialize desires; centre where Shiva and Shakti unite; see Chakra; see Granthi see Yam; see Kalpa Taru. अनाहत चक्र

Anahata Kshetram /Anaahata Kshetram/ literally 'field of anahata', trigger point of anahata chakra at the sternum. अनाहत क्षेत्रम्

Anahata Nada /Anaahata Naada/ transcendental cosmic sound experienced only in the higher states of meditation; sound which can not be grasped or heard externally; that sound which is beyond sound; unstruck sound. अनाहत नाद

Anala fire, digestive power, bile. अनल

Ananda /Aananda/ pleasure, happiness; pure unalloyed bliss; state of consciousness (in yoga practice); in Vedanta: one of the three attributes of the ultimate principle; name of Shiva; see Sachchidananda. आनन्द

Ananda Abhava /Aananda Abhaava/ absence of spiritual bliss. आनन्द अभाव

Anandaghana /Aananda-ghana/ mass of bliss. आनन्दघन

Ananda Lahari /Aananda Laharee/ 'wave of bliss'; first 41 slokas of the hymn to Devi, *Saundarya Lahari,* said to be composed by Adi Shankaracharya. आनन्द लहरी

Anandam /Aanandam/ pleasing, delighting; blissful. आनन्दम्

Anandamaya /Aanandamaya/ the supreme state of bliss; the supreme consciousness; fullness of existence. आनन्दमय

Anandamaya Kosha /Aanandamaya Kosha/ the state of bliss attained in samadhi; subtler sphere of existence, consciousness; the innermost wrapper or sheath (kosha) of the embodied spirit; priya, moda and pramoda are the three types of bliss experienced in this kosha; see Pancha Kosha; see Karanasharira. आनन्दमय कोष

Ananda Samadhi /Aananda Samaadhi/ blissful absorption; a phase of samprajnata awareness characterized by a state of bliss; see Samprajnata Samadhi. आनन्द समाधि

Ananta endless, infinite, boundless, inexhaustible; name of Vishnu, of Vishnu's conch, and of the serpent Shesha on whom Vishnu rests. अनन्त

Ananta Amatra /Ananta Amaatra/ infinite and immeasurable. अनन्त अमात्र

Ananta Ananda /Ananta Aananda/ infinite bliss. अनन्त आनन्द

Ananta Drishti unlimited vision. अनन्त दृष्टि

Ananta Jyoti infinite light. अनन्त ज्योति

Anantam the sky, atmosphere; infinity; supreme state of existence; Brahman. अनन्तम्

Ananta Matra /Ananta Maatra/ having infinite signs; absolute. अनन्त मात्र

Anantapadmanabha /Ananta-padma-naabha/ a name of Vishnu; according to Hindu mythology, Vishnu sleeps in the primeval ocean on Shesha, the serpent with 1000 heads. During his sleep a lotus grows from his navel from which is born the creator Brahma, who fashions the world. अनन्तपद्मनाभ

Ananta Vrata worship of Vishnu performed in Bhadrapada, the sixth lunar month of the Hindu almanac. अनन्त व्रत

Ananya having no other. अनन्य

Ananya Bhakti exclusive devotion to any single aspect of the Lord; when the meditation and the object of meditation become one. अनन्य भक्ति

Anarabdha Karya /Anaarabdha Kaarya/ works which have not yet begun to produce their effects. अनारब्ध कार्य

Anartha worthless; harmful, a calamity, misfortune. अनर्थ

Anasakti /Anaasakti/ non-attachment, dispassion, indifference to all sense experience and pairs of opposites; a high state of wisdom (jnana). अनासक्ति

Anatman /Anaatman/ not-self, another, the perishable body; something different from atman. अनात्मन्

Anatman Vada /Anaatman Vaada/ state of so-called non-self in Buddhism paralleled in yoga by the experience of asamprajnata samadhi. अनात्मन् वाद

Anavachhinna /Anavachchhinna/ unlimited, uninterrupted. अनवच्छिन्न

Anavachhinna Chaitanya / Anavachchhinna Chaitanya/ undivided intelligence which is the real self. अनवच्छिन्न चैतन्य

Anavadhana /Anavadhaana/ non-attention. अनवधान

Anavasada /Anavasaada/ cheerfulness; non-dejection. अनवसाद

Anavastha unsettled, unstable; fallacy arising from the absence of finality or conclusion. अनवस्थ

Anavastha Dosha moving backward into infinity; infinite regression. अनवस्थ दोष

Anavasthita unsteady, unsettled; changed; dissolute. अनवस्थित

Anavasthitattwa /Anavasthitattva/ inability to continue the practice of yoga; feeling that one has reached the highest state of samadhi and therefore it is not necessary to continue. अनवस्थितत्त्व

Anavasthitva instability. अनवस्थित्व

Anavopaya /Anavopaaya/ (Anavaupaaya); the means by which the empirical individual (anu) uses his/her instruments (karanas) of senses, mind and energy (prana) for self-realization. Includes practice of shatkarma, asana, pranayama, pratyahara, mudra, bandha, disciplines concerning regulation of prana, rituals, japa, concentration, etc.; techniques for inner realization; the first or most gross of the four upaya sadhanas of tantra; see Upaya. अनवोपाय

Anga limb or part of the body; a constituent part; a step. अङ्ग

Anga Nyasa /Anga Nyaasa/ ritual performed to instal devatas at different parts of a person's body; invoking or activating a person's energy body. अंग न्यास

Angula a specific measurement; width of one finger. अङ्गुल

Anguli finger, toe. अङ्गुलि

Angushtha the thumb, the big toe. अङ्गुष्ठ

Angushtha Matra /Angushtha Maatra/ of the size of the thumb. अङ्गुष्ठ मात्र

Angiras /Angeeras/ name of a rishi (and his descendants), who composed many of the hymns in the *Rigveda* and founded the science of Brahma Vidya; certain hymns from the *Atharva Veda*. अङ्गीरस्

Anibadha /Anibaadha/ without obstacles. अनिबाध

Anima /Animaa/ subtlety; the power of making the body subtle; reducing the physical mass and density at will; one of the eight siddhis; see Siddhi. अणिमा

Anirvachaniya /Anirvachaneeya/ indescribable, inexpressible; neither existence or non-existence. अनिर्वचनीय

Anirvachaniya Satta /Anirvachaneeya Sattaa/ inscrutable being (maya). अनिर्वचनीय सत्ता

Anishta undesired; bad, evil. अनिष्ट

Anitya impermanent. अनित्य

Anjana /Anjanaa/ mother of Hanuman. अञ्जना

Anna food. अन्न

Annamaya Kosha sheath or body of matter; the sphere of existence created by food, maintained by food and which ultimately becomes food, i.e. the body; see Pancha Kosha; see Sthula Sharira. अन्नमय कोष

Anrita untruth, falsehood. अनृत

Antah, Antar inner, internal. अन्त:, अन्तर्

Antahchatushtaya fourfold internal organ or mind; the inner equipment in its four aspects: manas, buddhi, chitta and ahamkara; see Devata. अन्त:चतुष्टय

Antahkarana inner organ, instrument or tool of consciousness; mind; see Manas; see Buddhi; see Chitta; see Ahamkara. अन्त:करण

Antahkarana Pratibimba Chaitanya reflection of the intelligence in the mind. अन्त:करण प्रतिबिम्ब चैतन्य

Antahkarana Shastra /Antahkarana Shaastra/ psychology, science of the internal organ or mind. अन्त:करण शास्त्र

Antarakasha /Antar-aakaasha/ inner space which forms the substratum for our own individual creation. अन्तराकाश

Antaranga 'inner limb'; in raja yoga: sense withdrawal (pratyahara) leads to concentration (dharana), meditation (dhyana) and samadhi; internal organ, inner part, inner stage; mind; see Ashtanga Yoga; see Bahiranga. अन्तरङ्ग

Antaratma /Antar-aatmaa/ the indwelling self, inner soul, the heart; substance. अन्तरात्मा

Antaratman Sadhana /Antar-aatman Saadhanaa/ the innermost quest of the inner self by means of sense withdrawal (pratyahara), concentration (dharana), meditation (dhyana) and samadhi. अन्तरात्मन् साधना

Antardhauti inner cleaning. अन्तर्धौति

Antardrishti inner vision; a kind of intuitive knowledge. अन्तर्दृष्टि

Antarjyoti inner light, brightness; illuminated faculty of mind developed by samyama i.e. moving between concentration, meditation and samadhi. अन्तर्ज्योति

Antarkumbhaka internal breath retention; suspension of breath after full inhalation; see Kumbhaka. अन्तर्कुम्भक

Antarlakshya internal aim to be aspired for in concentration (dharana); introversion; introspection. अन्तर्लक्ष्य

Antarmouna inner silence; meditative technique belonging to the fifth step of raja yoga (pratyahara); consists of six stages: 1. awareness of sense perception, 2. awareness of spontaneous thought process, 3. posing and disposing of thoughts at will, 4. awareness of spontaneous thoughts and disposal of thoughts at will, 5. freedom from thought, 6. awareness of sleep state consciousness (prajna); see Pratyahara; see Prajna. अन्तर्मौन

Antarmukha introspective; gaze turned inwards. अन्तर्मुख

Antarmukha Vritti state in which the mind is turned inward and withdrawn from objects; see Pratyahara. अन्तर्मुख वृत्ति

Antarvaha Sharira /Antarvaha Shareera/ the subtle body of a yogi through which entry into the bodies of others is accomplished. अन्तर्वाह शरीर

Antarveshtini /Antarveshtinee/ an important energy flow (nadi) which is very delicate; nadi in which the pure and resplendent shakti called kundalini is located. अन्तर्वेष्टिनी

Antaryajna internalization of the yajna process. अन्तर्यज्ञ

Antaryamin inner ruler; the supreme being present in every object of creation and guiding all creatures. अन्तर्यामिन्

Antara in the middle, between; inner, internal, within; interval; location, place; distance. अन्तर

Anu fine; minute; atomic, an atom of matter, 'an atom of time'; the 54,675,000th part of a muhurta (of 48 minutes); name of Shiva, 'the subtle one'; name of the fingers preparing the soma juice; in poetry the 4th part of a matra; in Vaisheshika, a positional reality that has no length, breadth or thickness; limited, conditioned or empirical individual; see Anavopaya. अणु

Anu Matrika /Anu Maatrika/ having the size of an atom, containing the atomic elements (matra) of the body. अणु मात्रिक

Anupaya /Anoopaya/ (Anu-upaaya); the fourth upaya of tantra, attainment of spiritual experience without need of means or effort – possible for very advanced aspirants only; see Upaya. अणूपाय

Anu Renu atomic dust (as seen in sunbeams). अणु रेणु

Anuvadin /Anu-vaadin/ one who believes in and teaches atomism; see Vaisheshika. अणुवादिन्

Anu one of the prepositions in Sanskrit. अनु

Anubhava direct perception or cognition, knowledge derived from personal observation or experiment; experience; intuitive consciousness (self-realization); personal spiritual experience. अनुभव

    Anubhava Advaita actual living experience of oneness. अनुभव अद्वैत

    Anubhava Gamyam obtainable by direct perception (through samadhi). अनुभव गम्यम्

    Anubhava Vakya /Anubhava Vaakya/ self-realized statement, i.e. 'Aham Brahmasmi'; see Aham Brahmasmi; see Maha Vakya. अनुभव वाक्य

    Anubhavi Guru /Anubhavee Guru/ preceptor who has personal spiritual realization. अनुभवी गुरु

Anubhuta /Anubhoota/ perceived, understood. अनुभूत

Anudatta /Anudaatta/ lowest of the three tones used for chanting Sanskrit mantras aloud; see Udatta; see Swarita. अनुदात्त

Anugraha divine grace, kindness, assistance. अनुग्रह

Anuloma in a natural direction, with the grain. अनुलोम

    Anuloma Pranayama /Anuloma Praanaayaama/ pranayama in

which inhalation is performed through both nostrils and exhalation alternately through either nostril. अनुलोम प्राणायाम

Anumana /Anumaana/ inference; one of the three means of correct knowledge (pramana) enumerated by Patanjali in the *Yoga Sutras*; knowledge which is preceded by perception; see Pramana; see Vritti. अनुमान

Anumanika /Anumaanika/ relating to a conclusion; derived from an inferential perception. अनुमानिक

Anumanta giver of the sanction to the movements of nature. अनुमन्त

Anumati permission, consent, approval. अनुमति

Anupada following the feet closely. अनुपद

Anupalabdha unobtained; unperceived; unascertained. अनुपलब्ध

Anupalabdhi one of the eight proofs of knowledge of the existence of non-existence or the negative. अनुपलब्धि

Anusandhana /Anusandhaana/ enquiry; investigation. अनुसन्धान

Anushasana /Anushaasana/ complete instruction; command; laying down rules or precepts; a law; advice, persuasion; subtle management. अनुशासन

Anushaya repentance, remorse, regret; the result or consequence of bad deeds which cling very closely and so cause the soul to enter other bodies after enjoying temporary freedom from recurring births. अनुशय

Anushthana /Anushthaana/ a resolve to performa mantra sadhana with absolute discipline for a requisite period of time; a fixed course of sadhana; systematic performance of religious practices undertaken usually for some definite period of time, e.g. 40 days. अनुष्ठान

Anuvrata obedient, devoted. अनुव्रत

Anuvritti turning round and round; following; having respect for one's own thought. अनुवृत्ति

Anuvyakhyana /Anuvyaakhyaana/ exposition, gloss, commentary; part of a brahmana which explains difficult aphorisms (sutras); see Brahmana. अनुव्याख्यान

Anuvyavasaya /Anuvyavasaaya/ perception of a sentiment or judgement. अनुव्यवसाय

Anyonya one another, each other, mutual. अन्योन्य

Ap, Apas /Aapa, Aapas/ water; the liquid state of matter; in Sankhya philosophy, the fourth mahabhuta with the special property of taste; a religious ceremony; see Pancha Mahabhuta. आप, आपस्

Apas Tattwa /Aapas Tattva/ water element; water principle. आपस् तत्त्व

Apamana /Apamaana/ disrespect, disgrace. अपमान

Apana Chaitanya /Apaana Chaitanya/ awareness of apana vayu. अपान चैतन्य

Apana Vayu /Apaana Vaayu/ one of the five energies (vayus or pranas), moving downwards from the navel to the perineum, governing the lower abdominal region and responsible for elimination and reproduction; downward moving breath; see Vayu; see Pancha Prana. अपान वायु

Apara another; ordinary; opposite of para. अपर

Apara Brahman lower Brahman, Brahman with attributes or qualities (saguna Brahman), personal God (Ishwara). अपर ब्रह्मन्

Apara Vairagya /Apara Vairaagya/ lower kind of vairagya or dispassion denoting detachment from the objects of pleasure; see Vashikara; see Para Vairagya. अपर वैराग्य

Apara Vidya /Apara Vidyaa/ intellectual (or lower) knowledge of the Vedas; intellectual knowledge. अपर विद्या

Apara /Aparaa/ all knowledge except spiritual knowledge; worldly knowledge; 'aparaa' is the feminine of apara – other; ordinary; inferior; lower. अपरा

Aparadha /Aparaadha/ fault, mistake. अपराध

Aparadha Bhava /Aparaadha Bhaava/ devotion with a sense of guilt. अपराध भाव

Aparadha Kshamapana Stotra /Aparaadha Kshamaapana Stotra/ tantric prayer to Lord Shiva to forgive faults and failures, composed by Adi Shankaracharya. अपराध क्षमापन स्तोत्र

Aparichhinna /Aparichchhinna/ without any limitations; infinite; never-ending, continuous. अपरिच्छिन्न

Aparigraha freedom from covetousness; abstention from greed; non-receiving of gifts conducive to luxury; without possessions or belongings; one of the five yamas described by Patanjali in the *Yoga Sutras* as a preliminary discipline of yoga; see Yama. अपरिग्रह

Aparimita Drishti the view transcending the limitation of space, time and causation; unmeasured view. अपरिमित दृष्टि

Aparinama /Aparinaama/ unchangeable, unalterable. अपरिणाम

Aparoksha not invisible, perceptible to the senses; not distant or remote; direct, immediate. अपरोक्ष

Aparokshanubhava Swarupa /Aparoksha-anubhava-Svaroopa/ the essence of direct intuitive perception; direct realization. अपरोक्षानुभव स्वरूप

Aparokshanubhuti /Aparoksha-anubhooti/ direct, actual experience; state of intuitive experience; literally 'not indirect experience'. अपरोक्षानुभूति

Aparokshatva feeling of directness or immediacy. अपरोक्षत्व

Apavada /Apavaada/ exception; negation, rejection; refutation, as of a wrong imputation or belief; contradiction. अपवाद

Apavarga release, liberation; release from the bondage of embodiment; completion; see Moksha. अपवर्ग

Apekshika /Aapekshika/ relative. आपेक्षिक

Aprajna /Apraajna/ ignorant; unlearned. अप्राज्ञ

Aprakrita unmanifested; unperceived; not published; concealed, hidden. अप्रकृत

Aprama /Apramaa/ false or incorrect notion. अप्रमा

Apramatta careful, watchful, vigilant; not dull or intoxicated. अप्रमत्त

Aprana /Apraana/ without prana, the principle of life. अप्राण

Apta /Aapta/ reached, obtained; intimate; relative, friend. आप्त

Apta Kama /Aapta Kaama/ one whose desires have been fulfilled; one who has renounced all worldly desires and attachments; a realized sage. आप्त काम

Apta Vakya /Aapta Vaakya/ evidence of the wise; testimony of the trustworthy; Veda or shruti. आप्त वाक्य

Apurna /Apoorna/ imperfect; not full, incomplete. अपूर्ण

Apurva /Apoorva/ unseen; strange, extraordinary; the hidden force of a karma which will bring its fruits in the future. अपूर्व

Aradhana /Aaraadhanaa/ to be fully immersed in worship of the deity with intense reverence. आराधना

Arambha /Aarambha/ beginning. आरम्भ

Arambha Avastha /Aarambha Avasthaa/ beginning stage; according to *Hatha Yoga Pradipika* the first state of hearing the inner nada attained after piercing Brahma granthi. आरम्भ अवस्था

Arambhakopadana /Aarambhakopaadaana/ (Aarambhaka-upaadaana); material cause that gives birth to an effect which is an essentially different entity, e.g. atoms of the Vaisheshika school. आरम्भकोपादान

Arani piece of wood used in kindling fire by friction during yajna (fire ceremonies); sacrificial wood. अरणि

Aranya forest; the name of one of the 10 orders of sannyasins founded by Adi Shankaracharya; see Dashnami Sampradaya. अरण्य

Aranya /Aaranya/ jungle or forest-born; wild. आरण्य

Aranyaka /Aaranyaka/ output of forest life; being in or relating to a forest; wild; third part of the Vedas. These texts are contemplative ancient scriptures containing subtle mystical interpretations of vedic rituals composed in the forest by rishis who had renounced worldly life; transition from ritual to philosophy; see Veda. आरण्यक

Aranyakula Ashrama /Aaranyakula Aashrama/ see Vanaprastha Ashrama. आरण्यकुल आश्रम

Arati /Aaratee/ rite of worship involving waving of lights with reverence before a deity. आरती

Aravinda name of a famous yogi from Pondicherry (whose name is pronounced 'Aurobindo' by Bengalis). He was concerned with the transformative power of yoga on all levels of the human being. अरविन्द

Archana /Archanaa/ offering of flowers, etc. at the time of worship; honouring; reverence or respect paid to deities and superiors. अर्चना

Ardha half, forming a half. अर्ध

Ardhamatra /Ardha-maatraa/ half syllable. अर्धमात्रा

Ardhanarishvara /Ardhanaareeshvara/ (Ardhanaree-eeshvara); form of Shiva which is half-male and half-female; Shiva and Shakti united in one form; concept of ida and pingala nadis in yoga philosophy. अर्धनारीश्वर

Arghya respectful offering of water to the gods or to guests; valuable; see Shodashopachara. अर्घ्य

Arjana gained; earned. अर्जन

Arjavam /Aarjavam/ straightforwardness, being truthful and innocent. आर्जवम्

Arjuna name of the third Pandava, who was the son of Indra and Kunti; in the *Bhagavad Gita* he received a divine revelation from Lord Krishna; white or clear colour. अर्जुन

Arjunavishadayoga /Arjuna-vishaada-yoga/ 'yoga of the despondency of Arjuna', the first chapter of the *Bhagavad Gita* in which Arjuna explains the reasons he does not want to fight against his family even in a just war. अर्जुनविषादयोग

Arohana /Aarohana/ ascending; ascending energy flow in the subtle body; counterpart of avarohana. आरोहण

Arta /Aarta/ devotee who prays for relief from personal calamities or pain. आर्त

Artha accomplishment; attainment in all spheres of life; material need; wealth; in yoga philosophy, the object of meditation; the basis for the mind; see Purushartha. अर्थ

Artharthi /Arthaarthee/ devotee who prays to fulfil a personal desire. अर्थार्थी

Artha Tattwa /Artha Tattva/ the real nature of anything. अर्थ तत्त्व

Arudha /Aarudha/ mounted, ascended; seated on. आरूढ

Arundhati /Arundhatee/ name of the wife of Vashistha (one of the seven rishis). Like her husband, she was the guide and controller of Raghu's line in her own right; the morning star personified as the wife of Vashistha; one of the Pleiades (a group of stars). अरुन्धती

Arundhati Darshana Nyaya /Arundhatee Darshana Nyaaya/ the star Arundhati is rarely visible to the naked eye; therefore, to point it out a very big star nearby is shown. That star is then rejected and a smaller star is pointed out and so on, until the actual Arundhati is located. This method of leading from the gross to the more subtle is called Arundhati Darshana Nyaya; see Adhyaropa; see Apavada. अरुन्धती दर्शन न्याय

Arundhi /Arundhee/ ascent, rise, elevation. अरुन्धी

Arupa /Aroopa/ formless, shapeless; the pradhana or prakriti of Sankhya philosophy and the Brahman of Vedanta. अरूप

Arurukshu /Aarurukshu/ one who wishes to 'climb' the steps of yoga. आरुरुक्षु

Arya /Aarya/ generic name used to refer to vedic people; a title given to a respectable person or head of a family. आर्य

Arya Samaj /Aarya Samaaja/ a reformist group founded by Swami Dayananda Saraswati, interested in reestablishing Vedic customs. आर्य समाज

Asadavarana /Asat-aavarana/ veiling power of maya which screens the existence of Brahman and makes us think there is no Brahman, one of the two aspects of avarana shakti; asadavarana is removed by direct knowledge (aparoksha jnana). असदावरण

Asadrisha unlike; unequalled. असदृश

Asakta unattached, unselfish. असक्त

Asakti /Aasakti/ attachment. आसक्ति

Asamartha not having a suitable attitude and aim; not capable; not having the intended meaning. असमर्थ

Asamavayin /Asamavaayin/ not intimately related; not inherent; not being the substance. असमवायिन्

Asambhavana /Asambhaavanaa/ spiritual doubt, one of the obstacles (pratibandha) that stands in the way of self-realization; lack of respect; improbability; impossibility of comprehending. असम्भावना

Asamprajnata Samadhi /Asamprajnaata Samaadhi/ stage of samadhi where the traces of the mind (samskaras) become active according to their intensity; state of identification of the individual consciousness with the universal state of existence and consciousness; samadhi which is experienced between the different phases of samprajnata samadhi. A dynamic state of laya (dissolution) or nirodha (cessation) where awareness and willpower drop and the nature of the samskaras is the guiding factor; see Samprajnata Samadhi; see Samskara. असम्प्रज्ञात समाधि

Asamprayoga not coming into contact; incorrect application. असम्प्रयोग

Asamshakti in Vedanta, the fifth of seven levels of wisdom (jnana bhumika), where there is the highest degree of non-attachment to objects of the world and the world is like a dream; see Brahmavidvara. असंशक्ति

Asamskrita uncultured. असंस्कृत

Asamvedana /Asamvedanaa/ non-receptivity of the mind; imperishable state of quiescent wisdom (jnana); thoughtless state (nirvikalpa samadhi). असंवेदना

Asamyagdarshana (A-samyak-darshana); incorrect or imperfect vision; consciousness of the objective universe. असम्यग्दर्शन

Asana /Aasana/ in raja yoga, a physical posture in which one is at ease and in harmony with oneself; the third limb of yoga as described by Patanjali in the *Yoga Sutras*; seat; posture for meditation or for health; in hatha yoga, a specific body posture to balance and channel energy (prana), open the chakras and remove energy blocks; see Shodasho-pachara. आसन

Asanavidhi /Aasana vidhi/ rite or service performed by a devotee taking his seat to conduct puja. आसन विधि

Asanga non-attachment; freedom from ties. असङ्ग

Asanga Bhavana /Asanga Bhaavanaa/ feeling or mental attitude of non-attachment. असङ्ग भावना

Asantosha discontent, disgust. असन्तोष

Asara /Asaara/ without essence; dry; barren. असार

Asat not being or existing, not manifest; in Vedanta, the passive aspect of the ultimate principle, Brahman. असत्

Asevita not attended upon, not served; not enjoyed. असेवित

Asha /Aashaa/ hope; expectation. आशा

Ashasya /Aashasya/ to be obtained by a boon; to be wished; desirable; blessing, benediction. आशस्य

Ashabda not expressed in words; without any sound. अशब्द

Ashabdam the inexpressible, i.e. Brahman; in Sankhya philosophy, the primary germ of nature. अशब्दम्

Ashada /Aashaada/ fourth lunar month according to the Hindu almanac, corresponding to June/July. Its full moon is celebrated as the Guru Purnima festival; see Grishma; see Masa; see Ritu; see Guru Purnima. आषाढ

Ashana /Ashanaa/ hunger; desire to consume. अशना

Ashanti /Ashaanti/ restlessness, distraction; absence of peace of mind; non-cessation. अशान्ति

Ashaya /Aashaya/ receptacle, abode; place where the residue of karmas and unfulfilled desires or experiences are stored in a particular state of mind; karmic stock; mind; heart; intention. आशय

Ashcharyavat /Aashcharyavat/ marvellous, wonderful; applied to the indweller of the body. आश्चर्यवत्

Ashirvada /Aasheervaada/ blessing, benediction. आशीर्वाद

Ashrama /Aashrama/ hermitage, hut, cell, dwelling or abode of ascetism and spiritual practice; stage, order, or period of life, of which there are four: brahmacharya or studentship, grihastha or household life, vanaprastha or forest-dwelling, sannyasa or total renunciation; the name of one of the 10 orders of sannyasins founded by Adi Shankaracharya; see Dashnami Sampradaya; see Varna Ashrama. आश्रम

Ashramadharma /Aashrama-dharma/ the special duties of each order of life; the duties of one leading a hermit's life. आश्रमधर्म

Ashraya /Aashraya/ that on which things depend, to which things are closely connected; resting place, asylum, support, help; dependence. आश्रय

Ashrita /Aashrita/ having recourse; depending on the body; to live in; see Dehamashrita. आश्रित

Ashtama eighth. अष्टम

Ashtadhyayi /Asthtaa-dhyaayee/ literally 'eight chapters', the name of Panini's treatise on Sanskrit grammar. अष्टाध्यायी

Ashtakshara Mantra /Ashta-akshara Mantra/ mantra with eight syllables, Om Namo Narayanaya. अष्टाक्षर मन्त्र

Ashtalokapala /Ashtaloka-paala/ guardians of the eight directions. अष्टलोकपाल

Ashtami /Ashtamee/ eighth lunar day (tithi) of the dark and bright fortnight on the lunar calendar. अष्टमी

Ashtanga Yoga /Ashta-anga Yoga/ the eight limbs of yoga described by Patanjali in the *Yoga Sutras*, viz. 1. yama, 2. niyama, 3. asana, 4. pranayama, 5. pratyahara, 6. dharana, 7. dhyana, 8. samadhi; see Antaranga; see Bahiranga Sadhana. अष्टाङ्ग योग

Ashtashraddha /Ashta-shraaddha/ eight funeral rites performed for all worldly relations, including one's previous self; ceremony performed when taking initiation into sannyasa. अष्टश्राद्ध

Ashubha evil, inauspicious. अशुभ

Ashubha Vasana /Ashubha Vaasanaa/ impure desire or tendency. अशुभ वासना

Ashuddha impure, not purified; incorrect, wrong. अशुद्ध

Ashuddha Manah /Ashuddha Manah/ impure mind, lower mind with evil impressions. अशुद्ध मन:

Ashwa /Ashva/ horse; symbolic expression for the number 'seven'; temporary. अश्व

Ashwamedha Yajna /Ashvamedha Yajna/ horse sacrifice; an elaborate vedic ceremony undertaken by kings to attain a son or sovereignty. अश्वमेध यज्ञ

Ashwina /Aashvina/ seventh lunar month of the Hindu almanac, containing Ashwina Navaratri. Corresponds to September/October; see Sharada; see Masa; see Navaratri Anushthana. आश्विन

Ashwinau /Ashvinau/ the two physicians of the gods, who are respected as the twin sons of the Sun by a nymph in the shape of a mare called Ashwini; presiding deities of the nostrils; also called Ashwini Kumara. अश्विनौ

Ashwini /Ashvinee/ the first of 27 nakshatras or lunar mansions (consisting of three stars); a nymph, considered in later times to be the mother of the Ashwinau and the wife of the Sun. अश्विनी

Ashwini Mudra /Ashvinee Mudraa/ a yogic practice to redirect energy upwards; mudra involving contraction of the anal sphincter as a horse does; see Mudra. अश्विनी मुद्रा

Ashwattha /Ashvattha/ holy fig or pipal tree, a huge tree whose roots and branches spread extensively. Lord Buddha achieved enlightenment beneath it; sacred tree regarded as the dwelling place of Lord Vishnu. अश्वत्थ

Asiddha not perfected, unrealized. असिद्ध

Asmat pertaining to us or me. अस्मत्

Asmi I am, I exist. असि

Asmita /Aasmitaa/ state where the ego and the sense of individuality are completely finished and there is only pure awareness. आस्मिता

Asmita /Asmitaa/ sense of doership; egoism; one of the five causes of affliction (kleshas) described by Patanjali in the *Yoga Sutras*; awareness of 'I am' superimposed on the body, action and mind;

feeling of 'I' identified with an action; see Klesha. अस्मिता

Asmitanasha /Asmitaa-naasha/ destruction of egoism or I-ness. अस्मितानाश

Asmita Samadhi /Asmitaa Samaadhi/ a state of samprajnata samadhi attained by dissolution of the ego; merging of body, mind and soul; samadhi with the seed of individual self-awareness; superconscious state immediately below seedless samadhi (nirbija samadhi) with only the feeling of 'I am', or 'I exist', 'Aham Asmi'; see Samprajnata Samadhi. अस्मिता समाधि

Asmriti forgetfulness; state of unconsciousness. अस्मृति

Asparshana non-contact, avoiding contact (with anything). अस्पर्शन

Asteya honesty, not stealing; one of the yamas of Patanjali's *Yoga Sutras*; see Yama. अस्तेय

Asthi bone found in the body tissues; bone. अस्थि

Asthira wavering and unsteady. अस्थिर

Asti being, existent, present; often used at the beginning of a tale or narrative in the sense of 'so it is', or merely as an expletive; Brahman. अस्ति

Astibhatipriya /Asti-bhaati-priya/ asti means existence, bhati means consciousness, priya means bliss, the eternal qualities inherent in Brahman; see Sachchidananda. अस्तिभातिप्रिय

Astika /Aastika/ theist; theistic philosophy. आस्तिक

Astra projectile weapon, like an arrow or a spear. अस्त्र

Astradhari /Astra-dhaaree/ weapon holder. अस्त्रधारी

Asura demon, evil spirit; common name for the enemies of gods; see Daitya. असुर

Asuramaya /Asura-maayaa/ demonical magic. असुरमाया

Asurya demonical. असुर्य

Asurya /Asoorya/ sunless. असूर्य

Asuya /Asooyaa/ envy; jealousy; intolerance; detraction; calumny; anger, indignation. असूय

Atadroopa Pratishtha /Atadroopa Pratishthaa/ (A-tat-roopa Pratishthaa); knowledge of false identity; inability to link name with form. अतद्रूप प्रतिष्ठा

Atadvyavritti /Atadvyaavritti/ (Atat-vyaavritti); process of knowing the truth through something opposed to it, e.g. the self distinct from the three gross, subtle and causal bodies. अतद्व्यावृत्ति

Atadvyavritti Samadhi /Atadvyaavritti Samaadhi/ (Atat-vyavritti Samaadhi); samadhi that does not care for or require the aid of others; samadhi attained through the negation of anatman (anything other than atma). अतद्व्यावृत्ति समाधि

Atala first centre of the instinctive or animal body below mooladhara chakra; see Patalam. अतल

Atattvika /Ataattvika/ not real. अतात्त्विक

Atharvana the eldest son of Brahma and his descendants. His incantations are found in the *Atharva Veda*. अथर्वण

Atharva Veda fourth vedic text containing the tantric concepts and the collection of spells; see Veda. अथर्व वेद

Atigraha object of sense; hold, seize, take, support. अतिग्रह

Atilaghava /Ati-laaghava/ exceeding lightness. अतिलाघव

Atindriya /Ateendriya/ (Ati-indriya); beyond the reach of the senses. अतीन्द्रिय

Atisarva superior to all. अतिसर्व

Atithi guest; the practice of feeding a stranger or unknown guest is known as atithi yajna and is one of the pancha mahayajna (duties of a householder). अतिथि

Atma, Atman /Aatmaa, Aatman/ the self beyond mind and body; also called principle of life, supreme consciousness, spirit, soul, etc.; the seer of turiya (reality) according to *Mandukya Upanishad*; see Paramatma. आत्मा, आत्मन्

Atmabhava /Aatma-bhaava/ feeling of unity with all; seeing the atman (soul) equally in all beings. आत्मभाव

Atmabodha /Aatma-bodha/ *Knowledge of the Self*, a preliminary text by Adi Shankaracharya. आत्मबोध

Atmabodhakara /Aatma-bodhakara/ *Knowledge of the Self* according to Goraksha. आत्मबोधकर

Atma Chintana /Aatma Chintana/ introspection; reflection on the self or the atman. आत्म चिन्तन

Atma Drohin /Aatma Drohin/ self-deceiving; suicidal. आत्म द्रोहिन्

Atma Ghata /Aatma Ghaata/ slaughter of the self, suicide (physical or otherwise); worldliness; ignorance of the nature of

the self. आत्म घात

Atmahan /Aatmahan/ killers of the self; suicide. आत्महन्

Atmajna /Aatma-jna/ one who knows the self; seer with self-knowledge. आत्मज्ञ

Atma Jnana /Aatma Jnaana/ direct knowledge of the self; see Brahma Jnana. आत्म ज्ञान

Atma Krida /Aatma Kreedaa/ one who rejoices in one's own self. आत्म क्रीड़ा

Atma Labha /Aatma Laabha/ attaining realization of the self. आत्म लाभ

Atmanatmaviveka /Aatma-anaatma-viveka/ discrimination between the self and the not-self. आत्मानात्मविवेक

Atmanishtha /Aatma-nishtha/ one who constantly seeks for spiritual knowledge; established in the essential nature of the self. आत्मनिष्ठ

Atmanivedana /Aatma-nivedana/ dedicating one's entire self to the divine; self-surrender. आत्मनिवेदन

Atma Prakasha /Aatma Prakaasha/ the shining forth or light of the self. आत्म प्रकाश

Atma Priya /Aatma Priya/ beloved. आत्म प्रिय

Atma Puri /Aatma Puree/ city of the soul. आत्म पुरी

Atma Samyama Yoga /Aatma Samyama Yoga/ yoga of self-restraint. आत्म संयम योग

Atmashakti /Aatma-shakti/ one's own power or ability; inherent power. आत्मशक्ति

Atma Shatkam /Aatma Shatkam/ group of six verses written by Adi Shankaracharya describing the soul in the state of samadhi. आत्म षट्कम्

Atmashrayi /Aatma-aashrayee/ dependent on the self for existence. आत्माश्रयी

Atmashuddhi /Aatma-shuddhi/ inner purity. आत्मशुद्धि

Atmavatta /Aatma-vatta/ self-control, wisdom, self-possession. आत्मवत्ता

Atma Vibhuti /Aatma Vibhooti/ spiritual wealth consequent upon self-realization. आत्म विभूति

Atma Vichara /Aatma Vichaara/ enquiring into the self. आत्म विचार

Atmavid, Atmavit /Aatma-vid, Aatma-vit/ a wise person, sage, knower of the self. आत्मविद्, आत्मवित्

Atmavidya /Aatma-vidyaa/ knowledge of the inner self. आत्मविद्या

Atmavinigraha /Aatma-vinigraha/ self-control. आत्मविनिग्रह

Atmayoni /Aatma-yoni/ self-born; name of Brahma. आत्मयोनि

Atmic Triveni /Aatmika Trivenee/ Triveni is the place near Prayaga where the river Ganges (Ganga) joins the Yamuna and the underground Saraswati river. Ajna chakra is the atmic triveni where ida, pingala and sushumna nadis meet at the eyebrow centre, and meditation at this centre is the real bath for sannyasins and yogins; see Kumbhamela. आत्मिक त्रिवेणी

Atmiya /Aatmeeya/ one's own, belonging to oneself. आत्मीय

Atri name of one of the seven rishis, the father of Dattatreya. अत्रि

Atyanta /too much; extreme. अत्यन्त

Atyantabhava /Atyanta-abhaava/ complete non-existence; extreme unreality. अत्यन्ताभाव

Atyantika /Aatyantika/ final, ultimate. आत्यन्तिक

Atyantika Pralaya /Aatyantika Pralaya/ immediate liberation; liberation of the individual wherein there is complete annihilation of the phenomena subjectively. आत्यन्तिक प्रलय

Aum, Om universal mantra, in Patanjali's *Yoga Sutras*: repetition of Aum and meditation on its meaning is the practice resulting in union with Ishwara; in Vedanta, Aum is regarded as Shabda Brahman and as the seed of the Vedas; in *Mandukya Upanishad*, the 'A' of Aum is explained as the waking state of consciousness, the 'u' as the subconscious, the 'm' as the unconscious and the whole reverberation to represent the superconscioius state; see Om; Tryakshara ; see Jagrat; see Swapna; see Sushupti; see Turiya. ॐ

Aupasana /Aupaasana/ relating to household fire; a fire used for domestic worship. औपासन

Aurobindo see Aravinda. अरविन्द

Aushadhi /Aushaddhee/ a herb; particular extraction from a certain herb; a medicinal plant; one of the methods to attain samadhi enumerated by Patanjali in the *Yoga Sutras*. औषधि

Aushadhipati /Aushadhee-pati/ name of soma, the Lord of plants; a physician; the moon. औषधीपति

Aushadhi Yoga /Aushadhee Yoga/ yoga in which herbal preparations are administered to restore health. औषधी योग

Avaccheda /Avachchheda/ a part, portion; boundary, limit; separation. अवच्छेद

Avacchinna Chaitanya /Avachchhinna Chaitanya/ consciousness limited by adjuncts. अवच्छिन्न चैतन्य

Avachetana /Ava-chetana/ subconscious. अवचेतन

Avadhana /Avadhaana/ attention, devotion, care, carefulness. अवधान

Avadhuta /Avadhoota/ one who is free from all worldly attachments or mental illusions; an ascetic who has renounced the world and is usually naked; the sixth order of sannyasa; the highest state of asceticism or tapas; book containing the teaching of sage Dattatreya; see Sannyasa. अवधूत

Avahana /Aavaahana/ invocation using mantras so the deity manifests during the time of worship. आवाहन

Avarana /Aavarana/ covering, concealing; veil or covering which hides or excludes part of the reality; veil of ignorance. आवरण

Avarana Abhava /Aavarana Abhaava/ absence of the veil. आवरण अभाव

Avarana Bhanga /Aavarana Bhanga/ destruction of the veil of ignorance. आवरण भङ्ग

Avarana Shakti /Aavarana Shakti/ veiling power of maya; avidya in the individual; mental ignorance which veils the real nature of things; see Maya; see Vikshepa Shakti; see Asadavarana; see Abhavarana. आवरण शक्ति

Avarohana descending passage in the subtle body; descending spinal passage; counterpart of arohana. अवरोहण

Avastha /Avasthaa/ state of consciousness or condition of the mind; position; circumstances. अवस्था

Avasthana /Avasthaana/ standing; residing, dwelling; situation, position. अवस्थान

Avasthantargataprati /Avasthaa-antargatraprati/ state of the effect being resolved or involved into the cause. अवस्थान्तर्गतप्रति

Avasthasthiti /Avasthaa-sthiti/ permanent, abiding, changelessness. अवस्थास्थिति

Avasthatraya /Avasthaa-traya/ three states of consciousness: jagrata or waking, swapna or dream and sushupti or deep sleep. अवस्थात्रय

Avastu non-material, non-substance; nothing; without the characteristics of something bound by time and space; unsubstantial. अवस्तु

Avatara /Avataara/ descent, advent or incarnation of God. There are 10 avataras of Vishnu: Matsya (the fish), Kurma (the tortoise), Varaha (the boar), Narasimha (the man-lion), Vamana (the dwarf), Parashurama (Rama with an axe), Rama (hero of the epic *Ramayana*), Krishna (hero of the epic *Mahabharata* and teacher of Arjuna in the *Bhagavad Gita*), Buddha and Kalki; see Bhagavata. अवतार

Avekshanam looking towards or at, seeing; guarding, taking care of, attending to; supervision, inspection; attention, observation; regarding, considering. अवेक्षणम्

Avekshitavya to be observed attentively. अवेक्षितव्य

Avetri not-knower. अवेतृ

Avidya /Avidyaa/ ignorance; lack of conscious awareness; mistaking the non-eternal for the eternal; confined cognition; the chief of the five kleshas or sources of trouble and confusion described by Patanjali's *Yoga Sutras*. In Vedanta, it is a mistake that considers the non-eternal, impure, evil and non-atman to be eternal, pure, good and atman; illusion personified or Maya; one of the five restricting cloaks of maya; see Kanchuka; see Klesha. अविद्या

Avidya Nivritti /Avidyaa Nivritti/ removal of ignorance; liberation (moksha). अविद्या निवृत्ति

Avidya Samskara /Avidyaa Samskaara/ impression of basic ignorance. अविद्या संस्कार

Avikari /Avikaaree/ immutable Brahman. अविकारी

Avinashi /Avinaashee/ indestructible. अविनाशी

Avirati non-dispassion; incessant, continuity, uninterruptedness; sensual indulgence. अविरति

Avirodha consistency, compatibility. अविरोध

Avis /Aavis/ a particle meaning before the eyes, openly, evidently. आविस्

Avishkaranam /Aavishkaranam/ manifestation, making apparent or visible; innovation, invention. आविष्करणम्

Avishta /Aavishta/ entered; possessed (by an evil spirit); full of; overpowered, overcome. आविष्ट

Avrittachakshu /Aavritta-chakshu/ one whose gaze is turned inwards; introvertedness. आवृत्त चक्षु:

Avritti /Aavritti/ turning towards; return, coming back; recurrence or repetition in general; repetition of birth and death, worldly existence. आवृत्ति

Avyabhichara Bhakti /Avyabhichaara Bhakti/ unswerving devotion, steadfast in devotion. अव्यभिचार भक्ति

Avyabhicharin /Avyabhichaarin/ not going astray; unfailing; steady; permanent; faithful. अव्यभिचारिन्

Avyagra steady, cool, not agitated or ruffled; not engaged or occupied. अव्यग्र

Avyakta not manifest or apparent; uncreated; primary matter which has not yet entered into real existence; undeveloped; invisible, imperceptible; indistinct; inarticulate; undetermined; unknown. अव्यक्त

Avyaktadrishti view from the standpoint of the infinite; eternal whole. अव्यक्तदृष्टि

Avyaktam another name for Prakriti; in Sankhya philosophy, the primary germ of nature, the primordial element or productive principle from which all the phenomena of the material world are developed; see Sarvakarana. अव्यक्तम्

Avyakta Prakriti unmanifest nature. अव्यक्त प्रकृति

Avyavahara /Avyavahaara/ free from worldly activities or concern. अव्यवहार

Avyaya not liable to change, imperishable, immutable; eternal,

everlasting; Brahman, Vishnu. अव्यय

Ayam Atma Brahma /Ayam Aatmaa Brahma/ literally 'this soul is Brahman' or 'this self is the absolute', the great statement of the identity between the individual and supreme soul found in the *Mandukya Upanishad* of the *Atharva Veda*; see Maha Vakya. अयम् आत्मा ब्रह्म

Ayama /Aayaama/ length; expansion, extension; stretching; restraint, control, stopping. आयाम

Ayana movement; the sun's passage southward and northward from the tropics of Cancer and Capricorn. अयन

Ayukta not devoted or pious; inattentive; negligent; unfit; untrue; not a yogi. अयुक्त

Ayus /Aayus/ life, duration of life; vital power; food. आयुस्

Ayurveda /Aayurveda/ science of health or medicine, the vedic system of medical diagnosis and treatment. The two most ancient and outstanding authorities are Charaka and Sushruta; see Dosha. आयुर्वेद

Ayurvedic, Ayurvedin /Aayurvedika, Aayurvedin/ belonging to medicine; well-versed in medical science, a physician. आयुर्वेदिक, आयुर्वेदिन्

Ayurvriddhi /Aayurvriddhi/ long life, longevity. आयुर्वृद्धि

B

> **Pronunciation**
>
> ब् b – as in rub
> भ् bh – as in abhor

Badarayana /Baadaraayana/ founder of Vedanta philosophy as expounded in the *Shariraka Sutra,* also known as the *Brahma Sutra* or *Vedanta Sutra.* Some scholars contend that Badarayana is identical with Vyasa, the celebrated sage who is regarded as the original compiler and arranger of the Vedas and other portions of sacred Hindu literature. He is believed to be an incarnation of Vishnu; see Vyasa. बादरायण

Baddha bound, caught, restrained, tied. बद्ध

Badhita /Baadhita/ obstructed, refused, contradicted; oppressed. बाधित

Badrinath /Badreenaath/ also known as Valley of the Gods, a high altitude valley in the Himalayas where Jyotirmatha is situated; see Jyotirmatha. बद्रीनाथ

Bahir outside, external. बहिर्

  Bahiranga external stage. बहिरङ्ग

  Bahiranga Lakhsya concentration upon an external object or point in space. बहिरङ्ग लक्ष्य

  Bahiranga Sadhana /Bahiranga Saadhanaa/ the first stages of yoga: yama, niyama, asana and pranayama are the outward quest and keep the seeker in harmony with the community and nature; see Ashtanga Yoga. बहिरङ्ग साधना

Bahirkumbhaka external breath retention; see Kumbhaka. बहिकुम्भक

Bahirmukha external, extrovert. बहिर्मुख

  Bahirmukha Vritti the outgoing mode or tendency of the mind. बहिर्मुख वृत्ति

Bahirprajna /Bahir-prajnaa/ objective consciousness as in the waking state. बहिर्प्रज्ञा

Bahirvritti Nigraha restraint of the outgoing waves of the mind. बबहिर्वृत्ति निग्रह

Bahishkrita /Bahir-krita/ outcast; a form of antar dhauti in which the belly is filled with air, which is retained for an hour and a half and then sent downwards, ejecting and diluting stale and toxic gases trapped in the system; see Shatkarma. बहिष्कृत

Bahu many; great, enormous. बहु

  Bahudaka /Bahoodaka/ (Bahu-udaka); supported by many; second stage of sannyasa; literally 'having much water'; a mendicant who begs for food at a bathing ghat; see Sannyasa. बहूदक

  Bahusyam /Bahusyaam/ literally 'may I be many', enunciated by Brahman in the Vedas explain-

ing the cause of creation; see
Ekoham Bahusyam. बहुस्याम्

Bahutva plurality. बहुत्व

Bahuvirya /Bahu-veerya/ enormous power. बहुवीर्य

Bahya /Baahya/ external. बाह्य

Bahya Karana /Baahya Karana/
outer instrument, e.g. eye, ear
etc.; external sense organ. बाह्य करण

Bahya Kumbhaka /Baahya
Kumbhaka/ suspension of breath
after full exhalation; see Kumbhaka. बाह्य कुम्भक

Bahya Vishaya Pratyaksha
/Baahya Vishaya Pratyaksha/ external objective perception; direct cognition of sense object. बाह्य
विषय प्रत्यक्ष

Bahya Vritti Pranayama /Baahya
Vritti Praanaayaama/ the variety
of pranayama in which the breath
is forcefully exhaled and the
lungs are held for a time at their
lowest minimal air capacity. बाह्य
वृत्ति प्राणायाम

Baidyanath Dham see Vaidyanath
Dham. बैद्यनाथ धाम

Baikhari see Vaikhari. बैखरी

Baka type of heron or crane; hypo-
crite. बक

Bala /Baala/ young, child; boy. बाल

Balakriya /Baala-kriyaa/ activities
or conduct of children. बालक्रिया

Bala strength, power; violence,
force; army troops. बल

Balarama /Balaraama/ brother of
Lord Krishna, known for his

courage, and said to be an incarnation of Lakshmana. बलराम

Bali /Baali/ a celebrated monkey
chief and a very powerful monkey, who even placed Ravana under his armpit when they fought.
During his absence from Kish-
kindha while slaying the brother
of Dundubhi, his younger brother
Sugriva usurped his throne, considering him to be dead. When
Bali returned, Sugriva had to flee
and his wife was seized by Bali.
Sugriva sought Lord Rama's aid
and she was returned to her husband when Rama slew Bali. बालि

Bali an oblation. बलि

Baliyajna an oblation; the offering of necessary things to all creatures of the Lord. बलियज्ञ

Bali, Mahabali /Bali, Mahaa-bali/
son of Virochana, and a very powerful demon. Even the gods
(devas) were afraid of him since
he had acquired the power of
Indra. Kashyapa and Aditi, of
whom all the gods were offspring,
prayed to Vishnu for succour.
Vishnu descended on earth as
their son in the form of a dwarf
(Vamana), assumed the garb of a
mendicant, went to Bali and
asked for as much earth as he
could cover in three steps. Bali
was also the grandson of Prahlada
who was noted for his liberality,
and did not hesitate to fulfil this
apparently simple request. The
dwarf, however, soon assumed a
mighty form. His first step covered the earth, the second the
heavens, and not knowing where
to place the third, he planted it

on Bali's head. This blessing sent Bali and all his legions to Patala, allowing him to be its ruler; see Trivikrama; see Vamana; see Avatara. बलि, महाबलि

Bandha binding, tying; connection, union; psycho-muscular energy locks which close the pranic exits (like throat, anus, etc.); psychic locks that concentrate the flow of energy in the body at one point or plexus; postural contraction of the body; see Jalandhara Bandha; see Uddiyana Bandha; see Moolabandha; see Maha Bandha; see Mudra. बन्ध

Bandha Moksha bondage and liberation. बन्ध मोक्ष

Bansuri /Baansuree/ flute (the instrument most favoured by Lord Krishna); in nada yoga, hearing flute-like sounds internally indicates attainment of a higher state of consciousness. बाँसुरी

Basant see Vasanta. बसन्त

Basti, Vasti method of cleaning the intestines; yogic enema; a kriya by which abdominal activities are made to function better; one of the six hatha yoga techniques to purify and develop the body; see Shatkarma. बस्ति, वस्ति

Batuh a boy initiated by the upanaya ceremony. बटु

Bel see Bilva. बेल

Bhadra gracious, gentle; blessed, auspicious, fortunate; beautiful lover or husband. भद्र

Bhadrapada /Bhaadrapada/ sixth lunar month of the Hindu almanac, corresponding to August/September; see Varsha; see Masa; see Ritu. भाद्रपद

Bhaga /Bhaaga/ part, constituent. भाग

Bhaga Tyaga /Bhaaga Tyaaga/ logical method to establish the identity of jiva (individual state of consciousness or existence) and God (universal state of existence) by partly abandoning their surface attributes. भाग त्याग

Bhaga affluence, prosperity; fame, glory; beauty; excellence; lord. भग

Bhagavad Gita /Bhagavad Geetaa/ 'divine song', Lord Krishna's discourse to Arjuna delivered on the battlefield of Kurukshetra during the great Mahabharata war, it is one of the source books of Hindu philosophy, containing the essence of the Upanishads and yoga; see Prasthanatraya; see Sthitaprajna; see Mahabharata. भगवद् गीता

Bhagavan /Bhagavaan/ illustrious one; God, deity; an epithet of Vishnu, Shiva, Jina, Buddha etc. भगवान्

Bhagavata /Bhaagavata/ name of a sacred text dealing with the doctrines of creation and the sport or play (lila) of Bhagavan Vishnu in all his incarnations; see Puranam. भागवत

Bhagya /Bhaagya/ relating to destiny, fate; good fortune, welfare; entitled to share. भाग्य

Bhaiksha living on alms, begging, mendicancy. भैक्ष

Bhairava state of consciousness which precedes the ultimate experience of universal consciousness or Shiva; an order or tradition; name of Lord Shiva in his fierce aspect; derived from the root 'ravayati', which literally means 'to howl' or 'to wail', hence the vehicle of Bhairava is a dog; the cry of separation from universal consciousness which is almost within the aspirant's reach; experience of intoxicated bliss. भैरव

Bhairavi /Bhairavee/ female counterpart or shakti of Bhairava. भैरवी

Bhaja Govindam literally 'seek Govinda', a spontaneously composed song which is also a philosophical text by Adi Shankaracharya; also known as Mohamudgar; see Govinda. भज गोविन्दम्

Bhajana devotional song, praise, hymn; adoration, worship. भजन

Bhakta devotee. भक्त

Bhakti complete devotion to the higher reality of life; love for all beings; devotion as service; chanelling of emotion to a higher force. भक्ति

Bhakti Darshanam process of seeing, knowing and realizing the self through devotion to a higher principle of life. भक्ति दर्शनम्

Bhakti Marga /Bhakti Maarga/ the way or path to realization through adoration of a personal God; a higher principle of love expressed in positive actions. भक्ति मार्ग

Bhakti Yoga yoga of devotion, channelling emotiional energy to a higher reality of life; a systematic path with nine steps or stages expanding, strengthening and purifying the emotions. भक्ति योग

Bhaktiyoga (Bhakti-yoga); 'yoga of devotion', the 12th chapter of the *Bhagavad Gita* in which Arjuna asks if it is better to worship God with or without form. Lord Krishna explains that both are good, although worship of God with form is easier for embodied beings, and lists the qualities any devotee needs to become the beloved of God. भक्तियोग

Bhala /Bhaala/ forehead, brow; splendour, lustre. भाल

Bhalu /Bhaalu/ the sun. भालु

Bhamini /Bhaminee/ a beautiful young woman. भामिनी

Bhana /Bhaana/ manifestation, appearance. भान

Bhandara /Bhandaara/ storehouse. भण्डार

Bhanga /Bhaanga/ intoxicating drink prepared from hemp. भाङ्ग

Bhanga breaking, shattering, tearing down; interruption; obstacle; disturbance. भङ्ग

Bhanu /Bhaanu/ light, lustre; the sun. भानु

Bharadvaja /Bharadvaaja/ the sage to whom Yajnavalkya related the story of Rama in Tulsidas' *Ramacharitamanas*; father of Drona, the military preceptor of the Kauravas and Pandavas. भरद्वाज

Bharata /Bhaarata/ the original name of India, the 'land engulfed in light'; descended from the Bharatas. भारत

Bharata name of the son of Dushyanta and Shakuntala, who became a universal monarch. India was called Bharata after him; name of an ancient sage reputed to have been the founder of the science of music and dramaturgy. भरत

Bharati /Bhaaratee/ female descendant of Bharata; without bondage; adept in Brahma vidya; an incarnation of the goddess Saraswati and the wife of Mandana Mishra whom Adi Shankaracharya defeated in a debate; the name of one of the 10 orders of sannyasins founded by Adi Shankaracharya; see Dashnami Sampradaya; see Ubhaya Bharati; see Sureshwara. भारती

Bhasa /Bhaasa/ light, lustre; name of a poet. भास

Bhasha /Bhaashaa/ speech, language; dialect. भाषा

Bhaskara /Bhaaskara/ making light, shining; the sun. भास्कर

Bhasma ash from a sacrificial fire; sacred ash smeared on the body. भस्म

Bhasma Nishtha /Bhasma Nishthaa/ one who loves bhasma. भस्म निष्ठा

Bhastra /Bhastraa/ bellows used to fan a fire; leather bottle. भस्त्रा

Bhastrika Pranayama /Bhastrikaa Praanaayaama/ 'bellows breathing', a pranayama where air is forcibly drawn in and out as in a blacksmith's bellows. भस्त्रिका प्राणायाम

Bhati /Bhaati/ light, splendour; perception or knowledge; to shine. भाति

Bhautika pertaining to, or composed of elements; material, physical; belonging to created or living beings. भौतिक

Bhava /Bhaava/ becoming, being, existence; feeling; love; condition; state, inclination or disposition of mind. भाव

Bhava Advaita /Bhaava Advaita/ unity in feeling. भाव अद्वैत

Bhavanartha /Bhaavanaartha/ the mental state or awareness for developing a state of samadhi. भावनार्थ

Bhavana Shakti /Bhaavanaa Shakti/ power of imagination. भावना शक्ति

Bhava Samadhi /Bhaava Samaadhi/ absorption in meditation due to emotional cause, e.g. kirtan; superconscious state of existence attained by intense emotion. भाव समाधि

Bhava birth, production, worldly existence or worldly life. भव

Bhava Padartha /Bhava Padaartha/ a thing that exists. भव पदार्थ

Bhavapashavimukti /Bhava-paasha-vimukti/ state of liberation; according to *Goraksha Shatakam*, it is the goal of human life. भवपाशविमुक्ति

Bhava Rupa /Bhava Roopa/ positive nature of factual being. भवरूप

Bhava Sagara /Bhava Saagara/ literally 'ocean of becoming'; the world of change; the world is always in a state of flux and knows no rest whereas the true aim of human life is said to be the realization of peace. भव सागर

Bhaya second basic instinct, fear; fear of death; see Pravritih; see Klesha. भय

Bheda pass through, pierce; differentiate; purify. भेद

Bhedabheda /Bheda-abheda/ unity in difference; a particular line of approach to the supreme reality in which unity and multiplicity are intermingled; state of oneness that is not pure and has in it the appearance of multiplicity. भेदाभेद

Bheda Buddhi the intellect that creates differences; the relative (vyavaharika) buddhi that diversifies everything as opposed to the absolute (paramarthika) buddhi that unifies everything. भेद बुद्धि

Bhedahamkara /Bheda-ahamkaara/ the differentiating ego, the sense of separateness. भेदाहङ्कार

Bheda Jnana /Bheda Jnaana/ consciousness of difference; worldly consciousness. भेद ज्ञान

Bhedana to pierce; breaking through, passing through; to discriminate, differentiate. भेदन

Bheka frog; timid person. भेक

Bhiksha /Bhikshaa/ alms; offerings. भिक्षा

Bhikshu beggar, mendicant, monk. भिक्षु

Bhima /Bheema/ the second Pandava, son of Vayu and Kunti; younger brother of Hanuman; fearful, formidable. भीम

Bhima Nada /Bheema Naada/ terrific sound; sending forth a sound; lion; name of one of the seven clouds at the destruction of the world. भीम नाद

Bhimasena /Bheemasena/ one-man army; another name of Bhima. भीमसेन

Bhoga experience and craving for pleasure; enjoyment, delight; object of pleasure; food; festival. भोग

Bhogabhumi /Bhoga-bhoomi/ land of experience or enjoyment; see Karmabhumi. भोगभूमि

Bhogya object of experience or enjoyment. भोग्य

Bhojanam food offered to a guest. भोजनम्

Bhokta /Bhoktaa/ one who enjoys. भोक्ता

Bhoktritva enjoyership; see Kartritva. भोक्तृत्व

Bhoochari Mudra see Bhuchari Mudra. भूचरी मुद्रा

Bhoota see Bhuta. भूत

Bhrama illusion, delusion, confusion, error; circular motion, a whirlpool; wandering. भ्रम

Bhramati move to and fro, wander about, flutter; be confused or agitated; to err. भ्रमति

Bhramara a bee, a large black bee. भ्रमर

Bhramara Keelaka wasp, the 24th guru of Dattatreya. भ्रमर कीलक

Bhramari Pranayama /Bhraamaree Praanaayaama/ 'humming of bees'; tranquillizing pranayama in which the ears are plugged and a deep soft sound like the humming of bees is made. भ्रामरी प्राणायाम

Bhramsha a definite fall from the principles of yoga or spiritual life. भ्रंश

Bhranti /Bhraanti/ wandering; confusion; mistake; false idea or impression, wrong notion, delusion. भ्रान्ति

Bhrantidarshana /Bhraanti-darshana/ mistaken notion. भ्रान्तिदर्शन

Bhrantija /Bhraanti-ja/ born of delusion or misconception. भ्रान्तिज

Bhrantimatra /Bhraanti-maatra/ mere illusion or delusion. भ्रान्तिमात्र

Bhrantisukha /Bhraanti-sukha/ illusory pleasure, deluding happiness. भ्रान्तिसुख

Bhrasta /Bhrashta/ fallen from the way of yoga or spiritual life. भ्रष्ट

Bhru /Bhroo/ eyebrow. भ्रू

Bhrukuti space between the eyebrows. भ्रूकुटि

Bhrumadhya /Bhroo-madhya/ trigger point for ajna chakra located at the eyebrow centre. भ्रूमध्य

Bhrumadhya Dristhi /Bhroomadhya Dristhi/ a form of concentrated gazing (trataka) in which the attention is fixed between the eyebrows. भ्रूमध्य दृष्टि

Bhu /Bhoo/ earth. भू

Bhuchari Mudra /Bhoocharee Mudraa/ gazing at the invisible point left when the fourth finger is removed from its position at the nosetip. This tranquillizing mudra induces pratyahara, culminating in awakening ida nadi signalled by a vision of blue light; gazing at the ground, looking into the earth; see Mudra. भूचरी मुद्रा

Bhu Devi /Bhoo Devee/ earth goddess. भू देवी

Bhuh Loka /Bhooh Loka/ terrestrial plane of existence, also called jiva loka; see Loka. भू: लोक

Bhumi /Bhoomi/ the earth, ground, place; degree; situation. भूमि

Bhuman Earth, world; all existing things. भूमन

Bhumika /Bhoomikaa/ step or stage; state; degree; a preface or introduction to a book. भूमिका

Bhu Samadhi /Bhoo Samaadhi/ suspension of breath (kumbhaka) where all vital functions appear to have ceased. भू समाधि

Bhuja arm, hand; trunk of an elephant; bough. भुज

Bhuja Pida /Bhuja Peedaa/ pressure on the arm or shoulder. भुज पीड़ा

Bhujanga a serpent, a snake. भुजङ्ग

Bhukti material enjoyment. भुक्ति

Bhuma /Bhooma/ the unconditioned; infinite; Brahman. भूम

Bhunakti eat; enjoy (also carnally); possess (the land); rule; reap (the fruits of deeds); suffer. भुनक्ति

Bhupura /Bhoopura/ the outer square and protective force of a yantra. भूपुर

Bhuta /Bhoota/ existing, real; an element or elemental; state of existence, being; what has come into being; an entity as opposed to the unmanifested; any of the five elementary constituents of the universe: earth, water, fire, air, space; see Mahabhuta. भूत

Bhutadi /Bhootaadi/ (Bhoota-aadi); the tamasic manifestation of ahamkara; according to the *Vishnu Purana*, the attachment to worldly life based on the bhuta is born out of ignorance. भूतादि

Bhutajanya /Bhoota-janya/ born of the elements. भूतजन्य

Bhutajaya /Bhoota-jaya/ conquest over the elements or the body. भूतजय

Bhuta Loka /Bhoota Loka/ the world of primordial matter. भूत लोक

Bhutamatra /Bhoota-maatra/ created beings. भूतमात्र

Bhutapati /Bhoota-pati/ the Lord of beings; name of Shiva. भूतपति

Bhutashakti /Bhoota-shakti/ power in matter; subtle material elements; permanent atoms. भूतशक्ति

Bhutashuddhi /Bhoota-shuddhi/ purification of the elements of the body. भूतशुद्धि

Bhuta Siddhi /Bhoota Siddhi/ control over all states of matter (elements, entities, bodies). भूत सिद्धि

Bhutatanmatra /Bhoota-tanmatraa/ the root elements of matter; see Tanmatra. भूततन्मात्रा

Bhutatma /Bhoota-atmaa/ the lower self. भूतात्मा

Bhuta Yajna /Bhoota Yajna/ an oblation or offering to all created beings; see Pancha Maha-yajna. भूत यज्ञ

Bhuta Bhavishya Vartamana /Bhoota Bhavishya Vartamaana/ past, present and future. भूत भविष्य वर्तमान

Bhuti /Bhooti/ power, might; prosperity, welfare; ornament; being, existence. भूति

Bhuva the higher etheric or astral world. भुव

Bhuvah Loka, Bhuvarloka intermediate realm between earth and heaven, astral plane of existence; see Loka. भुव:लोक, भुवर्लोक

Bhuvana a being; mankind; world, earth; abode, residence. भुवन

Bija /Beeja/ seed, source; origin. बीज

Bija Mantra /Beeja Mantra/ seed sound, repeated mentally, the seed thus planted in the mind germinates into one-pointedness; a basic mantra or vibration; sacred syllable. बीज मन्त्र

Bijakshara /Beeja-akshara/ the root letter or seed letter which contains the latent power of the mantra. बीजाक्षर

Bilam a hole, cavity, burrow; gap, pit; aperture, opening, outlet; bowl of a spoon or ladle. बिलम्

Bilva a tree sacred to Shiva, its fruit aid digestion, its leaves help alleviate diabetes and it promotes virility and fertility, used in tantric rituals for Shiva and Devi. The *Atharva Veda* states its wood is so sacred it should not be burned. बिल्व

Bimba disc (of the moon); orb, globe; mirror, reflection, image; fruit of a gourd called mimordica monadelpha. बिम्ब

Bindu point; dot denoting the 'n' or 'm' vowel sounds in Sanskrit;

seed, source, drop; the basis from which emanated the first principle (maha tattwa) according to the tantra shastra; psychic centre located in the brain; the most important psychic centre in nada yoga; top of the head, where Hindu brahmins wear their tuft of hair; semen. बिन्दु

Bindu Visarga literally the drop of specially secreted fluid at the top back of the head; centre or source of individual creation from where psychic vibrations first emanate; the flow of bindu; see Visarga. बिन्दु विसर्ग

Bodha, Bodhi spiritual wisdom, knowledge, intelligence; awakening. बोध, बोधि

Bodhaikata /Bodhaikataa/ (Bodha-ekataa); oneness of consciousness. बोधैकता

Bodhisattwa /Bodhi-sattva/ one whose essence is perfect knowledge; one who does not leave the body after reaching nirvana, but waits in order to serve and help mankind. बोधिसत्त्व

Brahma, Brahman /Brahmaa, Brahman/ 1. God as creator, one of the trinity of Brahma, Vishnu, and Maheshwara (or Shiva); 2. Hiranyagarbha or cosmic intelligence; eternal, omnipresent principle of existence or ultimate reality. The all-pervading 'some-thing' or 'nothing' from which all time, space and creatures are uninterruptedly being created. According to Vedantins, Brahman is both the efficient (nimitta) and the material (upadana) cause of the visible universe, from which all manifest things are produced and into which they are absorbed; 3. the sacred and mystic syllable Aum (Om); 4. the Vedas; see Aum; see Veda; see Bahusyam; see Anantapadmanabha. ब्रह्मा, ब्रह्मन्

Brahmaksharayoga /Brahma-akshara-yoga / 'yoga of the imperishable consciousness', another name for the eighth chapter of the *Bhagavad Gita*; see Aksharabrahmayoga. ब्रह्माक्षरयोग

Brahma Chakra lowermost psychic centre in the spinal column, more often called mooladhara chakra. ब्रह्म चक्र

Brahmacharin /Brahmachaarin/ one who is constantly revelling in Brahman (reflecting on the pure self, the supreme state of existence); student vowed to celibacy and continence; a person in the first quarter of life; see Ashrama. ब्रह्मचारिन्

Brahmacharya conduct suitable for proceeding to the highest state of existence, especially continence or absolute control of sensual impulses. One of the yamas described by Patanjali in the *Yoga Sutras* as resulting in indomitable courage (virya); see Yama. ब्रह्मचर्य

Brahmacharya Ashrama /Brahmacharya Aashrama/ first

stage of life up to 25 years according to the ancient vedic tradition, devoted to study and learning; see Ashrama. ब्रह्मचर्य आश्रम

Brahma Chintana constant meditation on Brahman. ब्रह्म चिन्तन

Brahma Dhyana /Brahma Dhyaana/ meditation on the concept of Brahman. ब्रह्म ध्यान

Brahmadhyasa /Brahma-adhyaasa/ meditating, reflecting, or conversing on Brahman; study of the Vedas, etc. aimed at realization of Brahman; see Nididhyasana. ब्रह्माध्यास

Brahmadvara /Brahma-dvaara/ the door or gate of Brahma, where kundalini enters sushumna nadi; see Sushumna Nadi. ब्रह्मद्वार

Brahmagola the universe. ब्रह्मगोल

Brahma Granthi the psychic/muscular 'knot' of creation, situated in mooladhara chakra, symbolizing material and sensual attachment. It is the knot of ignorance (avidya), desire (kama) and action (karma); see Granthi. ब्रह्म ग्रन्थि

Brahma Jnana /Brahma Jnaana/ realization or immediate knowledge of Brahman. ब्रह्म ज्ञान

Brahmakaravritti /Brahmaakaara-vritti/ the flow of mind towards Brahman; identifying with the supreme to the exclusion of all other thoughts. ब्रह्माकारवृत्ति

Brahma Loka the world of Brahma; also called satya loka; see Loka. ब्रह्म लोक

Brahma Mimamsa /Brahma Meemaamsaa/ another name for Uttara Mimamsa. ब्रह्म मीमांसा

Brahma Muhurta /Brahma Muhoorta/ the two hours around sunrise (in India between 4 a.m. and 6 a.m.) best suited to yoga sadhana; see Sandhya. ब्रह्म मुहूर्त

Brahmana /Braahmana/ of the priestly caste; a person whose life is dedicated to the study of the Vedas and dispensation of the knowledge of Brahman and is thus qualified to act as a priest in vedic rituals; one of the four guilds or divisions of the caste system in India; integral part of the Vedas which elucidates the path of ritual to be followed by householders and explains the meaning and use of vedic hymns; see Varna; see Yaju; see Veda. ब्राह्मण

Brahma Nadi /Brahma Naadee/ subtlest and innermost of the three energy or pranic flows within sushumna nadi through which kundalini ascends; another name for sushumna nadi; energy current that flows through the spinal canal according to hatha yoga. ब्रह्म नाड़ी

Brahmananda /Brahma-aananda/ bliss of the infinite absolute; supreme transcendental joy. ब्रह्मानन्द

Brahmanda /Brahma-anda/ literally 'Brahma's egg', the cosmic egg, the macrocosmos. ब्रह्माण्ड

Brahmanishtha one who is established in the direct knowledge of Brahman. ब्रह्मनिष्ठ

Brahmanubhava /Brahma-anubhava/ self-realization; absolute experience. ब्रह्मानुभव

Brahmanya Prana /Braahmanya Praana/ the cosmic breath. ब्राह्मण्य प्राण

Brahmaprapti /Brahma-praapti/ absorption into the supreme state of existence. ब्रह्मप्राप्ति

Brahmapuranam /Brahma-puraanam/ name of one of the group of 18 Puranas (ancient scriptures); see Puranam. ब्रह्मपुराणम्

Brahmarandhra crown of the head; fontanelle; opening in the crown of the head, through which the soul is said to escape on leaving the body. ब्रह्मरन्ध्र

Brahmarshi /Brahma-rishi/ a member of the priestly caste (brahmana) who has attained realization; a sage. ब्रह्मर्षि

Brahmasamstha grounded in Brahman; sannyasin. ब्रह्मसंस्थ

Brahmashrotriya one who has knowledge of the Vedas and the Upanishads. ब्रह्मश्रोत्रिय

Brahmasthiti being established or dwelling in Brahman. ब्रह्मस्थिति

Brahma Sutras /Brahma Sootras/ classical vedantic scriptures written by Vyasa and commented upon by Adi Shankaracharya in his *Brahma Sutra Bhashya*; see Prasthanatraya. ब्रह्म सूत्र

Brahmatejas the effulgent splendour of Brahman. ब्रह्मतेजस्

Brahmavadin /Brahma-vaadin/ discoursing on sacred texts; con-

noisseur of vedic texts. ब्रह्मवादिन्

Brahma Varchasa magnetic brahmic aura; divine glory or splendour. ब्रह्म वर्चस

Brahma Vidya /Brahma Vidyaa/ science of the self; knowledge of Brahman (the supreme existence); study to attain real knowledge; see Angiras. ब्रह्म विद्या

Brahma, Vishnu, Shiva the three aspects of the divine personality associated with creation, preservation and dissolution of the universe; the Hindu trinity; see Trimurti. ब्रह्मा, विष्णु, शिव

Brahmavit literally 'one who knows Brahman'; in Vedanta the name of one who has reached the fourth state of wisdom (jnana bhumika); see Sattwapatti. ब्रह्मवित्

Brahmavidvara (Brahmavit-vara); in Vedanta the name of one who has reached the fifth state of wisdom (jnana bhumika); see Asamshakti. ब्रह्मविद्वर

Brahmavidvarishtha (Brahmavit-varishtha); in Vedanta the name of one who has attained the seventh state of wisdom (jnana bhumika); see Turiya; see Jivanmukta. ब्रह्मविद्वरिष्ठ

Brahmavidvariya /Brahmavidvareeya/ (Brahmavit-vareeya); in Vedanta the name of one who has attained the sixth state of wisdom (jnana bhumika); see Padarthabhavana. ब्रह्मविद्वरीय

Brahma Yajna teaching and reciting the Vedas, one of the five daily sacrifices to be performed by a householder, also called Rishi yajna; see Pancha Mahayajna; see Brahmana. ब्रह्म यज्ञ

Brahma Yoga wherein one finds oneself and the whole universe as Brahman. ब्रह्म योग

Brahmin see Brahmana. ब्राह्मिण

Brahmi Sthiti /Braahmee Sthiti/ state of God-realization; the fixed, unchanging, expansive, self-aware state. ब्राह्मी स्थिति

Brahmi Vritti /Braahmee Vritti/ aklishta (not painful) vritti that leads to identification with the drashta (witnessing consciousness or Brahman); spiritual aspect of the vrittis, the self-aware, individual consciousness; see Chitta Vritti. ब्राह्मी वृत्ति

Brahmopasana /Brahmopaasanaa/ (Brahma-upaasanaa); study of the Vedas. ब्रह्मोपासना

Brihaspati guru of the gods; the planet Jupiter; ajna chakra. बृहस्पति

Brihat large, big, absolute. बृहत्

Brihadaranyaka /Brihadaaranyaka/ (Brihat-aaranyaka); literally 'the great teaching from the forest'; name of an Upanishad from the *Shatapatha Brahmana* of the *Yajurveda*. It discusses the identity of the individual atma (soul) in relation to the universal self, different modes of worship, religion and meditation; see Aham Brahmasmi. बृहदारण्यक

Brihat Brahmanda /Brihat Brahmaanda/ great macrocosmos. बृहत् ब्रह्माण्ड

Brihattva vastness, largeness, absoluteness. बृहत्व

Brindavan see Vrindavana. बृन्दावन

Budh to be aware of, to know; intellect, reason, discrimination, judgement, knowledge, opinion, intention; the higher intelligence concerned with wisdom. बुध

Buddha the enlightened one; see Nirvana; see Shunyavada; see Vijnana Pada; see Vishuddhi Marga. बुद्ध

Buddhi discerning, discriminating aspect of mind; the faculty of valuing things for the advancement of life; principle of universal intuition in which the meditator becomes joined in the super-reflective state of samadhi; a faculty which enhances discriminative power; see Bheda Buddhi. बुद्धि

Buddhi Shakti intellectual power. बुद्धि शक्ति

Buddhi Shuddhi purity of intellect. बुद्धि शुद्धि

Buddhi Tattwa /Buddhi Tattva/ principle of intelligence. बुद्धि तत्त्व

Buddhi Vyapara /Buddhi Vyaapaara/ functioning of the intellect. बुद्धि व्यापार

Buddhi Yoga the practice of wisdom in living. बुद्धि योग

C

Pronunciation
च् ch – as in check
छ् chh – as in churchhill

Chadanam /Chhaadanam/ a cover, concealing screen; a leaf; clothing. छादनम्

Chaitanya the consciousness that knows itself and knows others; absolute consciousness; consciousness, mind, intelligence, spirit. चैतन्य

Chaitanya Jyoti eternal flame of spirit. चैतन्य ज्योति

Chaitanya Mahaprabhu /Chaitanya Mahaaprabhu/ India's inspired bhakta (devotee) from Bengal. चैतन्य महाप्रभु

Chaitanya Purusha one who has attained the state of spiritual consciousness. चैतन्य पुरुष

Chaitanya Samadhi /Chaitanya Samaadhi/ the state of superconsciousness marked by absolute self-awareness and illumination, as distinct from jada samadhi, in which there is no such awareness. चैतन्य समाधि

Chaitra first lunar month of the year according to the Hindu almanac, containing the Chaitra Navaratri festival. Corresponds to March/April; see Vasanta; see Masa; see Navaratri. चैत्र

Chakora a bird like a partridge, said to feed on moon-beams. चकोर

Chakra wheel or vortex; centre of energy or psychic centre; confluence point of energy flows (nadis). The main chakras threaded in the region of the spinal column on the sushumna nadi relate to many levels of the human being. On a physical level the main areas of influence are: mooladhara chakra, pelvic plexus; swadhisthana chakra, coccygeal plexus; manipura chakra, solar plexus; anahata chakra, cardiac plexus; vishuddhi chakra, pharyngeal plexus, also connected with the thyroid gland; and ajna chakra, plexus of command at the top of the spinal column, also connected with the pineal gland. Bindu visarga, sometimes known as bindu chakra, is at the top of the back of the head. Sahasrara chakra, the 1000-petalled lotus, is the upper cerebral centre connected with the pituitary gland. The chakras are subtle and not easily cognizable. Though they interact with the various plexi and glands, it should not be assumed that these alone are the chakras. Of the 28 planes of consciousness or regions, the highest seven are called loka, the next seven are chakra, the next seven patalam and the lowest seven naraka; see Loka; see Patalam;

see Naraka. चक्र

Chakra Sharira /Chakra Shareera/ body of the chakras. चक्र शरीर

Chakra Shuddhi purification of the psychic centres. चक्र शुद्धि

Chakrayudha /Chakra-aayudha/ the weapon or discus of Vishnu or Krishna named Sudarshana. चक्रायुध

Chakshus eye, one of the five organs of knowledge (jnanendriya); sight; light; lustre; see Devata. चक्षुस्

Chala /Chhala/ fraud, deceit, pretext, guise. छल

Chamatkara /Chamatkaara/ admiration; surprise; show, spectacle. चमत्कार

Chanchala unsteady; moving; shaking, trembling, tremulous; inconstant. चञ्चल

Chanchalatva fickleness; tossing of the mind. चञ्चलत्व

Chanchalavritti natural wavering tendency of the mind. चञ्चलवृत्ति

Chanda fierce; violent; passionate, angry, wrathful; passionate. चण्ड

Chandala /Chaandaala/ untouchable, an outcast. चाण्डाल

Chandana sandalwood tree associated with divine qualities of fragrance and coolness. चन्दन

Chandas /Chhandas/ delight, pleasure; desire, wish; free will, wilful conduct; meaning, intention; fraud; holy song; metre; prosody; the science of the sacred texts auxiliary to the vedic hymns, it deals with the arrangements of the consonants into the words of mantras, words into lines and lines into lyrics, and is regarded as one of the six vedangas; see Vedanga. छन्दस्

Chandasa /Chhaandasa/ a person familiar with vedic texts. छान्दस

Chandoga /Chhandoga/ chanter of holy songs. छन्दोग

Chandogya Upanishad /Chhaandogya Upanishad/ name of an Upanishad from the *Sama Veda* teaching the origin and significance of the mantra Aum; see Tat Twam Asi. छान्दोग्य उपनिषद्

Chandi /Chandee/ a manifestation of Durga, Chandi is invincible in battle against demonic forces; see Durga Saptashati. चण्डी

Chandisthan /Chandeesthaana/ (Chandee-sthaana); 'the place of Chandi'; an ancient shaktipeeth on the banks of the Ganga in today's Munger district, where the 'eye' of Sati is worshipped. When his wife, Sati, died, Shiva became wild with grief and carried her body around India. Various parts fell in different places, where shaktipeeth are presently established. In Chandhisthan, her eye is worshipped. It is said Chandi was worshipped at Chandisthan by the emperor Karna. From a neighbouring hill, he would then distribute his weight in gold to the people; see Karna. चण्डीस्थान

Chandi Yajna /Chandee Yajna/ a sacrifice performed in honour of the goddess Chandi, at which the *Durga Saptashati* is chanted; see Durga; see Shata Chandi Maha Yajna. चण्डी यज्ञ

Chandra moon; shining, bright; representing mental energy. चन्द्र

Chandra Bheda Pranayama
/Chandra Bheda Praanaayaama/
pranayama that pierces and purifies ida nadi. चन्द्र भेद प्राणायाम
Chandragupta name of a king.
चन्द्रगुप्त
Chandra Nadi /Chandra Nadee/
pranic current connected with the
left nostril and the lunar force,
another name for ida nadi. चन्द्र
नाड़ी
Chandrayana Vrata
/Chaandraayana Vrata/ an observance which begins with 15
morsels of food being consumed
on a full moon day, decreasing
by one morsel daily, until no food
is taken on new moon day, then
again increasing by one daily,
until 15 morsels of food are consumed on a full moon day. चान्द्रायण
व्रत
Chapalata /Chapalataa/ activity;
craving; fickleness. चपलता
Charu a preparation of boiled rice,
milk, sugar and ghee offered into
the fire for gods; a sattwic regi-
men usually undertaken by yoga
practitioners and celibates. चरु
Charvaka /Chaarvaaka/ a system of
Indian philosophy that accepts
only perceivable phenomena as
valid. It is named after Charvaka,
a materialistic philosopher said
to have been a pupil of Brihaspati, the guru of the gods. चार्वाक
Chatra /Chhaatra/ pupil, disciple.
छात्र
Chatur four. चतुर्
Chaturashramya
/Chatur-aashramya/ the four periods of life; see Ashrama. चतुराश्रम्य
Chaturmasa /Chaatur-maasa/ the

four months of the monsoon traditionally used for sadhana. This
auspicious period begins on the
day after the full moon of Ashada
(i.e. Guru Purnima) and com-
prises the lunar months of
Shravana, Bhadrapada, Ashwina
and Kartika; see Masa. चातुर्मास
Chatursampradaya /Chatur-
sampradaaya/ four denomina-
tions. चतुर्सम्प्रदाय
Chaturvarga the four aims of
human life, viz. material security
(artha), fulfilment of desire
(kama), righteousness (dharma)
and spiritual liberation (moksha);
see Purushartha. चतुर्वर्ग
Chedana /Chhedana/ cutting, tearing; splitting, dividing. छेदन
Chesta /Cheshtaa/ motion, movement; effort, exertion; gesture,
action; behaviour. चेष्टा
Chetana /Chetanaa/ consciousness;
unmanifest aspect of consciousness and energy. चेतना
Chetanavastha /Chetana-
avasthaa/ the conscious state of
mind; sentience; feeling. चेतनावस्था
Chetas consciousness; sense; reasoning faculty. चेतस्
Chetasa Jnana /Chetasa Jnaana/
power of telepathy gained by advanced yogis. चेतस ज्ञान
Chetati observe; comprehend;
know. चेतति
Chhanachhan Nada /Chhanachhan
Naada/ an imitative sound, expressive of the noise of falling
drops. छनछन नाद
Chhanna covered; hidden, concealed; secret. छन्न
Chhaya /Chhaayaa/ shade; reflection; lustre; light. छाया

Chhaya Siddhi /Chhaayaa Siddhi/ power or ability gained through concentration on one's shadow. छाया सिद्धि

Chhayopasana /Chhaayopaasanaa/ (Chhaaya-upaasanaa); a tantric practice in the *Shiva Swarodaya*, involving close observation of one's shadow and chanting mantras in order to divine the future. छायोपासना

Chikitsa /Chikitsaa/ process of treatment; medical therapy. चिकित्सा

Chikitsya to be treated; medically curable. चिकित्स्य

Chinna /Chhinna/ removed; limited; torn; chopped; destroyed. छिन्न

Chinta /Chintaa/ thinking, thought; care, anxiety. चिन्ता

Chit thought; perception; intelligence, intellect; understanding; the heart/mind; pure knowing beyond the division of subject and object; in Vedanta, one of the three attributes of the ultimate principle; the soul, spirit and the animating principle of life; Brahman, the pure consciousness that lies behind all phenomena; see Sachchidananda. चित्

Chidabhasa /Chidaabhaasa/ (Chit-aabhaasa); reflected consciousness; the reflection of intelligence. चिदाभास

Chidagni (Chit-agni); the soul, spirit, the animating principle of life. चिदग्नि

Chidakasha /Chidaakaasha/ (Chit-aakaasha); the space or sphere within, where the capacity of sense perception is internalized to observe the process and reactions of individual awareness; the inner space visualized in meditation behind the closed eyes or in the region of ajna chakra; the state of pure, unbounded consciousness; Brahman in its aspect of limitless knowledge or unbounded intelligence; the pure consciousness (chit) is, like space (akasha), an all-pervading continuum; mind conceived as all-pervading space; see Akasha. चिदाकाश

Chidakasha Dharana /Chidaakaasha Dhaaranaa/ (Chit-aakaasha Dhaaranaa); concentration on the inner space of consciousness; a meditative technique in which one concentrates on visualization or watches one's reactions on the physical, mental and psychic planes of personality. चिदाकाश धारणा

Chidambara (Chit-ambara); place of pilgrimage in South India; chit means consciousness, and ambara means atmosphere or garment; name of a god who covers all with his consciousness; name of Shiva. चिदम्बर

Chiddharma (Chit-dharma); desire to do. चिद्धर्म

Chinmatra /Chinmaatra/ (Chit-maatra); mere consciousness, consciousness alone. चिन्मात्र

Chinmaya (Chit-maya); supreme intelligence. चिन्मय

Chinmayi /Chinmayee/ (Chit-mayee); permeated, as it were, by consciousness. चिन्मयी

Chinmudra /Chinmudraa/ (Chit-mudraa); psychic gesture (mudra)

of consciousness, a hand position with palm upwards on the knee and the index finger locked into the base of the thumb; see Mudra. चिन्मुद्रा

Chitsamanya /Chit-saamaanya/ the basic universal consciousness. चित्सामान्य

Chit Shakti the power of pure consciousness; mental force governing the subtle dimensions; intellectual capacity. चित शक्ति

Chitswarupa /Chit-svaroopa/ of the very form of pure intelligence or consciousness. चितस्वरूप

Chitra bright; clear; various; strange; wonderful; variegated colour; a picture. चित्र

Chitra Nadi, Chitrini Nadi /Chitraa Naadee, Chitrinee Naadee/ the second of three energy currents (nadis) lying within sushumna nadi, which are dormant until the balancing of ida and pingala nadis allows sushumna to flow. Once they awaken, new states of understanding come naturally. चित्रा नाडी, चित्रिणी नाडी

Chitta individual consciousness, including the subconscious and unconscious layers of mind; thinking, concentration, attention, enquiry; the stuff of the mind; storehouse of memory or samskaras; one of the four parts of the antahkarana or inner instrument; seat of consciousness, and as such includes the conscious, subconscious, unconscious and superconscious. चित्त

Chittaprasada /Chitta-prasaada/ serenity of mind. चित्तप्रसाद

    Chittaprasadana /Chitta-prasaadana/ peace or tranquillity of mind. चित्तप्रसादन

Chitta Shakti mental force governing the subtle dimensions. चित्त शक्ति

Chitta Shuddhi purification of the mind; purity of consciousness, the power of individual consciousness at all levels. चित्त शुद्धि

Chitta Vidya /Chitta Vidyaa/ psychology; science of the mind and the different states of consciousness. चित्त विद्या

Chitta Vikshepa distraction; confusion; perplexity. चित्त विक्षेप

Chitta Vimukti freedom from the bondage of the mind. चित्त विमुक्ति

Chitta Vritti disposition or state of the mind; inclination; feeling, emotion; in yoga philosophy the inward working of the mind, its mental vision or inward purpose; in raja yoga Patanjali lists five main categories of chitta vritti in the *Yoga Sutras*: 1. right knowledge (pramana), 2. wrong knowledge (viparyaya), 3. imagination (vikalpa), 4. sleep (nidra), 5. memory (smriti). They can be painful (klishta), leading to an increase in karmic stock and the necessity for embodiment, or not painful (aklishta); see Brahmi Vritti; see Vritti. चित्त वृत्ति

D

Pronunciation

ड् *d* – *as in dunk;* ढ् *dh* – *as in redhead*
द् *d* – *as in the;* ध् *dh* – *as in adhere*

Dadhichi /Dadheechi/ name of a celebrated sage who offered his bones to the gods when requested. With these bones, the architect of the gods made a thunderbolt with which Indra defeated Vritra and other demons. दधीचि

Dahana burning, consuming by fire. दहन

Daharakasha /Dahara-aakaasha/ deep space, encompassing mooladhara, swadhisthana and manipura chakras; see Akasha. दहराकाश

Daharakasha Dharana /Dahara-aakaasha Dhaaranaa/ concentration on the symbols of chakras and tattwas within the deep space; see Pancha Tattwa Dharana. दहराकाश धारणा

Daitya class of mighty beings in whom the diabolical quality predominates; belonging to the class of demons; a giant. दैत्य

Daiva belonging to gods; divine, celestial; fate; royal; relating to desires. दैव

Daiva Samskara /Daiva Samskaara/ samskaras that purify vijnanamaya and anandamaya koshas; see Samskara. दैव संस्कार

Daivasurasampadvibhagayoga /Daiva-asura-sampad-vibhaaga-yoga/ 'yoga of the division between the divine and the demonical', the 16th chapter of the *Bhagavad Gita*, clarifying how these qualities manifest in people's lives and after death, and recommending scriptures as guidelines for conduct. देवासुरसम्पद्विभागयोग

Dakini /Daakinee/ the goddess in mooladhara, the basic lotus. डाकिनी

Daksha celebrated lord of created beings (Prajapati), one of the 10 sons of Brahma; able, competent, expert, skilful; suitable; upright, honest. दक्ष

Dakshina situated on the right side; the right hand or arm; situated to the south, southern; sincere, straightforward, honest; epithet of Shiva or Vishnu. दक्षिण

Dakshina Itara literally 'other than dakshina'; left; left side of the body; northern. दक्षिण इतर

Dakshina Nadi /Dakshina Naadee/ another name for pingala nadi. दक्षिण नाडी

Dakshina Pashchima south-western. दक्षिण पश्चिम

Dakshinapati 'Lord of the south', an epithet of Yama, the god of death. दक्षिणपति

Dakshina Uttara turned or lying to the south and the north. दक्षिण उत्तर

Dakshina Vrittam the meridian line. दक्षिण वृत्तम्

Dakshinayana /Dakshinaayana/ southern 'path' of the sun when, due to the tilt of the earth and its elliptical orbit, the sun appears to move south towards the Tropic of Capricorn. The six months of this southern journey are from mid-July to mid-January. It is not regarded as a good time to die as one will be reborn on earth. This path is also called pitriyana and dhumamarga; one of two pre-scribed paths of meditation; see Uttarayana. दक्षिणायन

Dakshina /Dakshinaa/ offering to the guru. दक्षिणा

Dama control of the outer senses; self-command through self-re-straint and curbing the passions; drawing the mind away from evil deeds or curbing its evil propen-sities; taming, subduing; punish-ment, fine; one of the sixfold vir-tues; see Shadsampatti. दम

Damyati /Daamyati/ to be tamed; to be calm or tranquil; to sub-due, conquer or restrain. दाम्यति

Damani /Damanee/ a layer within a nadi or channel for the passage of energy; overpowering; tran-quil; passionless. दमनी

Damaru /Damaroo/ an hour-glass shaped hand drum; one of the accoutrements of Lord Shiva. डमरू

Dambha hypocrisy; pride; arro-gance; ostentation. दम्भ

Dana /Daana/ gift, donation; liber-ality, unconditional giving; puri-fication; protection; posture; see Yajna. दान

Danadanyoh /Daanaadaanayoh/ simultaneous give and take. दानादानयो:

Danda stick, staff, club, handle; power, force; sovereignty; the sceptre of a king; the rod as a symbol of authority and punish-ment; name of Yama; name of Vishnu; trunk of an elephant; the staff of a sannyasin or ascetic; stem or stalk from a lotus or tree, etc.; see Tridandin; see Eka-dandin. दण्ड

Dandashakti sceptre; the rod of power or punishment. दण्डशक्ति

Dandin one of the priestly caste (brahmana) or a sannyasin with a staff; a Jaina ascetic; an epithet of Yama, the god of death. दण्डिन्

Dandaka name of a celebrated dis-trict in the Deccan, situated be-tween the rivers Narmada and Godavari (a vast region said to be tenantless in the time of Rama). दण्डक

Danta Dhauti method of cleaning the teeth; see Shatkarma. दन्त धौति

Danti /Daanti/ self-restraint; sub-jection, control. दान्ति

Darpa pride; arrogance; insolence; rashness; vanity, conceit. दर्प

Darpana looking-glass, mirror; eye; kindling, inflaming. दर्पण

Darshana a glimpse, seeing, observ-ing; sight, vision; knowing, un-derstanding; philosophical sys-tem of the vedic tradition, so

called because it is based on rev-
elations or truths that were 'seen'
in a higher state of consciousness; see Shaddarshana. दर्शन

Darshanarthi /Darshana-arthee/
one who seeks darshan. दर्शनार्थी

Dashnami Sampradaya /Dasha-
naamee Sampradaaya/ 10 orders
of sannyasa, viz. Aranya, Ashrama, Bharati, Giri, Parvat, Puri,
Sagara, Saraswati, Tirtham and
Vanam, connected with the
Advaita Vedanta tradition established by Adi Shankaracharya in
order to protect, preserve and
propagate spiritual knowledge.
दशनामी सम्प्रदाय

Dasharatha king of the solar dynasty, father of Shri Rama,
Lakshmana, Bharata and Sha-
trughna, and husband of Kaushalya, Sumitra and Kaikeyi; see
Shravana. दशरथ

Data /Daataa/ benefactor; one who
gives. दाता

Dattatreya /Dattaatreya/ an ancient
sage who learned from 24 gurus,
the son of Atri and Anusuya, considered to have been an incarnation of Brahma, Vishnu and
Shiva; see Saptodharini. दत्तात्रेय

Daya /Dayaa/ sympathy, pity, clem-
ency, tenderness, compassion. दया

Deepa see Dipa. दीप

Deerghakala see Dirghakala. दीर्घकाल

Deha body; mass; person. देह

Dehabhimana /Deha-abhimaana/
egoistic attachment to the body.
देहाभिमान

Dehadhyasa /Deha-adhyaasa/
false identification with the body.
देहाध्यास

Dehamashrita /Dehamaashrita/

embodied. देहमाश्रित

Dehasamya /Deha-saamya/ body
stillness. देहसाम्य

Dehashuddhi purity or purification of the body. देहशुद्धि

Dehatma Buddhi /Deha-aatma
Buddhi/ the intellect that makes
one identify the self with the
body. देहात्म बुद्धि

Dehavat, Dehavaan embodied; a
person. देहवत्, देहवान्

Dehavidya /Deha-vidyaa/
anatomy, physiology. देहविद्या

Dehi /Dehee/ one who has a body;
the conscious embodied self; jiva
or individual self. देही

Dehin the soul, spirit (en-
shrined in the body). देहिन्

Desha place. देश

Deshakalasambandha /Desha-
kaala-sambandha/ extended in
space and located in time, having connection with space and
time, space-time relation.
देशकालसम्बन्ध

Deshatita /Deshaateeta/
spaceless; beyond space. देशातीत

Deva luminous being; a god or divine being. देव

Devadatta one of the minor
pranas which provides for the in-
take of extra oxygen in a tired
body by causing a yawn; name of
the conch-shell of Arjuna; a certain person (used in speaking of
men indefinitely); see Upaprana.
देवदत्त

Devadvishah /Deva-dvishah/ haters of light; haters of gods. देवद्विष:

Devakulya /Deva-kulyaa/ another
name for the river Ganges
(Ganga), which is known as the
river of the gods. देवकुल्या

Deva Loka plane of light; sphere of higher consciousness of existence; heaven. देव लोक

Devanagri /Deva-naagaree/ the script of the gods; the script used to write Sanskrit. देवनागरी

Devarupa, Devarupin /Deva-roopa, Deva-roopin/ of divine form or beauty. देवरूप, देवरूपिन्

Devata /Devataa/ form of divine dignity or power; divine being representing the higher state of evolution; illumined form; divinity, deity; the presiding deities or illumining powers of the five sense organs (jnanendriyas) are Surya, sun (eyes), Digdevata, space (ears), the Ashwinau twins, earth (nose), Vayu, air (skin) and Varuna, water (tongue); the presiding deities of the five organs of action (karmendriyas) are Vahni, fire (vocal cords), Indra, king of the gods (hands), Vishnu, Vishnu (legs), Mrityu, Lord of death (anus) and Prajapati, Lord of created beings (genitals); the four illumining powers of a person's inner instrument or mind (antahkarana) are Chandra (manas), Brahma (buddhi), Vasudeva (chitta) and Rudra (ahamkara); see Vasu. देवता

Deva Tattwa /Deva Tattva/ first tattva: the divine element. देव तत्त्व

Deva Yajna a sacrifice to the superior gods made by oblations to fire; one of the five daily sacrifices to be performed by a householder; see Pancha Mahayajna. देव यज्ञ

Devayana /Deva-yaana/ the path of the gods; the path of light that can be taken by the spirit after leaving the physical body; see Uttarayana. देवयान

Devendra (Deva-indra); king of the gods. देवेन्द्र

Devi /Devee/ female deity, goddess; name of Durga, Saraswati and others; see Shakta. देवी

Devi Bhagavatam /Devee Bhaagavatam/ a subsidiary text of the *Shiva Purana* that speaks of the female deity a collection of stories about Devi; see Durga Saptashati; see Puranam. देवी भागवतम्

Devisukta /Devee-sukta/ prayer to the goddess. देवीसूक्त

Dhairya firmness; durability; strength; constancy; steadiness; calmness; gravity; patience; inflexibility. धैर्य

Dhananjaya minor prana responsible for decomposition of the body after death; another name of Arjuna; see Upaprana. धनञ्जय

Dhanu bow. धनु

Dhara /Dhaaraa/ stream or current of water; flow; drop; series; edge; margin. धारा

Dharana /Dhaaranaa/ concentration or complete attention; sixth stage of ashtanga yoga described by Patanjali's *Yoga Sutras* as holding or binding of the mind to one point; bearing, supporting; moulding; keeping in memory; see Raja Yoga. धारणा

Dharana Shakti /Dhaaranaa Shakti/ power of grasping and retaining ideas. धारणा शक्ति

Dharana Yoga /Dhaaranaa Yoga/ the yoga of concentration, before the stage of meditation (dhyana)

and samadhi. धारणा योग

Dharatala /Dharaatala/ fifth centre of the instinctive or animal body below mooladhara chakra; see Patalam. धरातल

Dharitri /Dharitree/ 'she who holds', a name for the planet Earth. धरित्री

Dharma the natural role we play in life; ethical law; duty; the laws or fundamental support of life; usage, practice, custom; religion; virtue, righteousness, good work; regarded as one of the four aims of human existence; see Purushartha. धर्म

Dharmameghasamadhi /Dharma-megha-samaadhi/ state of superconsciousness or samadhi called 'cloud of virtue', as it showers nectar drops of immortality through the knowledge of Brahman when the deep impressions (vasanas) are entirely destroyed. The cloud of virtue is the name given to samadhi in the ashtanga yoga of Patanjali's *Yoga Sutras*. धर्ममेघसमाधि

Dharma Shastra /Dharma Shaastra/ manual of laws, law book relating to duties of mankind; a class of works handed down by tradition and regarded as the last word in social and other conflicts. The dharma shastras are monographs compiled to make an orderly presentation of knowledge gleaned from the Vedas. Topics include: 1. classification of society based on functional responsibilities, 2. duties of people in each class, 3. duties of kings, 4. duties of men and women, 5. the social code, 6. civil rules, 7. definition of sin and corresponding punishments; see Smriti. धर्म शास्त्र

Dhatu /Dhaatu/ layers of tissue in the body; element; metal; the vital force in humans which yogis conserve through celibacy, developing vitality (ojas) and brilliance (tejas). धातु

Dhauta washed, cleaned of, purified. धौत

Dhauti cleansing practices involving gentle washing with air, water, cloth or a specially prepared stick; process for the purification and cleaning of the alimentary canal, the stomach and sphincter muscles; one of the six hatha yoga cleansing techniques; see Shatkarma; see Bahishkrita; see Danta Dhauti; see Hridaya Dhauti; see Kapala Dhauti; see Kapala Randhra Dhauti; see Karna Dhauti; see Mula Dhauti; see Shankhaprakshalana; see Vamana Dhauti; see Vastra Dhauti; see Vatasara Dhauti. धौति

Dhenu cow; the Earth. धेनु

Dhenuka name of a demon killed by Balarama. धेनुक

Dhimat /Dheemat/ wise, prudent. धीमत्

Dhivasana /Dhee-vaasanaa/ the mind that has assumed its finest stage and which then contains in bud-like form all the impressions of actions. धीवासना

Dhoop see Dhupa. धूप

Dhritarashtra /Dhritaraashtra/ literally 'whose empire is firm'; father of the Kauravas and blind from birth, his blind attachment to his sons led his kingdom to civil war. He ordered the clairvoyant Sanjay to describe his sons' battle against Lord Krishna and Arjuna's brothers (the Pandavas). The description is recorded as the *Bhagavad Gita*. धृतराष्ट्र

Dhriti firmness, steadiness, equanimity. धृति

Dhruva firm, steady, constant, permanent, certain; the Pole Star; a child devotee of Lord Vishnu. ध्रुव

Dhuma /Dhooma/ smoke. धूम

Dhumamarga /Dhooma-maarga/ the path of smoke, as distinguished from the path of light (devayana), it can be taken by the spirit in its journey to heaven and re-birth; see Dakshinayana; see Pitriyana. धूममार्ग

Dhumralingam /Dhoomra-lingam/ smoky or ill-defined lingam which symbolizes the astral body and our self-concept in mooladhara chakra; see Linga. धूम्रलिंगम्

Dhupa /Dhoopa/ incense; see Shodashopachara. धूप

Dhwani /Dhvani/ sound, noise; thunder; tone. ध्वनि

Dhyana /Dhyaana/ spontaneous state after deep concentration or meditation; the seventh of the eight steps described in raja yoga; the intermediate internal process where the power of attention becomes so steadily fixed upon the object of meditation that other thoughts do not enter the mind; natural expression of the sattwic state; see Raja Yoga; see Sattwa. ध्यान

Dhyanabindu /Dhyaana-bindu/ name of an Upanishad which teaches that meditation, especially on the mantra Aum, can cut through mountains of karma. ध्यानबिन्दु

Dhyanagamya /Dhyaana-gamya/ attainable through meditation. ध्यानगम्य

Dhyanayoga /Dhyaana-yoga/ 'yoga of meditation', the sixth chapter of the *Bhagavad Gita*, which explains the techniques of meditation resulting in mastery of the senses, self-control and the vision of the self in all beings. ध्यानयोग

Dhyanika /Dhyaanika/ pertaining to dhyana or meditation. ध्यानिक

Dhyeya object of meditation or worship; purpose behind action. ध्येय

Dhyeyarupa /Dhyeya-roopa/ the form for the purpose of meditation. ध्येयरूप

Dhyeyatyaga /Dhyeya-tyaaga/ renunciation of object in meditation; absolute experience or nirvikalpa samadhi. ध्येयत्याग

Digambara (Dik-ambara); naked, literally 'space clothed' (dik means space or direction, ambara means cloth), an epithet applied particularly to those Jaina monks who claim to be from the original tradition which forbade clothing; see Shvetambara. दिगम्बर

Digvijaya (Dik-vijaya); victory (over all directions). दिग्विजय

Diksha /Deekshaa/ initiation, consecration; preparation for a sacrifice or a ceremony; dedication of oneself to a particular object; ceremony or religious rite in general; birth of a new vision. दीक्षा

Dikshana /Deekshana/ initiation, consecration. दीक्षन

Dikshapatra /Deekshaa-patra/ letter of initiation. दीक्षापत्र

Dikshate /Deekshate/ to concentrate or prepare oneself for the performance of a sacred rite; to dedicate oneself to; to initiate or introduce a pupil; to invest with the sacred thread; to practise self-restraint. दीक्षते

Dikshakti power of illusion that produces the consciousness of space. दिक्शक्ति

Dinachara /Dina-achaara/ daily conduct, daily activity. दिनाचार

Dipa /Deepa/ small lamp fed with ghee, waved as an offering in front of the deity, light used in ceremonial worship; see shodashopachara. दीप

Dirgha /Deergha/ long. दीर्घ

Dirghakala /Deergha-kaala/ for a long period of time, a necessary element in yoga practice according to Patanjali's *Yoga Sutras*. दीर्घकाल

Dirghaswapna /Deergha-svapna/ literally 'long dream', usually refers to the unreal nature of the world. दीर्घस्वप्न

Dishtam unseen power in karma that links up the act and its fruit; destiny or fate. दिष्टम्

Diti mother of all the demons or daityas. दिति

Divya divine power; ordeal. दिव्य

Divya Bhava /Divya Bhaava/ divine feeling. दिव्य भाव

Divya Chakshu divine eye, associated with the third eye or the eye of Shiva; see Ajna Chakra. दिव्य चक्षु

Divya Drishti divine sight; the so-called third or divine eye, located between the eyebrows or in ajna chakra; intuition; clairvoyance. दिव्य दृष्टि

Divya Loka plane of divine or transcendental experience. दिव्य लोक

Dola a swing; swinging; doubt. डोल

Dosha three humours of the body described in ayurveda: mucus (kapha), bile (pitta) and wind (vata). Their imbalance prevents the flow of energy in sushumna nadi and thus one is bound to the dualities. Hatha yoga techniques are designed to correct this. दोष

Drashta /Drashtaa/ witness, uninvolved observer, onlooker, seer; the consciousness which knows what is going on; atman or purusha; see Sakshi; see Kutastha. द्रष्टा

Drashta Bhava /Drashtaa Bhaava/ witnessing attitude. द्रष्टा भाव

Drashtu seer within, responsible for all experiences and for all knowledge; the witness of all actions that makes possible the perception of time, space and causality. द्रष्टु

Draupadi /Draupadee/ great devotee of Lord Krishna, daughter of king Drupada of Panchala and wife of the five Pandava brothers. द्रौपदी

Dravya substance; money; liquid. द्रव्य

Dravyadvaita /Dravya-advaita/ unity of substance or matter. द्रव्याद्वैत

Dravyagrahana appropriation of things. द्रव्यग्रहण

Dravya Yajna offering wealth to the needy without expectation of return. द्रव्य यज्ञ

Dridha fixed, firm, strong, certain, unshaken. दृढ

Dridhabhoomi solid foundation; well-founded in any state of yoga. दृढभूमि

Dridhasamskara /Dridha-samskaara/ well-grounded mental impression. दृढसंस्कार

Dridhasushupti undisturbed deep sleep state. दृढसुषुप्ति

Drik seer, perceiver; vision. दृक्

Drish to see, look at, observe, view; to behold, perceive, regard, consider; to search; to see by divine intuition. दृश्

Drishta seen, observed; visible; well-known; manifest; real. दृष्ट

Drishtanta /Drishtaanta/ instance, example, illustration. दृष्टान्त

Drishti seeing, viewing; knowing, knowledge; eye, faculty of seeing, sight. दृष्टि

Drishtisamya /Drishti-saamya/

stillness of vision. दृष्टिसाम्य

Drishtisrishtivada /Drishti-srishti-vaada/ doctrine holding that the existence of the world is purely the outcome of the faculty of perception, and that actually nothing exists beyond imagination. दृष्टिसृष्टिवाद

Drishtvanta having seen. दृष्ट्वन्त

Drishyaprapancha phenomenal world that is visible to the eye. दृश्यप्रपञ्च

Drona teacher of the arts of war, especially archery, to the Pandava and Kaurava princes. द्रोण

Duhkha uneasy, uneasiness; difficult; unpleasant; grief, pain, suffering. दुःख

Duhkha Jihasa /Duhkha Jihaasaa/ wish to avoid pain and sorrow. दुःख जिहासा

Duradrishti /Doora-drishti/ distant vision; television. दूरदृष्टि

Duratma /Duraatmaa/ evil-natured, mean. दुरात्मा

Durga impossible; inaccessible; difficulty, distress. दुर्ग

Durga /Durgaa/ remover of difficulties, the beautiful goddess who slays the difficult and even impossible enemies and rides the lion or tiger; a name of the wife of Shiva; the higher state of human consciousness and evolution; see Chandi; see Shakta. दुर्गा

Durgasaptashati
/Durgaasaptashatee/ (Durgaa-saptashatee); part of the Puranic literature which tells the story of Durga's creation from the combined power (shakti) of the gods so that she could overcome all enemies in battle. It tells of her glories and victories over the demonic forces and forms part of the *Devi Mahatmya* of the *Markandeya Purana*; see Chandi Yajna; see Puranam. दुर्गासप्तशती

Durvasa /Durvaasaa/ name of a very irascible sage whose anger has become proverbial. दुर्वासा

Dwadashanta /Dvaadasha-anta/ literally 'the end of 12'; two poles or points of rest between which the breath travels. द्वादशान्त

Dwaita /Dvaita/ dual. द्वैत

Dwaitadwaitavivarjita
/Dvaita-advaita-vivarjita/ beyond monism and dualism; destitute of oneness, duality and multiplicity. द्वैताद्वैतविवर्जित

Dwaitavada /Dvaita-vaada/ dualism; doctrine of dual existence propounded by Madhvacharya. द्वैतवाद

Dwaitya /Dvaitya/ duality, difference, diversity. द्वैत्य

Dwandwa /Dvandva/ pairs of opposites like pain and pleasure; duality; couples. द्वन्द्व

Dwandvata /Dvandvataa/ state of duality. द्वन्द्वता

Dwandvatita /Dvandva-ateeta/ beyond the pairs of opposites like heat and cold, hunger and thirst, pleasure and pain. द्वन्द्वातीत

Dwapara Yuga /Dvaapara Yuga/ the third aeon of the world, consisting of 864,000 years according to *Suryasiddhanta*; see Yuga. द्वापर युग

Dwara /Dvaara/ door, gateway, entrance, opening, aperture; way; means. द्वार

Dwarakarana /Dvaara-kaarana/ intermediate cause of the universe, as the unchanging Brahman cannot be an independent cause; that which is not actually the cause but simply a conveying factor of the chief cause, which is often found to inhere in the effect. द्वार कारण

Dwarka, Dwarika /Dvaarkaa, Dvaarikaa/ the harbour city of Lord Krishna, which has been rediscovered under the ocean next to the modern city in western India, where Sharada Matha is situated; see Sharada Matha. द्वारका, द्वारिका

Dwesha /Dvesha/ repulsion, aversion; hatred, enmity, dislike, repugnance, antagonism; one of the five causes of suffering (kleshas) described by Patanjali's *Yoga Sutras* as aversion to the unpleasant; see Klesha. द्वेष

Dweshya /Dveshya/ enemy. द्वेष्य

Dwiguna /Dviguna/ consisting of two strings; double, twofold. द्विगुण

Dwija /Dvija/ twice born; person of any of the three varnas, viz. priestly caste (brahmana), kingly and warrior caste (kshatriya) or merchant caste (vaishya); brahmana; person who has been given second birth by initiation (diksha). द्विज

E

Pronunciation

ए e – *as in grey*
ई ee – *as in fleet*

Eekshanam see Ikshanam. ईक्षणम्
  Eekshita see Ikshita. ईक्षित
Eershya see Irshya. ईर्ष्या
Eesha see Isha. ईश
  Eeshaa see Ishaa. ईशा
  Eeshana see Ishaana. ईशान
  Eeshitvam see Ishitvam. ईशित्वम्
Eeshwara see Ishwara. ईश्वर
  Eeshwara Pranidhana see Ishwara Pranidhana. ईश्वर प्रणिधान
  Eeshwara Prayatna see Ishwara Prayatna. ईश्वर प्रयत्न
Ejana trembling, shaking. एजन
Eka one, single, alone, only; the same, unchanged; firm; supreme, prominent. एक
  Ekadamstra, Ekadanta /Ekadamshtra, Ekadanta/ literally 'one-tusked', epithet of Ganesha. एकदंष्ट्र, एकदन्त

Ekadandin name of a class of sannyasins with one staff (otherwise called hamsa); see Danda. एकदण्डिन्
Ekadasi /Ekaadashee/ 11th day of the lunar fortnight, a time when mantra chanting and dietary restraint are held to be beneficial. एकादशी
Ekadesha spot or place; part or portion (of a whole); one-sided. एकदेश
Ekadrish, Ekadrishti one vision; one-eyed; name of Shiva; name of a philosopher; a crow. एकदृष, एकदृष्टि
Ekagra /Ekaagra/ one-pointed, fixed on the object or point only, where the mental faculties are all focused on a single point; closely attentive. एकाग्र
  Ekagramati /Ekaagramati/ fixing one's mind on one object. एकाग्रमति
  Ekagrata /Ekaagrataa/ one-pointedness of mind, fourth of the five states of mind where pure sattwa guna predominates enabling concentrated or meditative states of mind; see Manas. एकाग्रता
  Ekagra Vasana /Ekaagra Vaasanaa/ desires concentrated in respect of only one person or one thing. एकाग्र वासना
Ekakala /Eka-kaala/ one time; at the same time, simultaneously. एककाल
Ekakshara /Eka-akshara/ monosyllabic; the sacred syllable Aum. एकाक्षर

Ekamanas /Eka-manas/ having the mind concentrated on one object. एकमनस्

Ekanta /Ekaanta/ solitary; aside, apart; absolute; invariable, perpetual. एकान्त

Eka Pada /Eka Paada/ one foot or single foot; name of Vishnu and Shiva. एक पाद

Ekapinga, **Ekapingala** a name of Kubera, the god of wealth. एकपिङ्ग, एकपिङ्गल

Ekarasa oneness of aim or feeling; the only flavour or pleasure. एकरस

Ekartha /Eka-artha/ the same thing, object or intention; the same meaning. एकार्थ

Ekarupa /Eka-roopa/ likeness, similarity; uniformity. एकरूप

Ekasamaye simultaneously, at one time. एकसमये

Ekatam solely; invariably, always; absolutely; quite; wholly. एकतम्

Ekatattwabhyasa /Eka-tattva-abhyaasa/ the study of the single element, first principle or material condition (force) that pervades the innermost self of all beings. एकतत्त्वाभ्यास

Ekatra together. एकत्र

Ekatvat /Ekatvaat/ due to oneness. एकत्वात्

Ekavira /Eka-veera/ single force, one invincible force. एकवीर

Ekibhava /Ekee-bhaava/ combination, association; common nature or property. एकीभाव

Ekoham Bahusyam /Eko'ham Bahusyaam/ (Ekah-aham Bahusyaam); 'may I, the One, become many', the primal idea which manifested itself from Brahman, the one undivided being, prior to creation. एकोऽहं बहुस्याम्

Eshana /Eshanaa/ desire, wish. एषणा

Eshana Traya /Eshanaa Traya/ three mundane desires of humankind, viz. desire for wealth or prosperity (vitteshana), desire for progeny (putreshana) and desire for fame or popularity (lokeshana). एषणा त्रय

Eshin desiring, wishing. एषिन्

Evam similarly; exactly; just so; thus. एवम्

Evam Vid knowing so. एवम् विद्

Evam Vidha /Evam Vidhaa/ of such a kind. एवम् विधा

G

Gan /Gaana/ song, verse. गान

Gatu /Gaatu/ song, singer; celestial chorister. गातु

Gabhasti ray of light, sunbeam or moonbeam; the sun; epithet of Swaha, the wife of Agni. गभस्ति

Gabhira /Gabheera/ deep (in all senses); profound; grave, serious, earnest; mysterious. गभीर

Gabhiratman /Gabheera-aatman/ the supreme soul. गभीरात्मन्

Gada /Gadaa/ mace, club. गदा

Gagana the sky, firmament, atmosphere. गगन

Gaganachara moving in the air. गगनचर

Gaganadhvaja literally 'the flag in the sky', denoting the sun, a planet, a celestial being. गगनध्वज

Gaganaravinda /Gagana-aravinda/ literally 'sky-lotus', denoting something unreal or non-existent, the world, or an impossibility. गगनारविन्द

Gaganasindhu an epithet of the river Ganges (Ganga). गगनसिन्धु

Gaganasparshana air, wind. गगनस्पर्शन

Gaganasthita situated in the sky. गगनस्थित

Gaja elephant; the number eight; a demon killed by Shiva. गज

Gaja Karani /Gaja Karanee/ vomiting up the contents of the stomach as a cleansing practice; see Shatkarma. गज करणी

Gala throat, neck. गल

Gam go, depart, go away; move. गम्

Gamana going, motion; approaching; obtaining, attaining. गमन

Gana crowd, group; troop; Shiva's attendants. गण

Ganapati chief of a troop; name of the god Ganesha who is the son of Shiva and Parvati. गणपति

Ganapatya /Gaanapatya/ worshipper of Ganapati (Ganesha); see Panchaupasana; see Panchaupasaka. गाणपत्य

Ganesha (Gana-eesha); 'Lord of the ganas (Shiva's attendants)', name of the elephant-headed deity who is the auspicious son of Shiva and Parvati. Shiva beheaded him when he blocked his path following Parvati's instruction to allow no one in while she was bathing. Shiva then relented and gave his son an elephant's head. Ganesha is the scribe of the *Mahabharata*, deity of mooladhara chakra and regarded as the remover of obstacles and a god of fertility; see Vinayaka; see Shripancha. गणेश

Gandha smell, odour, perfume; see Pancha Tanmatra; see Shodashopachara. गन्ध

Gandha Tanmatra /Gandha Tanmaatra/ subtle principle of the root element of odour, the tanmatra associated with mooladhara chakra; see Pancha Tanmatra. गन्ध तन्मात्र

Gandharva celestials who engage in musical arts, dancing and singing; celestial musician; singer in general; being belonging to the higher state of existence. गन्धर्व

Gandharvanagara city of the Gandharvas; the appearance of mansions and cities (as in a mirage); any fanciful conception; the world. गन्धर्वनगर

Gandiva /Gaandeeva/ bow of Arjuna presented by Soma to Varuna, by Varuna to Agni and by Agni to Arjuna. गाण्डीव

Ganga /Gangaa/ the river Ganges, the most sacred river in India; the Ganges personified as a goddess, the eldest daughter of Himavat; see Triveni. गङ्गा

Ganita counting. गणित

Ganja a ruin; a treasury; a granary, a place where grain is stored for sale. गञ्ज

Garbha womb; belly; embryo; act of conception; inside, middle, or interior of anything; offspring of the sky. गर्भ

Garbhagriha most sacred room; sanctuary or body of a temple; sanctum. गर्भगृह

Garbhodaka (Garbha-udaka); the primeval waters. गर्भोदक

Gargi / Gaargee/ female sage whose questions and debates are recorded in *Brihadaranyaka Upanishad*. गार्गी

Garima /Garimaa/ heaviness; the power of increasing the weight of the body at will, one of the eight major siddhis; see Siddhi. गरिमा

Garuda name of the king of the birds, an eagle who is a son of Kashyapa and Vinata and the elder brother of Aruna. He is an implacable enemy of serpents. After his mother lost a dispute with her rival Kadru, she became Kadru's slave according to the conditions of the wager. Garuda brought down the heavenly beverage (amrita) to purchase her freedom after struggling with Indra. Vinata was then released, but the amrita was taken away from the serpents by Indra. Garuda is represented with a white face, an aquiline nose, red wings and golden body as the vehicle of Vishnu. गरुड

Garva pride, egoism, arrogance. गर्व

Gata gone for ever, passed away; dead, departed to the next world; being in, situated in; past. गत

Gatagati /Gata-aagati/ going and coming; passage after death. गतागति

Gati going, moving; gait; access; course, path, way; manner; event; success; state, condition, position, situation; mode of existence. गति

Gatha /Gaathaa/ folklore; stories

describing the significance of sacrificial rituals in the Brahmana scriptures; see Brahmana. गाथा

Gatram /Gaatram/ limb or member of the body; the body. गात्रम्

Gaudapada /Gaudapaada/ the great yogi and philosopher who was the guru of Govindapada, who was the guru of Adi Shankaracharya. गौडपाद

Gaudapada Karika /Gaudapaada Kaarikaa/ the commentary on *Mandukya Upanishad* written by Gaudapada, historically the first available systematic treatise on Advaita Vedanta, also known as the *Mandukyakarika*. गौडपाद कारिका

Gauna secondary; indirect. गौण

Gaunabhakti culture of devotion through rituals as a preliminary course on the path of love. गौणभक्ति

Gautama name of the propounder of the Nyaya system of philosophy; see Shaddarshana. गौतम

Gautama Buddha the founder of Buddhism. गौतम बुद्ध

Gayatram /Gaayatram/ a hymn composed and recited in the Gayatri metre. गायत्रम्

Gayatri /Gaayatree/ a vedic metre of 24 syllables; a most famous and sacred mantra suitable for everyone, repeated by every person of the priestly caste (brahmana) at the time of their morning and evening devotion (sandhya); vedic goddess, mother of the Vedas; female counterpart of the Sun; see Savitri. गायत्री

Gayatri Pravesha /Gaayatree Pravesha/ entering into the spirit of the Gayatri mantra (also called upanayanam). गायत्री प्रवेश

Gayatri Vidya /Gaayatree Vidyaa/ process of meditation taking Gayatri as the symbol of Brahman. गायत्री विद्या

Geru, Gairika red-brown or fire-coloured dye extracted from the mud of the river Ganges (Ganga). गेरु, गैरिक

Ghanaprajna /Ghanaprajnaa/ massive and undifferentiated consciousness. घनप्रज्ञा

Ghanta /Ghantaa/ bell. घण्टा

Ghanta Nada /Ghantaa Naada/ the sound of a bell. घण्टा नाद

Ghata /Ghaata/ a blow or stroke; killing; destruction. घात

Ghataka /Ghaataka/ killing, destroying; killer, destroyer, murderer. घातक

Ghatin /Ghaatin/ one who strikes, kills, destroys. घातिन्

Ghata mud pot. घट

Ghata Avastha /Ghata Avasthaa/ 'vessel stage', the second state of hearing the inner nada according to *Hatha Yoga Pradipika*; state of nada yoga attained when shakti enters the chitrini nadi within sushumna. घट अवस्था

Ghatastha Yoga a name of the yoga of Rishi Gheranda, in which he describes the body as a mud pot which needs to be fired by the practice of yoga in order to strengthen and purify it so that one may practise sadhana and attain knowledge of reality. घटस्थ योग

Gheranda Samhita /Gheranda Samhitaa/ traditional text on hatha yoga by Rishi Gheranda. It explains seven limbs (sapta anga) of yoga: shatkarma, asana, mudra, pratyahara, pranayama, dhyana and samadhi; see Ghatastha Yoga. घेरण्ड संहिता

Ghora terrific, dreadful, horrible; violent. घोर

Ghorarupa /Ghora-roopa/ of frightful appearance. घोररूप

Ghrana /Ghraana/ nose, one of the five jnanendriya (organs of knowledge). घ्राण

Ghrina /Ghrinaa/ disgust, aversion, contempt. घृणा

Ghrita clarified butter (ghee), fat, butter; water. घृत

Ghritachi /Ghritaachee/ ladle used for pouring ghee into the sacrificial fire; night; name of Saraswati; name of an apsara (nymphs in Indra's heaven). घृताची

Ghurna /Ghoorna/ shaking, moving to and fro; to revolve, to spin. घूर्ण

Ghurnavayu /Ghoorna-vaayu/ whirlwind. घूर्णवायु

Giri hill; the name of one of the 10 orders of sannyasins founded by Adi Shankaracharya, originally living in hilly country; see Dashnami Sampradaya. गिरि

Gita /Geetaa/ song; name given to certain sacred writings in verses (often in the form of a dialogue), but it appears to be especially recognized as referring to the *Bhagavad Gita*. गीता

Gna see Jna. ज्ञ

Go cow, cattle; the stars; the sky; thunderbolt of Indra; ray of light; a heaven; an organ of sense. गो

Gokula birthplace of Krishna. गोकुल

Gopa cowherd; guardian. गोप

Gopala /Gopaala/ cowherd; master of the senses; another name of Krishna, particularly referring to his childhood days in the countryside of Vrindavan; see Radha; see Bansuri. गोपाल

Gopati Lord of cows and stars; leader; bull; sun; moon; king; chief of herdsmen. गोपति

Gopayati guards, protects, conceals. गोपयति

Gopi /Gopee/ milkmaid; the gopis of Vrindavan are still sung of as the devotees of Gopala. गोपी

Gopi Chandana /Gopee Chandana/ clay brought from sacred places. गोपी चन्दन

Goraksha cowherd; name of a famous yogi and author of hatha yoga texts. गोरक्ष

Goraksha Ashtakam important ancient yogic text of the hatha yoga sect, ascribed to yogi Gorakhnath (Goraksha) who glorified his work as a guide to knowledge of the self. गोरक्ष अष्टकम्

Goshala /Goshaalaa/ cowshed. गोशाला

Govinda herdsman; a name of Lord Krishna who controls or enchants the mind and senses; a name of Brihaspati, guru of the gods; chief. गोविन्द

Gotra family race, family name; spiritual lineage; hurdle; cowshed; hen-coop. गोत्र

Govardhan Matha one of the four major matha established by Adi Shankaracharya in the four geographical quarters of India, situated in Puri in the eastern quarter of India. It was assigned the *Rigveda* with its maha vakya (great statement) 'Prajnanam Brahma' (Knowledge is Brahman). Its first head was Padmapadacharya. The Vanam and Aranyam orders of the Dashnami Sampradaya emanate from there. गोवर्द्धन मठ

Grahana taking; mentioning; understanding, comprehension, learning; to grasp, to hold. ग्रहण

Gramapati /Graama-pati/ chief of a village. ग्रामपति

Grantha binding, stringing together; treatise, composition; verse consisting of 32 syllables, written in the Anushtubh metre. ग्रन्थ

Granthi psychic knot; the three granthis on the sushumna nadi hinder the upward passage of kundalini, viz. Brahma granthi, Vishnu granthi and Rudra granthi. ग्रन्थि

Griha house. गृह

Grihastha Ashrama /Grihastha Aashrama/ the second stage of life according to the ancient vedic ashrama tradition, i.e. household or married life from 25 to 50 years of age; see Ashrama. गृहस्थ आश्रम

Grihini /Grihinee/ housewife. गृहिणी

Grihyasutra /Grihya-sootra/ manual of domestic rites. गृह्यसूत्र

Grishma Ritu /Greeshma Ritu/ the summer season comprised of the two months Jyeshtha and Ashada; see Ritu; see Masa. ग्रीष्म ऋतु

Gudha /Goodha/ hidden, covered, kept secret, concealed. गूढ

Guha hiding place; cave; the heart. गुह

Guhya secret. गुह्य

Guna quality; subordinate or constituent part; attribute, characteristic or property of all creation. According to Sankhya and yoga philosophy, prakriti (cosmic primordial matter or substance) is constituted of three different aspects called gunas, viz. sattwa, rajas and tamas. They are called an independent reality because they can be conceived (prameya), known (jneya) and named (abhidheya) independently of a substance in which they are inherent. The three gunas, which compose prakriti, undergo transformation from the unmanifest (avyakta) to the manifest (vyakta) state, produce matter and control it, thus creating the whole cosmos with all beings, time and space uninterruptedly. They relate directly to the human character; strength; see Sattwa; see Rajas; see Tamas. गुण

Gunadhana Samskara /Gunaadhaana Samskaara/ cultivating samskara that help to expand the good qualities already present. गुणाधान संस्कार

Gunamaya threads; consisting of gunas; possessing merits, virtuous. गुणमय

Gunanam multiplication, enumeration; describing merits or qualities. गुणनम्

Gunaniya /Gunaneeya/ multiplied; enumerated; advised. गुणनीय

Guna Rahita Akasha /Guna Rahita Aakaasha/ attributeless space; first of the five mental spaces; see Vyoma Panchaka Dharana. गुणरहित आकाश

Gunasamya /Guna-saamya/ state where the three gunas are found in equilibrium; supreme state of existence. गुणसाम्य

Gunashraya /Guna-aashraya/ dependent on the gunas; consort of the qualities. गुणाश्रय

Gunatita /Guna-ateeta/ freed from all properties; one who is freed and has gone beyond or crossed the three gunas of sattwa, rajas and tamas; see Sthitaprajna. गुणातीत

Gunatrayavibhagayoga /Gunatraya-vibhaaga-yoga/ 'yoga of the division of the three gunas', the 14th chapter of the *Bhagavad Gita*, which describes the distinct qualities of the gunas (sattwa, rajas and tamas), how they bind a human being, and the conduct of one able to transcend them. गुणत्रयविभागयोग

Gunavivechana discrimination in appreciating the merits of others; a just sense of merit. गुणविवेचन

Gunita multiplied; enumerated; heaped together, collected. गुणित

Gupta secret. गुप्त

Gupta Nadi /Gupta Naadee/ flow of energy which runs from the knees across the inside of the thighs into the perineum. गुप्त नाडी

Guru one who dispels the darkness caused by ignorance (avidya); teacher; preceptor; teacher of the science of ultimate reality who, because of extended practice and previous attainment of the highest states of meditation, is fit to guide others in their practice towards enlightenment; gu means darkness, ru means dispeller. गुरु

Guru Bhakta devotee of the guru. गुरु भक्त

Gurukula educational system of ancient India, where children lived in the ashram or family of the guru and were taught a comprehensive syllabus for life by the guru, including the vedanga. गुरुकुल

Guru Purnima /Guru Poornimaa/ holy day for worship of the guru or spiritual teacher when the disciple receives blessings from the guru. It is celebrated on the full moon of the lunar month Ashada, and Chaturmas sadhana begins the next day. गुरु पूर्णिमा

Guru Seva /Guru Sevaa/ service to the guru. गुरु सेवा

Gurutwam /Gurutvam/ quality of the guru; quality of being heavy. गुरुत्वम्

Guru Vritti conduct of a pupil towards the preceptor. गुरु वृत्ति

Gyana see Jnana. ज्ञान

H

Pronunciation

ह् h – as in hut

Ha first syllable of the word 'hatha', 'ha' stands for the sun and 'tha' stands for the moon; form of Shiva; water; sky; blood; an emphatic particle used to lay stress on the preceding word and translatable by 'verily', 'indeed', 'certainly'; often used expletively without any particular significance, especially in vedic literature. ह

Hakini /Haakinee/ the goddess in ajna chakra. हाकिनी

Halam plough. हलम्

Haladhara symbolic name of Balarama meaning 'holder of the plough'. हलधर

Ham bija mantra of the space element and therefore vishuddhi chakra; see Mahabhuta. (हं) हम्

Hamsa swan, goose, duck, flamingo. According to ancient texts, it is the vehicle of the god Brahma and the goddess Saraswati. In poetic convention it is represented as being able to separate milk from water, i.e. as possessing subtle discrimination; the title for a person able to distinguish between reality and unreality in spiritual development; third stage of sannyasa, emphasizing solitary sadhana; individual soul (jivatman); the sun; supreme existence, Brahman; Vishnu; Shiva; see Sannyasa. हंस

Hamsa Mantra correlate of the mantra soham, automatically and involuntarily uttered by the jiva with every act of inspiration and expiration. हंस मन्त्र

Hamsa Vidya /Hamsa Vidyaa/ ability to discriminate between real and unreal. हंस विद्या

Hamsa Yoga teaching of Lord Hari to Brahma and the Kumaras to clear their doubts, as recorded in *Shrimad Bhagavata*. हंस योग

Han to kill, slay, destroy, strike down; to strike or beat; to put down, to abandon; to remove, to take away. हन्

Hanuman /Hanumaana/ name of a powerful monkey chief, who was the son of Anjana by the god of wind named Marut, and hence is also called Maruti. He possessed extraordinary strength and powers which he manifested on several critical occasions on behalf of Shri Rama, the Lord of his heart. He was the chief minister of Rama's allied king Sugreeva, and played a very important part in the great war at Lanka. हनुमान

Hari the sun; a name of Vishnu, one of the gods of the Hindu trinity composed of Brahma, the creator, Vishnu, the preserver, and Shiva, the destroyer; the moon; horse of Indra. हरि

Harih Karta Hi Kevalam /Harih Kartaa Hi Kevalam/ literally 'the transcendental force (Hari) is the only doer'. हरि: कर्ता हि केवलम्

Harijana literally 'people belonging to Hari'; the 'untouchable' class in Hindu society was renamed thus by Mahatma Gandhi. हरिजन

Harishchandra name of a king of the solar dynasty who was famous for his liberality, probity and unflinching adherence to truth. He was put on 'fire' through tests by sage Vishvamitra to prove his noble qualities. Finally, the worthy king was elevated to heaven along with his subjects; see Saubham. हरिश्चन्द्र

Harin taking; attracting; wearing a garland of pearls; robbing, taking away, seizing; disturbing. हरिन

Harsha excitement, joy, pleasure; son of the god Kama. हर्ष

Hasta hand, one of the five organs of action (karmendriyas); the trunk of an elephant; name of the 13th lunar mansion consisting of five stars; see Devata; see Karmendriya. हस्त

Hata killed, slain; hurt, struck, injured; lost, perished; disappointed, frustrated. हत

Hatha the word 'hatha' is derived from two bija mantras 'ham' and 'tham'. 'Ha' represents the solar or pranic energy (pingala) and 'tha' the psychic or lunar energy (ida) in the human body, and the union of these two forces is hatha yoga. हठ

Hatharatnavali /Hatha-ratnaavalee/ traditional text giving the tantric aspects of yoga. हठरत्नावली

Hatha Vidya /Hatha Vidyaa/ the science of forced meditation. हठ विद्या

Hatha Yoga a system of yoga which specifically deals with practices for bodily purification; yoga of attaining physical and mental purity and balancing the prana (energy) in ida and pingala nadis so that sushumna nadi opens, enabling samadhi experiences; the purpose of hatha yoga is to purify the body and help to establish perfect harmony between the positive and negative forces; hatha yoga is the way towards realization through rigorous discipline. हठ योग

Hatha Yoga Pradipika /Hatha Yoga Pradeepikaa/ text on hatha yoga compiled by Yogi Swatmarama, usually translated as 'Light on Hatha Yoga', and which culminates in laya yoga techniques. हठ योग प्रदीपिका

Hatha Yogi /Hatha Yogee/ one who practises hatha yoga, or who is adept in it. हठ योगी

Havan /Havana/ fire ritual performed for incidental purposes (naimittika karma) using the essence of butter from cow's milk (ghee) as the oblation. हवन

Hemanta winter season comprised of two months, viz. Margashirsha and Pausha; see Ritu; see Masa. हेमन्त

Hetu cause, reason. हेतु

Himsa /Himsaa/ anything which disrupts the natural flow of human perception and consciousness; violence, killing, harm, injury. हिंसा

Hiranya golden. हिरण्य

Hiranyagarbha cosmic subtle body; the golden egg or womb of creation; golden seed of the unity of life. Hiranyagarbha is the first formation from the formless, the beginning of all time and space which spreads from the centre of the immeasurable present. The history of the universe and of human beings is unwinding from this everlasting, all pervading timeless centre. It is said that Brahman alone is creating himself from his own substance. According to *Yajnavalkya Smriti*, Hiranyagarbha was divided into two parts, so endowing tension and union, event, motion, evolution and the whole cosmos with endless possibilities and manifestations. One half is called prakriti or nature, the other half of the One is purusha, or the witness of all events, the cosmic mirror in which all pictures and actions are reflected and so become conscious. हिरण्यगर्भ

Hiranyakashipu a celebrated demon king and father of Prahlada, he was slain by Vishnu to save Prahlada, who was a great devotee of Lord Vishnu. हिरण्यकशिपु

Hiranyamaya made of gold, golden. हिरण्यमय

Hitanadi /Hita-naadee/ common name of several nerves leading from the heart, where the individual soul enters in deep sleep. हितनाडी

Hitopadesha (Hita-upadesha); collection of fables, literally 'salutary instruction'. हितोपदेश

Holika, Holi /Holikaa, Holee/ festival of colours or spring festival; beginning of the new year according to one of the Indian almanacs. होलिका, होली

Homa sacrificial fire which symbolizes the divine light on earth; ritualistic process in which oblations to the devata are offered into the fire while maintaining a sitting position. होम

Homadhenu sacred cows owned by rishis, whose milk was used to make ghee for the sacrificial offerings. होमधेनु

Hota /Hotaa/ priest who recites the *Rigveda* in a sacrifice, a priest adept in homa. होता

Hrid, Hridayam entrails; interior of the body; the heart; core. हृद्, हृदयम्

Hridaya heart; essential centre; see Amrita Nadi. हृदय

Hridaya Dhauti literally 'cleaning of the heart'; cleaning of the throat and chest internally by various means using techniques of hatha yoga; see Shatkarma. हृदय धौति

Hridaya Kamala lotus of the heart. हृदय कमल

Hridayakasha /Hridaya-aakaasha/ psychic space of the heart centre where the creative hues of emotion are observed, experienced between manipura and vishuddhi chakras, associated with anahata chakra; see Akasha. हृदयाकाश

Hridayakasha Dharana /Hridaya-aakaasha Dhaaranaa/ vedic meditative process involving concentration on anahata chakra and the heart space. हृदयाकाश धारणा

Hrita taken, seized, taken away; deprived; charmed. हृत

Hritamanasa /Hrita-maanasa/ whose mind is fascinated. हृतमानस

I

Pronunciation
इ i – as in hill
ई i –as in fleet

Iccha /Ichchhaa/ wish, desire; will. इच्छा

Iccha Bhojanam /Ichchhaa Bhojanam/ food asked for by a guest. इच्छा भोजनम्

Icchanivritti /Ichchhaa-nivritti/ indifference to desires; suppression of desires; tranquillity. इच्छानिवृत्ति

Iccha Shakti /Ichchhaa Shakti/ creative force or that desire which is the first manifestation of the greater mind; omnipotent desire-force. इच्छा शक्ति

Icchati /Ichchhati/ to seek, to endeavour to obtain; to wish, desire, intend. इच्छति

Ida Nadi /Idaa Naadee/ channel of lunar energy between the left nostril and the base of the spine, governing the left side of the body and the right side of the brain. The ida energy flow crisscrosses the spine through the major chakras between mooladhara and ajna, conducting the passive aspect of prana manifesting as mental force, lunar force or chitta shakti. Ida nadi and its counterpart pingala nadi have been related to ascending and descending tracts of the autonomic nervous system. These pathways function in yoga to open both the subconscious and superconscious mind; goddess, daughter of Manu; see Pingala Nadi. इडा नाडी

Idam this, here. इदम्

Idamta /Idamtaa/ this-ness. इदंता

Ihatya of this place; earthly; being here. इहत्य

Ikshanam /Eekshanam/ seeing, sight; a look; an eye. ईक्षणम्

Ikshita /Eekshita/ seen, regarded. ईक्षित

Ikshvaku /Ikshvaaku/ name of the celebrated ancestor of the solar kings who ruled in Ayodhya. He was the first of the solar kings and a son of Manu Vaivasvata. इक्ष्वाकु

Indira /Indiraa/ a name of Lakshmi, wife of Vishnu. इन्दिरा

Indivara /Indeevara/ blue lotus. इन्दीवर

Indivarini /Indeevarinee/ group of blue lotuses. इन्दीवरिणी

Indra king of the vedic gods, the ruler of heaven; lord of the senses; the mind or the soul; the rain god. इन्द्र

Indrajala /Indrajaala/ illusion or jugglery. इन्द्रजाल

Indrajalikamayasadrisha /Indra-jaalikaa-maayaa-sadrisha/ similar to the illusions created by jugglery; unreal ap-

pearance as in dreams.
इन्द्रजालिकामायासदृश

Indrani, Indra /Indranee, Indraa/ the wife of Indra. इन्द्राणी, इन्द्रा

Indranila /Indra-neela/ sapphire; bright blue colour. इन्द्रनील

Indriya power, force; sense organ; physical power or virility; power of the senses; see Jnanendriya; see Karmendriya; see Indra. इन्द्रिय

Indriyagochara /Indriya-agochara/ imperceptible. इन्द्रियागोचर

Indriyagochara perceptible to the senses. इन्द्रियगोचर

Indriya Jaya conquest, restraint or mastery of the senses by controlling desires. इन्द्रिय जय

Indriya Jnana /Indriya Jnaana/ sensory knowledge or the faculty of perception; consciousness. इन्द्रिय ज्ञान

Indriyamayatana /Indriyam-aayatana/ abode of the senses, i.e. the body. इन्द्रियमायतन

Indriya Nigraha restraint of the senses. इन्द्रिय निग्रह

Indriya Samyama to restrain the senses. इन्द्रिय संयम

Indriya Sannikarsha contact of a sense organ (either with its object or with the mind). इन्द्रिय सन्निकर्ष

Indriya Swapa /Indriya Svaapah/ insensibility, unconsciousness, stupor. इन्द्रिय स्वाप:

Indu the moon; the number one. इन्दु

Ira /Iraa/ the Earth; speech; goddess of speech; Saraswati. इरा

Irshya /Eershyaa/ envy, jealousy. ईर्ष्या

Isha /Eesha/ master, lord; name of an Upanishad; powerful, supreme; the all-pervasive deity of anahata chakra; pole of a carriage or plough. ईश

Ishaa /Eeshaa/ name of Durga. ईशा

Ishana /Eeshaana/ ruler, master, lord; name of Shiva; the Sun (as a form of Shiva); name of Vishnu. ईशान

Ishitvam /Eeshitvam/ superiority, greatness, lordship; one of the eight siddhis which gives the power to wilfully create and destroy; see Siddhi. ईशित्वम्

Ishwara /Eeshvara/ higher reality; unmanifest existence; non-changing principle or quality; principle of higher consciousness defined by Patanjali in the *Yoga Sutras* as a special purusha (soul) beyond the effect of karma (actions) and klesha (affliction); a state of consciousness beyond the physical and mental realms governing the entire physical universe; supreme being, lord, master; one who rules; powerful, able, capable; see Nashwara. ईश्वर

Ishwara Pranidhana /Eeshvara Pranidhaana/ cultivation of faith in the supreme or indestructible reality; one of the niyamas described by Patanjali in the *Yoga Sutras*; complete dedication of one's actions and will to the Lord; see Niyama. ईश्वर प्रणिधान

Ishwara Prayatna /Eeshvara Prayatna/ God's will. ईश्वर प्रयत्न

Ishta object of desire; the chosen ideal; the particular form of God one is devoted to; a sacrificial rite; worshipped, reverenced, beloved; liked, favourite, dear. इष्ट

Ishta Devata /Ishta Devataa/ personal deity, one's favourite god, one's tutelary deity, the aspect of God which is dear to you; see Sakara Ishta. इष्ट देवता

Ishta Mantra mantra of the chosen deity. इष्ट मन्त्र

Ishti wish, request, desire; seeking any desired object; desired rule or desideratum (something much desired). इष्टि

Itara Lingam, Itarakhya Lingam /Itara Lingam, Itaraakhya Lingam/ the consolidated black shivalingam seen in ajna chakra symbolizing the astral or subtle body; see Linga. इतर लिंगम्, इतराख्य लिंगम्

Iti through or thus. इति

Itihasa /Itihaasa/ legendary or traditional history; heroic history such as the great epics *Mahabharata* and *Ramayana*; historical evidence, tradition. इतिहास

J

Pronunciation

ज् *j* – as in joy; झ् *jh* – as in hedgehog
ज्ञ् *jn* – as in gnu

Ja born, produced; belonging; see Jan. ज

Jada cold, chilly; benumbed, rigid, paralyzed, motionless; senseless; dull-witted, stupid, non-intelligent; irrational; insentient. जड

Jada Prakriti unmanifest primordial nature which sustains all dimensions of creation, including tanmatras, mahabhutas and the aspects of mind (antahkarana). जड प्रकृति

Jada Samadhi /Jada Samaadhi/ state of samadhi induced by the hatha yogic process in which there is no awareness or illumination, as opposed to the chaitanya samadhi of the Vedantins. जड समाधि

Jado Jadabheda difference between various classes of matter. जडो जडभेद

Jagarana /Jaagarana/ waking, wakefulness, watchfulness, vigilance. जागरण

Jagartti /Jaagartti/ to be awake, watchful or attentive; to be roused from sleep; to foresee; to be provident. जागर्त्ति

Jagrat /Jaagrat/ first dimension of consciousness, witnessed by Vaishvanara according to *Mandukya Upanishad*; state of consciousness related to the senses and the phenomenal material universe. जाग्रत्

Jagradavastha /Jaagradavasthaa/ (Jaagrat-avasthaa); state of waking consciousness; consciousness of the objective universe; according to *Mandukya Upanishad*, the first state of consciousness, related to the 'A' of Aum; see Vaishvanara; see Avasthatraya. जाग्रदवस्था

Jagrita /Jaagrita/ conscious mind; sense of awakening. जागृत

Jagat world; universe; the material dimension; living creatures that can move; wind. जगत्

Jagachchakshus (Jagat-chakshus); literally 'eye of the universe', a name of the sun. जगच्चक्षुस्

Jagadadhara /Jagadaadhaara/ (Jagat-aadhaara); foundations of the world; time; air or wind. जगदाधार

Jagadamba /Jagadambaa/ (Jagat-ambaa); literally 'mother of the world', another name for Durga. जगदम्बा

Jagadatman /Jagadaatman/ (Jagat-aatman); the supreme spirit, the supreme consciousness; state of existence. जगदात्मन्

Jagadguru (Jagat-guru); world preceptor. जगद्गुरु

Jagadvyapara /Jagat-vyaapaara/ worldly business. जगद्व्यापार

Jagannatha /Jagannaatha/ (Jagat-naatha); lord of the world. जगन्नाथ

Jagannivasa /Jagannivaasa/ (Jagat-nivaasa); the supreme being; epithet of Vishnu; worldly existence. जगन्निवास

Jaimini disciple of Vyasa and the sage who wrote the Dharma Shastras; see Purva Mimamsa. जैमिनि

Jaina ancient religion noted for strict adherence to non-violence (ahimsa); see Jina. जैना

Jala /Jaala/ net, snare; web, cobweb; eye-hole, lattice, window; collection, assemblage, mass; not real, illusion; born, grown, arisen; caused, happened, living, living being; origin, race, sort, class. जाल

Jalandhara Bandha /Jaalandhara Bandha/ throat lock in which the chin rests forward upon the upper sternum, arresting the flow of breath in the throat; technique that frees the psychic blockages of Rudra granthi and controls the network of nadis, nerves and blood vessels flowing to the brain; see Bandha; see Granthi. जालन्धर बन्ध

Jala water; kind of fragrant medical plant; frigidity. जल

Jaladhara /Jala-dhaaraa/ waterfall. जलधारा

Jalakasha /Jala-akaasha/ space that is reflected together with clouds, stars, etc. in the water contained in a jar; space belonging to the water of a jar. जलाकाश

Jala Neti nasal cleansing using warm saline water); see Shatkarma. जल नेति

Jalpati to speak, converse; to murmur; to babble, gossip; to debate. जल्पति

Jambha jaws, tooth; eating, biting; a portion; the name of a demon killed by Indra. जम्भ

Jambhaka, Jrimbha a yawn; gaping. जम्भक, जृम्भ

Jambuka jackal. जम्बुक

Jamuna see Yamuna. जमुना

Jan to be born or produced; to rise, spring up or grow; to be, to become; to happen, take place or occur. जन्

Jana creature, living being; individual or person. जन

Janana birth, being born; causing, production, creation; appearance, manifestation, rise; life, existence. जनन

Janata /Janataa/ birth; number or assemblage of people, community, mankind. जनता

Janati to give birth. जनति

Janma birth; origin, production, creation; life, existence; birthplace; nativity. जन्म

Janmashtami /Janmaashtamee/ eighth day of the dark fortnight in the lunar month of Bhadrapada, birthday of Lord Krishna. जन्माष्टमी

Janmachakra the wheel of life. जन्मचक्र

Janmadhipa /Janmaadhipa/ (Janma-adhipa); epithet of Shiva; ruler of a constellation under which a person is born (in astrology). जन्माधिप

Janmakundali /Janma-kundalee/ diagram in a horoscope in which the positions of different planets at the time of one's birth are marked. जन्मकुण्डली

Janmapatra, Janmapatrika /Janma-patra, Janma-patrikaa/ literally 'birth paper' or 'birth letter'; a horoscope. जन्मपत्र, जन्मपत्रिका

Jantu creature, living being, man; the individual soul; animal in the lowest state of evolution. जन्तु

Jantumati /Jantu-matee/ literally 'mother of living beings', the Earth. जन्तुमती

Janus birth; creation, production; life, existence. जनुस्

Janyu birth, creature, living being; fire; the creator or Brahma. जन्यु

Janah Loka plane of rishis and munis; one of the seven higher planes of consciousness; see Loka. जनः लोक

Janaka father, progenitor; name of a famous king of Videha or Mithila, who was the foster-father of Sita. He was remarkable for his great knowledge, good works and holiness. जनक

Janmejaya name of a celebrated king of Hastinapura, son of Parikshita and great-grandson of Arjuna. जन्मेजय

Janati /Jaanaati/ to know, to understand, to learn, to acknowledge, to consider. जानाति

Janu /Jaanu/ the knee. जानु

Japa to rotate or repeat continuously without a break; repetition of a mantra or name of God; see Mantra. जप

Japarahitadhyana /Japa-rahita-dhyaana/ meditation without repetition of a mantra. जपरहितध्यान

Japasahitadhyana /Japa-sahita-dhyaana/ meditation with repetition of a mantra. जपसहितध्यान

Japa Yoga yoga of mantra repetition; system of union with the highest existence through repetition of a mantra or rotation of consciousness. जप योग

Jara /Jaraa/ old age; see Shadurmi. जरा

Jarayu /Jaraayu/ womb. जरायु

Jata /Jataa/ matted hair of sadhus and ascetics. जटा

Jata Mandala /Jataa Mandala/ matted locks of hair coiled on top of the head. जटा मण्डल

Jatayu /Jataayu/ a semi-divine bird, who was the son of Syeni and Aruna. While Sita was being carried away by Ravana, Jatayu heard her cries and fought desperately with the formidable giant to rescue her, but became mortally wounded and remained in that state until Rama passed, searching for Sita. The kind-hearted bird told Rama his wife had been carried away by Ravana, and then breathed his last. His funeral rites were duly performed by Rama and Lakshmana. जटायु

Jathara the digestive faculty; gastric fluid; belonging to or being in the stomach; abdominal area. जठर

Jathara Parivartana to and fro movement of the abdomen. जठर परिवर्तन

Jati /Jaati/ kinsman, relative; community; race, caste, lineage. जाति

Jatismarana /Jaati-smarana/ remembrance of incidents of one's previous births (whether spontaneously or through special voluntary effort). जातिस्मरण

Jatyantaraparinama /Jaatyantara-parinaama/ (Jaati-antara-parinaama); transformation of one genus or species into another; see Sajatiyabheda. जात्यन्तर परिणाम

Jaya victory, success, the exclamation 'Be victorious!'; control, mastery, e.g. 'asana jaya' means mastery over asana. जय

Jayadeva name of a poet, author of *Gita Govinda*. जयदेव

Jayashabda shout of victory; the exclamation 'Be victorious!' जयशब्द

Jayati to win (by conquest or in gambling); to conquer (with reference to passions); to conquer, defeat, overcome, subjugate; to surpass, excel; to be victorious, supreme or pre-eminent; to curb, restrain, control. जयति

Jighamsu /Jighaamsu/ an enemy; one desirous of killing, murderous. जिघांसु

Jighatsa /Jighatsaa/ the desire to eat, hunger; striving for; contending with. जिघत्सा

Jigisha /Jigeeshaa/ the desire for conquest or to subdue or overcome; emulation; rivalry; eminence; exertion; profession; habit of life. जिगीषा

Jignasu sannyasa /Jijnaasu sannyaasa/ aspirant; spiritual seeker; preliminary stage of sannyasa. जिज्ञासु संन्यास

Jihva /Jihvaa/ the tongue or the organ of taste and speech, one of the five jnanendriyas (organs of knowledge); see Devata. जिह्वा

Jina a follower of the Jaina doctrine, which emphasizes absolute non-violence (ahimsa) and the multi-faceted nature of reality. जिन

Jitendriya (Jita-indriya); one who has control over the indriyas or senses. जितेन्द्रिय

Jiva /Jeeva/ principle of life, vital breath; individual or personal soul; life, existence; creature, living being; living, existing, vivifying. जीव

Jiva Chaitanya /Jeeva Chaitanya/ individual consciousness. जीव चैतन्य

Jivajivabheda /Jeeva-jeeva-bheda/ difference between one individual and another. जीवजीवभेद

Jiva Loka /Jeeva Loka/ the world of living beings, the world of mortals, the world of earthly existence; living beings, mankind; another name for bhuh loka; see Loka. जीव लोक

Jivana /Jeevana/ life, existence; the principle of life; vital energy; water; livelihood, profession, means of existence; enlivening, animating, life-giving. जीवन

Jivanmukta /Jeevan-mukta/ a soul who is liberated while living; a person who, being purified by true knowledge of the supreme reality, is freed from future births and all ceremonial rites while yet embodied; in Vedanta, a person who has experienced all seven stages of wisdom (jnana bhumika). जीवन्मुक्त

> **Jivanmukti** /Jeevan-mukti/ final liberation in the present state of life; expanded state of awareness; see Videhamukti. जीवन्मुक्ति

Jivanta Prakriti /Jeevanta Prakriti/ the effulgent nature which sustains the dimension of time, space and object. जीवन्त प्रकृति

Jivasaphalya /Jeeva-saaphalya/ realization or attainment of the chief purpose of human existence; the fulfilment of human birth. जीवसाफल्य

Jivat /Jeevat/ living, alive. जीवत्

Jivatma /Jeeva-aatmaa/ individual or personal soul. जीवात्मा

Jivika /Jeevika/ living being; servant; Buddhist mendicant; any mendicant who lives by begging. जीविक

Jna to know (in all senses); to learn; to become acquainted with; to be aware of; to find out, ascertain or investigate; to comprehend, apprehend or understand; to feel; to experience; to recognize. ज्ञ

Jnana /Jnaana/ knowing, understanding; hearing; consciousness; cognizance; higher knowledge derived from meditation or from inner experience; wisdom; the organ of intelligence, sense, intellect. ज्ञान

Jnana Bhumika /Jnaana Bhoomikaa/ literally 'the foundation or basis for knowledge'; step, stage or degree in the attainment of knowledge; in the Vedanta tradition these seven stages are: shubhechha, suvichara, tanumanasi, sattwapati, asamshakti, padarthabhavana and turiya. ज्ञान भूमिका

Jnanabhyasa /Jnaana-abhyaasa/ repeated and uninterrupted practice of discriminating wisdom, the term generally used for the vedantic mode of sadhana. ज्ञानाभ्यास

Jnana Chakshu /Jnaana Chakshu/ literally the 'eye of wisdom' or intelligence, the mind's eye; immediate vision of reality. ज्ञान चक्षु

Jnanagni /Jnaana-agni/ fire of spiritual knowledge or wisdom. ज्ञानाग्नि

Jnanakanda /Jnaana-kaanda/ that inner or esoteric portion of the Vedas referring to true higher knowledge, or knowledge of the supreme state of existence as distinguished from knowledge of ceremonial rites. ज्ञानकाण्ड

Jnanakarmasannyasayoga /Jnaana-karma-sannyaasa-yoga/ 'yoga of wisdom, action and renunciation of the fruits of action', another name given for the fourth chapter of the *Bhagavad Gita*. ज्ञानकर्मसंन्यासयोग

Jnanakasha /Jnaana-aakaasha/ the ether or space of knowledge; Brahman. ज्ञानाकाश

Jnana Marga /Jnaana Maarga/ path of knowledge by which one finds realization; see Jnana Yoga. ज्ञान मार्ग

Jnana Maya /Jnaana Maya/ full of knowledge. ज्ञान मय

Jnana Mudra /Jnaana Mudraa/ hand gesture in which the tip of the index finger is brought in contact with the tip of the thumb, while the remaining three fingers are kept extended. The gesture is a symbol of intuitive knowledge and wisdom (jnana) as the index finger symbolizes the individual soul, the thumb signifies the universal soul, and their union symbolizes true knowledge; see Mudra. ज्ञान मुद्रा

Jnananishtha /Jnaana-nishthaa/ established in the knowledge of the self. ज्ञाननिष्ठा

Jnana Shakti /Jnaana Shakti/ power of knowing; the omnipotent universal force of knowledge. ज्ञान शक्ति

Jnanaswarupa /Jnaana-svaroopa/ of the very nature or embodiment of knowledge. ज्ञानस्वरूप

Jnanasya /Jnaanasya/ pertaining to knowledge. ज्ञानस्य

Jnana Tantra /Jnaana Tantra/ tantric text on higher knowledge. ज्ञान तन्त्र

Jnana Tapas /Jnaana Tapas/ penance consisting of the acquisition of true knowledge. ज्ञान तपस्

Jnana Tattwa /Jnaana Tattva/ true knowledge; knowledge of the real substance of the cosmos. ज्ञान तत्त्व

Jnanavibhagayoga /Jnaana-vibhaaga-yoga/ 'yoga of the division of wisdom', the fourth chapter of the *Bhagavad Gita*, in which it is declared that God is born in every age to protect righteousness and destroy evil, so have faith. ज्ञानविभागयोग

Jnanavijnanayoga /Jnaana-vijnaana-yoga/ 'yoga of wisdom and realization', the seventh chapter of the *Bhagavad Gita*, which explains that the lower nature of the divine manifests as the world via the five elements (mahabhutas) and that the higher conscious nature of the divine is the unmanifest. ज्ञानविज्ञानयोग

Jnana Yoga /Jnaana Yoga/ yoga of knowledge and wisdom attained through spontaneous self-analysis and investigation of abstract or speculative ideas; the path of knowledge; constant and serious thinking on the true nature of the self as taught by the guru; contemplation as the principal means of attaining the higher knowledge of reality; leading a discriminative lifestyle, living with wisdom. ज्ञान योग

Jnana Yogi /Jnaana Yogi/ one who practises the scheduled discipline of the path of knowledge; one who lives wisdom; one endowed with viveka and vairagya. ज्ञान योगी

Jnanendriya /Jnaanendriya/ (Jnaana-indriya); sensory organ; five subtle organs of perception, viz. ears (karna or shrotra), skin (twacha), eyes (chakshus), tongue (jihva) and nose (nasika or ghrana); see Karmendriya; see Devata. ज्ञानेन्द्रिय

Jnani /Jnaani/ one who expresses wisdom in daily life. ज्ञानी

Jnanodaya /Jnaanodaya/ (Jnaana-udaya); dawn of knowledge. ज्ञानोदय

Jnasa /Jnaasa/ to know, understand or be aware of; to recognize; to live in harmony; to watch or be on the alert. ज्ञास

Jnata /Jnaata/ known, understood. ज्ञात

Jnata /Jnaataa/ knower. ज्ञाता

Jnatiya /Jnateeya/ relationship. ज्ञातीय

Jneya /Jneya/ knowable, to be known or understood, object of knowing. ज्ञेय

Josha pleasure, satisfaction. जोष

Ju /Joo/ speed; atmosphere; female demon; epithet of Saraswati. जू

Jwala /Jvaalaa/ flame. ज्वाला

Jwalati /Jvalati/ blazes, shines. ज्वलति

Jyeshtha best; eldest; third lunar month according to the Hindu almanac, corresponding to May/ June; see Grishma; see Masa; see Ritu. ज्येष्ठ

Jyeshtha /Jyeshthaa/ a star. ज्येष्ठा

Jyoti, Jyotis light, brightness, fire. ज्योति, ज्योतिस्

Jyoti Mandir /Jyoti Mandira/ temple of light. ज्योति मन्दिर

Jyotirdhyana /Jyotirdhyaana/ (Jyotih-dhyaana); meditation on light; see Dhyana. ज्योतिर्ध्यान

Jyotirlinga natural oval-shaped stone worshipped as Lord Shiva, there are 12 jyotirlingas worshipped in different parts of India; symbol of pure consciousness; the effulgent shivalingam in sahasrara symbolizing the illumined state of consciousness; induces concentration of mind; see Linga. ज्योतिर्लिङ्ग

Jyotirmatha one of the four major matha established by Adi Shankaracharya in the four geographical quarters of India, situated in Badrinath in the north. It was assigned the *Atharva Veda* with its maha vakya (great statement) 'Ayam Atma Brahma' (soul is Brahman). Its first head was Trotakacharya. The Giri, Parvata and Sagara orders of the Dashnami Sampradaya emanate from there. ज्योतिर्मठ

Jyotirswarupa /Jyotirsvaroopa/ (Jyotih-svaroopa); of the form of light. ज्योतिस्वरूप

Jyotisha astronomy; the eye of the Vedas; a necessary tool in yoga to ascertain athe uspicious times for different techniques, etc.; one of the six sciences auxiliary to the Vedas; the branch of vedanga that deals with astronomical and astrological matters with respect to vedic karma; see Vedanga. ज्योतिष

Jyotishmati /Jyotishmatee/ luminous, full of light; supersensory perception. ज्योतिष्मती

Jyotishtoma literally 'praise of light'; a soma ceremony; knowledgable or wise person; true knower. ज्योतिष्टोम

Jyotsna /Jyotsnaa/ moonlight; light of the soul; light of consciousness; effulgence. ज्योत्स्ना

K

Pronunciation
क् k – as in king; ख् kh – as in inkhorn
क्ष् ksh – as in rickshaw

Kaikeyi /Kaikeyee/ princess of the Kekayas, a wife of Dasharatha, who caused the exile of Shri Rama. कैकेयी

Kailasa /Kailaasa/ name of a mountain peak of the Himalayas; residence of Shiva and Kubera. कैलास

Kaivalya final liberation; that state of consciousness which is beyond duality; perfect isolation; final emancipation; nirvana; the state that unifies all differences; see Kramamukti. कैवल्य

Kaivalya Pada /Kaivalya Paada/ fourth and last part of Patanjali's *Yoga Sutras* which explains the nature of liberation. कैवल्य पद

Kaivalyapragbharam /Kaivalya-praagbhaaram/ inclined towards oneness. कैवल्यप्राग्भारम्

Kaka /Kaaka/ crow, a symbol of alertness for the yogi. काक

Kakabhushundi /Kaaka-bhushundi/ a devotee of Lord Rama who in a previous life as a brahmin devotee of Lord Shiva showed disrespect for his guru. Lord Shiva therefore cursed him to be reborn as a crow for thousands of years. His humble and loving guru interceded for him and he was thus given the chance to have Lord Rama's darshan. His story is related in the *Ramacharitamanasa* by Tulsidasa. काकभुशुण्डि

Kaki /Kaakee/ crow's beak. काकी

Kaki Mudra /Kaakee Mudraa/ an important yogic practice for cooling the body; by virtue of this mudra one becomes disease-free like a crow; see Mudra. काकी मुद्रा

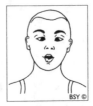

Kakini /Kakinee/ the goddess in anahata chakra, the heart lotus. काकिनी

Kala /Kaala/ black or dark blue colour; time (in general); proper time or portion of time; time considered as one of the nine substances; one of the five kanchukas (limiting aspects of energy) which creates the dimension of time and restricts the individual within it; one of the eight bhairavas or states of consciousness; the supreme spirit regarded as the destroyer of the universe; epithet of Shiva as a personification of the destructive principle or law of existence; Yama, the god of death; the planet Saturn; the weather. काल

Kala Bhairava /Kaala Bhairava/ Shiva in his terrible aspect as destroyer of the universe; a personification of the destructive principle; see Bhairava. काल भैरव

Kala Chakra /Kaala Chakra/ wheel of time. काल चक्र

Kala Loka /Kaala Loka/ dimension that comes under the influence of time and its secondary aspect, space. काल लोक

Kalanemi /Kaalanemi/ the rim of the wheel of time; the name of a demon. कालनेमि

Kalanirupana /Kaala-niroopana/ determination of time, chronology. कालनिरूपण

Kala Purusha /Kaala Purusha/ name of the god of time; dimension of existence beyond time. काल पुरुष

Kalaratri /Kaala-raatri/ literally 'dark night'; night of destruction at the end of the world; epithet of Durga. कालरात्रि

Kalatita /Kaala-ateeta/ beyond time. कालातीत

Kalena /Kaalena/ by time. कालेन

Kali /Kaalee/ goddess of destruction and wife of Lord Shiva; epithet of Parvati or Durga; divine mother; primal manifestation of Shakti who destroys time, space and object (i.e. ignorance); yogic state of consciousness; blackness, night; black ink; row of black clouds; dark blue colour; see Shakta. काली

Kalidasa /Kaalidaasa/ the most renowned dramatist and poet in Sanskrit literature, whose work *Abhijnana Shakuntala* is universally respected. He is said to have been a simple woodcutter who received great wisdom and poetic gifts due to his devotion for Kali; see Shakuntala; see Kartikeya. कालिदास

Kalika /Kaalikaa/ relating to time; depending on time; epithet of Durga. कालिका

Kala /Kalaa/ one of the five kanchuka (limiting aspect of energy) which restricts the creative power of individual consciousness and body; the manifest universe of time and space; ray or force which emanates from the nucleus of bindu due to vibrations caused by nada; part of a letter or word; art. कला

Kalasha copper vessel. कलश

Kali strife, quarrel, dissension, contention; war, battle; age personified; evil; black. कलि

Kali Yuga the age of Kali, which lasts 432,000 years and is the fourth and current era (yuga) of the world now more than 5,000 years old, the 'iron' age, dark, evil, difficult and full of strife; see Yuga. कलि युग

Kalinga name of a country and its inhabitants; district on the coast of Coromandel. कलिंग

Kaliya /Kaaleeya/ black sandalwood tree. कालीय

Kaliya /Kaaliya/ name of a tremendously large serpent who dwelt at the bottom of the river Yamuna, a place forbidden to Garuda, the enemy of serpents, due to a curse by the sage Saubhari. Kaliya was subdued by the child Krishna. कालिय

Kalki the tenth incarnation of Vishnu; see Avatara. कल्कि

Kalpa according to *Suryasiddhanta* a kalpa lasts 4,320,000,000 years (consisting of many mahayugas). Two kalpas make a day and a night of Brahma; ritual, ceremony; one of the six auxiliary sciences (vedanga) of the Vedas; the *Kalpa Sutras* are manuals that provide meticulous details of the processes and rules of yajna; see Yuga; see Vedanga. कल्प

Kalpana /Kalpanaa/ imagination, thought; an idea, fancy or image conceived in the mind; forming or arranging; composition; fixing or settlement; doing, performing; repairing; rejuvenation. कल्पना

Kalpanamatra /Kalpanaa-maatra/ mere imagination, existing only in imagination. कल्पनामात्र

Kalpanika /Kaalpanika/ existing only in fancy, fictitious, that which is imagined; falsely created. काल्पनिक

Kalpa Taru, Kalpa Vriksha 'wish-fulfilling tree'; a psychic centre activated when anahata chakra is awakened, resulting in the ability to materialize what is desired. कल्प तरु, कल्प वृक्ष

Kalyana /Kalyaana/ auspicious, beautiful, lovely, good; happiness, prosperity, virtue. कल्याण

Kama /Kaama/ emotional need for fulfilment; wish, object of desire; affection, love; the god of love. When the gods needed a commander for their forces in their war with Taraka, they sought Kama's aid in drawing Shiva's mind towards Parvati, for only her child would be able to vanquish the demon. Kama fulfilled the mission, but Shiva, being offended at the disturbance to his penance, burnt him to ashes with the fire of his third eye. Kama was reborn as Pradyumna, the son of Krishna and Rukmini, and married Rati; semen, virility; desire for sensual enjoyments considered as one of the four ends of life; see Purushartha; see Shadvairi. काम

Kamadhenu /Kaama-dhenu/ cow belonging to Indra, believed to yield whatever may be desired from her. कामधेनु

Kamagni /Kaama-agni/ fire of passion. कामाग्नि

Kamaja /Kaama-ja/ born of desire or passion. कामज

Kamakanchana /Kaama-kanchana/ lust and wealth, the two great barriers to self-realization. कामकञ्चन

Kamamaya /Kaama-maya/ full of desire and lust; infatuated due to lust. काममय

Kamarupa /Kaama-roopa/ 'of the

form of desire', so named after Kama. कामरूप

Kamarupi /Kaama-roopee/ taking any form at will. कामरूपी

Kamasankalpa /Kaama-sankalpa/ something to be gained; being desirous of something. कामसङ्कल्प

Kamashakti /Kaama-shakti/ force of lust and desire. कामशक्ति

Kamavashitva /Kaamavashitva/ fulfilment of every wish. कामवशित्व

Kami /Kaamee/ one who acts under the influence of passion or desire for pleasure. कामी

Kamyakarma /Kaamya-karma/ any action done with desire for the fruits thereof. काम्यकर्म

Kamala lotus; water; copper; medicament, drug. कमल

Kamalasanam /Kamala-aasanam/ lotus-seated; name of Brahma. कमलासनम्

Kamandalam, Kamandalu waterpot, earthen or wooden, carried by sannyasins or ascetics. कमण्डलम्, कमण्डलु

Kanchi Matha /Kaancchee Matha/ also known as the sarvajna peetha where only the most learned could sit. It is dedicated to Devi and Shri Vidya. Ubhaya Bharati was reputedly installed as its first head by Adi Shankaracharya. कञ्ची मठ

Kanchuka invisible cloak of maya which limits or restricts consciousness and creates the notion of duality; literally 'sheath' or 'envelope'; five in number, viz. 1. kalaa: limits the power to do all, 2. avidyavidya: limits the power to know all, 3. raga: creates like and dislike, 4. kaala: limits per-

petual existence by creating the notion of time, and 5. niyati: limits freewill. कंचुक

Kanda root of a plant; root of the nadis in the human body. *Hatha Yoga Pradipika* describes vajrasana, ashwini mudra and moolabandha as exciting kundalini to rise because they affect the subtle kanda situated close to the anus; see Ashwini Mudra; see Mulabandha. कन्द

Kanda /Kaanda/ bulbous root; knot; place where the three main nadis: sushumna, ida and pingala, unite and separate. काण्ड

Kandam /Kaandam/ section, a part in general; the portion of a plant from one knot to the other; stem, stock, branch; any division of a piece of work, such as a chapter of a book, like the seven kandas of the *Ramayana*. काण्डम्

Kandarpa a name of the god of love; love. कन्दर्प

Kantatwa /Kaantatva/ loveliness, beauty. कान्तत्व

Kanti /Kaanti/ loveliness, beauty; splendour; brilliance, effulgence; a quality of Devi; embellishment; desire, wish. कान्ति

Kantha throat, neck; the voice. कण्ठ

Kanthamula /Kantha-moola/ base of the neck, throat. कण्ठमूल

Kanya /Kanyaa/ young girl; virgin. कन्या

Kapala /Kapaala/ skull, cranium, forehead from the eyebrows to bindu; earthen frying pan used to roast flour as an oblation item. कपाल

Kapalabhati /Kapaalabhaati/ one of the six major cleansing techniques of hatha yoga (shat-karma), a process of clearing the cranial region using the breath or water to reduce phlegm (kapha); see Shatkarma. कपालभाति

Kapalabhati Pranayama /Kapaalabhaati Praanaayaama/ technique used to raise the pranic energy of the body and centre it at ajna chakra; here the inhalation is natural but the exhalation is vigorous; technique of purifying the frontal region of the brain by breathing rapidly through the nostrils with the emphasis on exhalation. कपालभाति प्राणायाम

Kapaladhauti /Kapaala-dhauti/ a type of dhauti also called bhalabhati in *Gherand Samhita*; three processes for cleansing excess mucus or phlegm from the head: 1. by rapid inhalation and exhalation through alternate nostrils (vatakrama), 2. by water drawn through the nostrils and ejected through the mouth (vyutkrama), 3. the reverse of vyutkrama (shitkrama); see Shatkarma. कपाल धौति

Kapala Randhra Dhauti /Kapaala Randhra Dhauti/ washing of the skull, regarded as the seat not only of the nerves and large brain, but also yogic power; see Shatkarma. कपाल रंध्र धौति

Kapalashodhana /Kapaala-shodhana/ variation of kapalabhati. कपालशोधन

Kapalika /Kaapaalika/ tantric sect whose practices involve the use of skulls. कापालिक

Kapha mucus, phlegm, one of the three humours (doshas) de-scribed in ayurveda; see Dosha. कफ

Kapila Muni name of the sage who founded the Sankhya philosophy. कपिल मुनि

Kapinjala the chataka bird which is supposed to drink only raindrops and dew. कपिञ्जल

Kapota dove; pigeon; bird. कपोत

Karana /Kaarana/ cause, reason; the unmanifested potential cause that in due time takes shape as the visible effect; material cause of the universe remaining during the period of dissolution, i.e. potential cosmic energy; the generative cause, creator, father; the origin; ground, motive; object; instrument; element, elementary matter; the body. कारण

Karanabrahman /Kaarana-brahman/ the highest and first manifestation of the absolute qualified by maya; Brahman with attributes; see Saguna Brahman. कारणब्रह्मन्

Karanajagat /Kaarana-jagat/ causal world. कारणजगत्

Karanasalila /Kaarana-salila/ primeval waters; the potential condition of the cosmic energy described figuratively as the water of an all-pervading ocean. कारणसलिल

Karanasharira /Kaarana-shareera/ causal body; also called anandamaya kosha; see Pancha Kosha. कारणशरीर

Karanavairagya /Kaarana-vairaagya/ dispassion caused by misery or disaster in life. कारणवैराग्य

Karanavastha /Kaarana-avasthaa/

causal state or condition. कारणावस्था

Karanaviveka /Kaarana-viveka/ slight discrimination caused accidentally. कारणविवेक

Kari /Kaaree/ that which produces. कारी

Karma, Karman action and result; action in the manifest and unmanifest dimension; work, deed; duty; in vedic parlance karma means sacrifice (yajna) at the physical level; law of cause and effect that shapes the destiny of each individual with actions inevitably bearing their fruit, as the law operates inexorably throughout the universe; pity, tenderness; it also implies devoted action to alleviate the suffering of the afflicted; each individual spirit (jiva) is under the influence of four types of karma; see Sanchita; see Prarabdha; see Agami; see Kriyamana; see Satkaryavada. कर्म, कर्मन्

Karmabandha bondage caused by karma. कर्मबन्ध

Karmabhumi /Karma-bhoomi/ land of action; the earth plane; see Bhogabhumi. कर्मभूमि

Karmadhyaksha /Karma-adhyaksha/ controller or ruler of actions; God; soul. कर्माध्यक्ष

Karma Kanda /Karma Kaanda/ the part of the Vedas that relates to sacrificial rules and ceremonial acts on the physical level; see Purva Mimamsa. कर्म काण्ड

Karma Marga /Karma Maarga/ the path of a dynamic person, leading towards self realization through action. कर्म मार्ग

Karma Mimamsa /Karma Meemaamsa/ another name for Purva Mimamsa. कर्म मीमांसा

Karmapara dependent on karma; advocating an action-oriented lifestyle. कर्मपर

Karmaphala fruit or result of action; the consequence of any deed in the shape of pain or pleasure; merit arising from due performance of karma. कर्मफल

Karma Sannyasa /Karma Sannyaasa/ householder sannyasa; renunciation combined with duty. कर्म संन्यास

Karmasannyasayoga /Karmasannyaasa-yoga/ 'yoga of renouncing (the fruits of) action', the fifth chapter of the *Bhagavad Gita*, which explains dissociating oneself from the doership or enjoyership of any karma by resting in Brahman. कर्मसंन्यासयोग

Karma Shakti power of action. कर्म शक्ति

Karmashaya /Karma-aashaya/ deep layers of consciousness where the karmas are stored in the form of impressions, symbols or archetypes; repository of karma; aggregate of works done. कर्माशय

Karmavada /Karma-vaada/ the doctrine of karma upholding that each action, good or bad, is inevitably followed by pain or pleasure as its sure effect. कर्मवाद

Karmavipaka /Karma-vipaaka/ fruits of past actions. कर्मविपाक

Karma Yoga the yoga that reveals the secret of action; action performed with meditative awareness; dynamic spirituality;

yogic path of selfless service; yogic discipline based on the law of cause and effect; gaining immunity to karma by dedicating one's actions to God; actions performed unselfishly for the welfare of others, without attachment to the fruit of one's action and renouncing the doership and enjoyership of any action. कर्म योग

Karmayoga 'yoga of action', the third chapter of the *Bhagavad Gita*, which explains that action done without selfish desire, purely as duty or sacrifice, does not bind but liberates. कर्मयोग

Karma Yogi /Karma Yogee/ one who practises karma yoga. कर्म योगी

Karmendriya (Karma-indriya); motor organs, five physical organs of action, viz. vocal cords (vach), hands (hasta), feet (pada), genital organ (upastha), anus (payu); see Jnanendriya; see Devata. कर्मेन्द्रिय

Karna the ear, one of the five organs of knowledge; to listen, to come to the ear, to become known; unacknowledged son of Kunti and Surya (the sun god), who nevertheless became famous for his courage, nobility, loyalty and generosity. He was a celebrated warrior on the side of the Kauravas in the *Mahabharata*, but was finally placed in an untenable position when Lord Krishna and his mother explained that Arjuna and the Pandavas were actually his brothers; see Jnanendriya; see Devata; see Kaunteya. कर्ण

Karna Dhauti methods of cleaning the ears; see Shatkarma. कर्ण धौति

Karna Pida /Karna Peedaa/ pressure around the ear. कर्ण पीडा

Karta /Kartaa/ doer, maker, creator, author, one who acts. कर्ता

Kartritva doership; see Bhoktritva. कर्तृत्व

Kartavya performing action with knowledge; that which ought to be done; duty. कर्तव्य

Kartavya Dharma duty as an expression of inherent nature. कर्तव्य धर्म

Kartika /Kaartika/ eighth lunar month of the Hindu almanac, corresponding to October/November and deemed auspicious for sadhana; see Sharada; see Masa; see Ritu. कार्तिक

Kartikeya /Kaartikeya/ the planet Mars; the god of war in Indian mythology, he was the son of Shiva and Parvati, also known as Kumara, whose birth forms the subject matter of *Kumarasambhava*, the epic poem written by Kalidasa; see Tarakah. कार्तिकेय

Karuna /Karunaa/ mercy, compassion, kindness. करुणा

Karunavishta /Karunaa-aavishta/ invaded by pity, sympathetic. करुणाविष्ट

Karunya /Kaarunya/ compassion, kindness. कारुण्य

Karya /Kaarya/ effect (correlate of karma); the physical body is described as the karya, whereas the causal body is described as the karana (cause); the world; Hiranyagarbha; what ought to be done or performed, duty; business affair; matter, thing, fact;

religious rite. कार्य

Karyabrahma /Kaarya-brahma/ Hiranyagarbha; Brahman expressed in karma. कार्यब्रह्म

Karya Karanasambandha /Kaarya Kaarana-sambandha/ relation between the cause and the effect. कार्य कारणसम्बन्ध

Karya Samiti /Kaarya Samiti/ working committee for selection of initiates for Naga sannyasa. कार्य समिति

Karya Shakti /Kaarya Shakti/ power to accomplish. कार्य शक्ति

Karya Tattwarthavit /Kaarya Tattva-arthavit/ one who knows the meaning of the essence of actions. कार्य तत्त्वार्थवित्

Karyavastha /Kaarya-avasthaa/ condition of an effect; karma-based state. कार्यावस्था

Karya Vimukti /Kaarya Vimukti/ liberation from activity; final emancipation. कार्य विमुक्ति

Kashaya /Kaashaaya/ red, dyed a reddish colour, a red cloth or garment; see Geru. काषाय

Kashaya /Kashaaya/ passion, emotion; subtle impressions produced by enjoyment which remain latent and later distract the mind from samadhi; hidden impressions; Kali yuga. कषाय

Kashi /Kaashee/ the modern Varanasi (Benares). काशी

Kashmir Shaivmata /Kaashmeer Shaivmata/ Kashmir Shaivism, a school of tantra based on the Trikashastra, a division of Shaivism found in North India; see Trika; see Prakasha; see Vimarsha. काश्मीर शैवमत

Kashta evil; sin, wickedness, bodily evil; hardship, difficulty; misery, suffering; painful, grievous; effort. कष्ट

Kashta Mouna observing silence in which even thoughts are not communicated to others. कष्ट मौन

Kashyapa tortoise; name of a rishi who was the father of gods and demons. He was the son of Marichi, who was a son of Brahma and bore an important share in the work of creation. It is said that Kashyapa married the 13 daughters of Daksha. By Aditi he begot the 12 gods (adityas) and by Diti the demons (daityas). With his other wives he had numerous and diversified progeny such as serpents, reptiles, birds and nymphs of the lunar constellation. The father of the gods, demons and all living beings, he is therefore often called Prajapati, the progenitor; see Takshaka. कश्यप

Katha /Kathaa/ story. कथा

Kathopanishad one of the principal Upanishads belonging to the *Taittiriya Brahmana* of the *Yajurveda*, written in verse and dialogue form, in which the seeker Nachiketa speaks with Yama, the god of death; see Satyameva Jayate. कठोपनिषद्

Kaula Tantra a sect of tantra in which the mother is recognized as the guru of the family lineage. कौल तंत्र

Kaunteya literally 'son of Kunti', usually applied only to Yudhisthira, Bhima or Arjuna, and not to Karna, her great yet unacknowledged first-born son; see Kunti. कौन्तेय

Kaupeena loin cloth. कौपीन

Kaurava, Kauravya relating to the Kurus; descendants of Kuru who fought the fratricidal Mahabharata war against their cousins, the Pandavas. कौरव, कौरव्य

Kaushala welfare; happiness; skilfulness. कौशल

Kaushalya /Kaushalyaa/ daughter of the king of Koshala, mother of Shri Rama and a wife of Dasharatha. कौशल्या

Kaustubha name of a celebrated jewel obtained with 13 other jewels during the churning of the ocean and worn by Vishnu on his breast. कौस्तुभ

Kavacha armour; a sectarian mark paint on the body consisting of lines, curves, circle and designs which bring an aspirant under the protection of a particular deity and protects one from negative forces. कवच

Kavi a wise person, sage; thinker; poet; Brahma; the sun; omniscient; praiseworthy; thoughtful, intelligent, clever. कवि

Kavya /Kaavya/ poem, poetry, poetical composition; happiness; wisdom; inspiration. काव्य

Kaya /Kaaya/ the physical body; a multitude. काय

Kayachikitsa /Kaaya-chikitsaa/ the third of the eight departments of medical science; treatment of diseases affecting the whole body. कायचिकित्सा

Kayakalpa /Kaaya-kalpa/ intensive purificatory practice; see Parakayapravesha. कायकल्प

Kayaklesha /Kaaya-klesha/ mortification and torment of the body; bodily suffering or pain. कायक्लेश

Kayasiddhi /Kaaya-siddhi/ perfection of the body through yoga. कायसिद्धि

Kaya Sthairyam /Kaaya Sthairyam/ practice of absolute steadiness and awareness of the physical body often performed as a preparation for pranayama or meditative states. कायस्थैर्यम्

Kayasthita /Kaaya-sthita/ corporeal, bodily. कायस्थित

Kayavyuha /Kaaya-vyooha/ group of bodies (created by the yogi to exhaust his/her prarabdha karma). कायव्यूह

Kayika /Kaayika/ relating to the body, bodily, corporeal. कायिक

Kendra centre; heart. केन्द्र

Keshava a name of Krishna. केशव

Kevala alone, mere; sole, only; unmingled, pure; entire, whole, wholly; spontaneous. केवल

Kevala Astitva state of absolute being. केवल अस्तित्व

Kevala Chaitanya pure consciousness or intelligence without thought. केवल चैतन्य

Kevala Kumbhaka spontaneous breath retention, the kumbhaka which occurs during samadhi when the consciousness transcends duality, also known as ajapa gayatri or kevala pranayama. केवल कुम्भक

Kevalamasti (Kevalam-asti); pure existence alone; pure consciousness; (He) alone is. केवलमस्ति

Kevalo'ham (Kevalah-aham); 'I am absolute'. केवलोऽहम्

Keyura /Keyoora/ ornament worn on the arm. केयूर

Khechari Mudra /Khecharee Mudraa/ literally 'the attitude of moving in space'; tongue lock; a hatha yoga practice in which the elongated tongue passes back into the pharynx to stimulate the flow of life-giving nectar (amrit), whereas in the milder raja yoga form the tongue is inserted in, or folded backwards towards, the upper cavity of the palate; see Mudra. खेचरी मुद्रा

Khyati /Khyaati/ reputation, fame; knowledge; awareness. ख्याति

Kirita /Kireeta/ diadem. किरीट

Kirtana /Keertana/ singing of God's name; practice in which a group of people sing a collection of mantras; see Mantra; see Bhava Samadhi. कीर्तन

Klesha pain, anguish, affliction, suffering, distress, trouble; five afflictions or causes of suffering described in Patanjali's *Yoga Sutras*, viz. ignorance (avidya), ego or sense of doership (asmita), attraction (raga), aversion (dwesha) and fear of death (abhinivesha); in yoga the five kleshas are the sources of all suffering or troubles, with ignorance (avidya) being considered the chief klesha; see Prasupta; see Tanu; see Udara; see Vichchhinna. क्लेश

Klishta painful; hard or difficult. क्लिष्ट

Kokila Indian cuckoo. कोकिल

Koorma see Kurma. कूर्म

Kosha body or realm of experience or existence; covering of the self which limits manifestation of the ultimate reality; pail, box, vessel in general; cash; treasure; see Pancha Kosha. कोष

Krama order; rules regarding rituals; step, proceeding, course; method, manner; series, succession. क्रम

Kramamukti progressive emancipation of devotees in which they proceed from this world to the world of Brahma, and from there attain kaivalya; the four steps are 1. samipya, 2. salokya, 3. sarupya, 4. sayujya; see Mukti. क्रममुक्ति

Kramati walks, steps; goes, goes over, passes, traverses; ascends; occupies (the space); undertakes; succeeds. क्रमति

Krikara Prana, Krikala Prana / Krikara Praana, Krikala Praana/ name of one of the subsidiary vital airs (pranas) whose function is to prevent substances going up the nasal passages and into the throat by bringing on sneezing and coughing, also induces hunger and thirst; see Upaprana. कृकर प्राण, कृकल प्राण

Kripa /Kripaa/ blessing; grace; mercy. कृपा

Krishna black, dark, dark blue; eighth incarnation of Vishnu, who took birth in Dwapara yuga as the son of Dewaki. He was brought up in Vrindavana by Yashoda and loved Radha, and his activities there are recorded in the *Bhagavata Purana*. He later reclaimed his inheritance and married the princess Rukmini. To uphold dharma he orchestrated the Mahabharata war. His teachings to his friend and disciple Arjuna during that war are immortalized in the *Bhagavad*

Gita. He is perhaps the most celebrated hero in Hindu mythology and seems to be an historical figure, as his capital Dwarka has been discovered at its legendary site; see Avatara; see Gopala; see Bhagavad Gita. कृष्ण

Krishnadvaipayana /Krishna-dvaipaayana/ the famous rishi also known as Vyasa or Veda Vyasa, author of the *Mahabharata,* Puranas and compiler of the Vedas. कृष्णद्वैपायन

Krishnajina /Krishna-ajina/ skin of the black deer; special kind of deerskin used as a seat during worship and yogic meditation. कृष्णाजिन

Kritanasha /Krita-naasha/ destruction of what has been done; destruction of actions done or the rewards of actions that have been done. कृतनाश

Kritartham (Krita-artham); a person whose purpose is fulfilled. कृतार्थम्

Krita Yuga another name for Satya yuga, the aeon of truth and purity, which lasts for 1,728,000 years according to *Suryasiddhanta*; see Yuga. कृत युग

Kriya /Kriyaa/ creative action or motion; in tantric literature kriya is used in the sense of activity that is eternally associated with knowledge and leads to perfection, in which knowledge and action are found to be identical; the six physical cleansing techniques (shatkarma) of hatha yoga: basti, dhauti, kapalabhati, nauli, neti and trataka. क्रिया

Kriyadvaita /Kriyaa-advaita/ oneness in action; practical living of oneness. क्रियाद्वैत

Kriyamana /Kriyamaana/ literally 'what is being done'; the effect of the deeds of the present life which are to be experienced in the future; the same as agami karma; see Karma. क्रियमाण

Kriya Nivritti /Kriyaa Nivritti/ relief from action; emancipation. क्रिया निवृत्ति

Kriya Shakti /Kriyaa Shakti/ power or faculty of acting. क्रिया शक्ति

Kriyavidhi /Kriyaa-vidhi/ rule of action; manner of performing any action. क्रियाविधि

Kriya Yoga /Kriyaa Yoga/ practices of kundalini yoga designed to speed the evolution of humanity; the employment of expedients or means; practical yoga with certain techniques which Patanjali's *Yoga Sutras* list as austerity or intensity (tapas), self-study (swadhyaya) and surrender to the divine (ishwara pranidhana); yoga of action; yoga of self-purification through external service or worship. क्रिया योग

Krodha anger, wrath, aggression; see Shadvairi. क्रोध

Krodhana wrathful, passionate, angry, irascible, hot-tempered. क्रोधन

Kruddha angry, furiousa. क्रुद्ध

Kruramati /Krooramati/ one with a cruel mind or intention. क्रूरमति

Kshama patient, enduring; adequate, competent, able, fit. क्षम

Kshama /Kshamaa/ patience, indulgence, forbearance; forgiveness; the earth; epithet of Durga. क्षमा

Kshana twinkling of an eye, moment, opportunity. क्षण

Kshanti /Kshaanti/ forgiveness. क्षान्ति

Kshara perishable; that which decays. क्षर

Kshatra power, supremacy, dominion, reigning or military order. क्षत्र

Kshatra Dharma /Kshaatra Dharma/ code of life and conduct of the warrior class. क्षात्र धर्म

Kshatriya the kingly or warrior caste, one of the four divisions of the caste system in India; one who protects others from injury; see Varna. क्षत्रिय

  Kshatriya Vidya /Kshatriya Vidyaa/ military science of the warrior caste. क्षत्रिय विद्या

Kshaya destruction; decay; fall, end. क्षय

Kshetra, Kshetram field, ground; place of origin, womb; sphere of action; the body; the mind; dimension; field of influence; place; chakra trigger points located in the frontal psychic passage. क्षेत्र, क्षेत्रम्

Kshetrajna the knower of the body, field or dimension; the soul; the immanent aspect of the supreme self. क्षेत्रज्ञ

Kshetrakshetrajnavibhagayoga /Kshetra-kshetrajna-vibhaaga-yoga/ 'yoga of the distinction between the field and the knower of the field', the 13th chapter of the *Bhagavad Gita* moves from desire and embodiment (the field) via humility, non-attachment and constancy in knowledge of the self, to seeing the supreme existing equally in all beings. क्षेत्रक्षेत्रज्ञविभागयोग

Kshina /Ksheena/ powerless, weak; thin, diminished, worn away. क्षीण

Kshinavritti /Ksheena-vritti/ a person who has weakened the modifications of mind (vrittis). क्षीणवृत्ति

Kshipati casts, throws (a glance), puts; strikes, insults, reviles; destroys; passes (time). क्षिपति

Kshipta wandering, dissipated or scattered state of mind (due to the overpowering force of rajas), the second of the five states of mind; see Manas. क्षिप्त

Kshiti Earth. क्षिति

Kshobha to shake or tremble, to be agitated or disturbed; to be unsteady; to stumble. क्षोभ

  Kshubhita shaken; agitated; afraid; enraged. क्षुभित

Kshudra little or minute; miserable; bad. क्षुद्र

  Kshudra Brahmanda /Kshudra Brahmaanda/ microcosm; human body. क्षुद्र ब्रह्माण्ड

Kshut hunger. क्षुत्

Kubera the god of wealth and treasure and the regent of the northern quarter with his abode in Kailash. He is represented as being bodily deformed, having three legs, only eight teeth and a yellow mark in place of one eye; see Yaksha. कुबेर

Kucharya /Kucharyaa/ evil conduct. कुचर्या

Kula family, lineage, race; collection, herd, troop, multitude; abode. कुल

Kuladharma duty to the family. कुलधर्म

Kula Kundalini /Kula Kundalinee/ the primordial cosmic energy located in the individual; see Kundalini. कुल कुण्डलिनी

Kumara /Kumaara/ child, boy, youth; prince; son; the four mental sons of Brahma, the creator, named Sanaka, Sanandan, Sanatana and Sanat Kumar; see Kartikeya. कुमार

Kumari /Kumaaree/ young girl; virgin. कुमारी

Kumari Pujanam /Kumaaree Poojanam/ worship of young girls. कुमारी पूजनम्

Kumbha a pot; in yoga it means closing the nostrils and mouth, to suspend the breath. कुम्भ

Kumbhamela /Kumbha-melaa/ huge bathing festival held at four auspicious places on the river Ganges (Ganga) every 12 years. The pot (kumbha) of nectar (amrit) that was found after churning the ocean was placed on Earth in these four places, viz. Nasik, Ujjain, Haridvar and Allahabad (the modern name for Prayaga). Millions of devotees attend the gatherings and the heads of the sannyasa traditions meet; see Atmic Triveni. कुम्भमेला

Kumbhaka internal or external retention of breath, a conscious process practised with shatkarma, asana, pranayama, mudra and bandha that aims at either retaining breath within the body (antarkumbhaka) or keeping it outside the body (bahir or bahya kumbhaka), and a spontaneous process accompanying samadhi states; see Kevala Kumbhaka. कुम्भक

Kumbhakarana so called because his ears were like pots (kumbha) in that whatever flowed into them never came out, i.e. he kept secrets. He was the brother of the demon king Ravana. While requesting a boon from the gods, instead of Indrapada (heaven) he asked for nidrapada (state of sleep), which was readily granted to him. It is said that he sleeps for six months at a time and then wakes up for only one day. कुम्भकरण

Kunda a kind of jasmine (white and delicate); epithet of Vishnu. कुन्द

Kunda cavity; vessel; pit; a pit made to kindle the sacrificial fire at a yajna or a copper pot to hold such a fire. कुण्ड

Kundala Kesha curly-haired. कुण्डल केश

Kundalini /Kundalinee/ literally 'coiled', circular, spiral, winding, coiling (like a serpent); spiritual energy; evolutionary potential related to the capacity and consciousness of human beings; the form of divine cosmic energy lying dormant in mooladhara chakra, epithet of

Varuna, regent of the ocean. कुण्डलिनी

Kundalini Shakti /Kundalinee Shakti/ Devi described as the potential energy of a human being dormant in mooladhara chakra, which, when awakened, works to awaken the chakras, resulting in progressive enlightenment; see Samarasatva; see Sushumna Nadi. कुण्डलिनी शक्ति

Kundalini Yoga /Kundalinee Yoga/ path of yoga which awakens the dormant spiritual force. कुण्डलिनी योग

Kunjal Kriya /Kunjal Kriyaa/ cleansing the stomach by voluntary vomiting using warm saline water, a form of dhauti; see Shatkarma; see Vamana Dhauti. कुञ्जल क्रिया

Kunti /Kuntee/ daughter of Yadava and the first wife of Pandu (who was unable to beget sons to continue the royal line). However, as a child, through devoted service to Sage Durvasa, Kunti received the power to invoke the deities Surya, Yama, Vayu and Indra for the births of Karna, Yudhisthira, Bhima and Arjuna respectively. She also invoked the Ashwinau to enable Pandu's other wife Madri to bear Nakula and Sahadeva. कुन्ती

Kurma /Koorma/ a tortoise; see Avatara. कूर्म

Kurma Nadi /Koorma Naadee/ psychic pathway in the throat. कूर्म नाडी

Kurma Prana /Koorma Praana/ minor prana responsible for opening and closing the eyes, blinking, and controlling the movement of the eyelids to prevent foreign matter or excessive light from entering the eye; see Upaprana. कूर्म प्राण

Kuru clan of the opponents of the Pandava princes in the *Mahabharata* epic. कुरु

Kusha sacred grass used for ritualistic purposes. कुश

Kutastha /Koota-stha/ absolute changelessness; the one who is found without exception in all creatures from Brahma, the creator, down to ants, and who is shining as the self, dwelling as the witness in all creatures; rock-seated; unchanging; another name for Brahman; established at the top; what stands above and beyond illusion; firm being; kuta means immoveable, stha means to stand. कूटस्थ

Kutastha Chaitanya /Kootastha Chaitanya/ inner self; individual consciousness destitute of egoism. कूटस्थ चैतन्य

Kutir /Kuteera/ small hut; simple dwelling. कुटीर

Kutichaka /Kuteechaka/ 'hut dweller', first stage of sannyasa where one lives simply and serves the guru for 12 years; see Sannyasa. कुटीचक

L

Labdha Chakshu endowed with supernatural sight. लब्ध चक्षु

Labha /Laabha/ gain, benefit. लाभ

Labhati catches, seizes; obtains, gets, meets with, finds, receives, has; perceives, sees, knows. लभति

Laghava /Laaghava/ according to *Hatha Yoga Pradipika*, it is the lightness of body gained through the practice of asana; according to *Gheranda Samhita* it is the lightness gained from pranayama. लाघव

Laghima /Laghimaa/ lightness; the power of making the body light; reducing the weight of the body at will; one of the eight major siddhis of yoga practice; see Siddhi. लघिमा

Laghu short form; light, not heavy; little, small, diminutive; easy, not difficult; soft, low, gentle; pleasant, desirable. लघु

Laghu Hasta light-handed; clever, dextrous, expert; active, agile. लघु हस्त

Laghu Kaya /Laghu Kaaya/ light-bodied. लघु काय

Laghukrama having a light step; going quickly. लघुक्रम

Laghu Shankhaprakshalana /Laghu Shankhaprakshaalana/ a light, short form of the practice of shankhaprakshalana, in which the digestive tract from mouth to anus is washed by drinking six glasses of saline water and practising a series of five asana; a modified form of dhauti; see Shatkarma. लघु शंखप्रक्षालन

Lajja /Lajjaa/ shyness, bashfulness, embarrassment; a quality of Devi. लज्जा

Lakini /Laakinee/ goddess of manipura chakra, benefactress of all. लाकिनी

Lakshana mark, sign, characteristic, name, indication; definition; kind, sort; aim, object. लक्षण

Lakshana Vritti the inherent power in a sound which gives rise to a thought of certain qualities like name, form, etc. that are directly or indirectly associated with it; indicative statement. लक्षण वृत्ति

Lakshya aim; stage; something to be looked at or observed; visible, perceptible; point of concentration; target. लक्ष्य

Lakshyartha /Lakshya-artha/ implied meaning; see Maha Vakya. लक्ष्यार्थ

Lakshmana a hero of the epic *Ramayana*, the brother of Rama whom he accompanied into exile; see Balarama. लक्ष्मण

Lakshmana Rekha /Lakshmana Rekhaa/ the protective line,

circle or boundary drawn by Lakshmana when he left Sita alone to search for Rama. Her sense of duty caused her to overstep the boundary, whereupon she was kidnapped by the terrorist Ravana. लक्ष्मण रेखा

Lakshmi /Lakshmee/ wealth; good fortune, good luck; loveliness, grace; success, accomplishment; the goddess of fortune, prosperity and beauty, and the wife of Vishnu, she is said to have sprung from the ocean along with other precious 'jewels' when it was churned for nectar by the gods and demons; creative power of manipura chakra; see Shakta. लक्ष्मी

Lalana /Lalanaa/ minor chakra at the back of the throat above the palate where nectar (amrit) can be collected as it falls from bindu visarga; the tongue; a wanton woman. ललना

Lalata /Lalaata/ forehead. ललाट

Lalita sportive, lovely, innocent, simple. ललित

Lalita /Lalitaa/ a wanton woman; epithet of Durga and Parvati; the goddess Lalita is red-coloured, denoting energy, and is hymned in the *Shri Lalita Pancharatnan* of Adi Shankaracharya as the prime cause of creation, protection and destruction of the universe; the esoteric goddess of Shri Yantra. ललिता

Lam bija mantra of the earth element and therefore mooladhara chakra; see Mahabhuta. लं (लम्)

Lambodara literally 'big-bellied'; epithet of Ganesha. लम्बोदर

Lanka /Lankaa/ name of the island residence of Ravana, presently called Sri Lanka. लङ्का

Laukika relating to phenomenal reality; worldly, terrestrial; common, ordinary, customary. लौकिक

Lauliki /Laulikee/ a hatha yoga practice which stimulates the digestive fire and manipura chakra; the name of nauli in *Gherand Samhita*; see Shat Karma. लौलिकी

Laulya fickleness, unsteadiness, inconstancy; eagerness, eager desire; greed; lustfulness, excessive passion or desire. लौल्य

Laxman see Lakshmana. लक्ष्मण

Laxmi see Lakshmi. लक्ष्मी

Laya dissolution, solution; disappearance, extinction, destruction; union, fusion, melting; sticking, adherence; lurking. लय

Laya Chintana concentration of the mind with a view to dissolving it; that kind of vedantic meditation where the mind is carried on progressively from grosser to subtler ideas until it is dissolved in the unmanifest Brahman, e.g. the bhutalaya chintana, the antahkaranalaya chintana and omkaralaya chintana. लय चिन्तन

Laya Kala /Laya Kaala/ the time of destruction (of the universe). लय काल

Laya Krama the order of the dissolution of the tattwas. लय क्रम

Laya Yoga yoga of conscious dissolution of individuality; a system of yoga where suspended animation takes place; the preferred technique for samadhi explained in the final chaper of *Hatha Yoga Pradipika*. लय योग

Leshavidya /Lesha-avidyaa/ trace of ignorance. लेशाविद्या

Lila /Leelaa/ literally 'play'; diversion, pleasure; activity of prakriti and its three gunas. लीला

Lilamati /Leelaa-matee/ a connotative name of the divine force for whom creation and dissolution are mere play or sport. लीलामती

Lilavilasa /Leelaa-vilaasa/ the splendour of the divine sport. लीलाविलास

Linga to be absorbed; mark, sign, characteristic; sign of gender, male organ; idol of Shiva; a naturally formed oval stone; often means the Shivalingam, an archetypal symbol; see Shivalingam; see Dhumralingam; see Itarakhya Lingam; see Jyotirlinga. लिङ्ग

Lingadeha astral body, subtle body. लिङ्गदेह

Lingamatra /Lingamaatra/ with mark or symbol. लिङ्गमात्र

Linga Purana /Linga Puraana/ ancient scripture describing the life of Shiva, the purushartha and the significance of Shivalingam worship. लिङ्ग पुराण

Lingasharira /Linga-shareera/ the subtle or psychic body that becomes particularly active during the dream state by creating a world of its own; the three sheaths of intelligence (vijnanamaya kosha), mind (manomaya kosha) and vital energy (pranamaya kosha) that constitute the subtle or psychic body. लिङ्गशरीर

Lingatman /Linga-atman/ subtle self. लिङ्गात्मन्

Lobha greed, desire; see Shadvairi. लोभ

Lobhana allurement, temptation. लोभन

Lubhayati desire, longing for. लुभयति

Lochana seeing, sight; the eye. लोचन

Loka open space, place, region; plane of existence, dimension; the world, earth; people, humankind; of the 28 planes of consciousness or regions, the highest seven are called loka, the next seven are chakra, the next seven patalam and the lowest seven naraka; seven divine regions explained as being above sahasrara chakra, viz. bhuh (or jiva), bhuvah, swah, mahah, janah, tapah and satya lokas; see Chakra; see Patalam; see Naraka; see Mahavyahriti. लोक

Loka Dwaya /Loka Dvaya/ both worlds (heaven and earth). लोक द्वय

Lokasangraha solidarity of the world; upliftment of society. लोकसङ्ग्रह

Lokayata /Lokaayata/ Charvaka or materialist philosophy. लोकायत

Lokeshana /Lokeshanaa/ (Loka-eshanaa); attachment to any expectations from people or the world; attachment to one's place or to one's past; desire for name and fame; desire for popularity; see Eshana Traya. लोकेषणा

Lola tremulous; moving to and fro like a swing or pendulum; fickle; greedy. लोल

M

Ma /Maa/ mother, divine mother; see Shakta. मा

Mada arrogance; see Shadvairi. मद

Madana love; the god of love. मदन

Madhu sweet, agreeable, delightful; sweet food or drink such as honey, milk, nectar, soma. मधु

Madhuparka a sweet made of honey, sugar, ghee, milk and curd, traditionally offered in worship; see Shodashopachara. मधुपर्क

Madhura sweet, pleasant, melodious; the feeling when the devotee looks upon God as their beloved. मधुर

Madhurya Bhava /Maadhurya Bhaava/ attitude of lover and beloved towards the Lord. माधुर्य भाव

Madhushala /Madhushaalaa/ literally 'place where honey is kept', refers to nectar (amrit) within the body of the seeker which brings about a state of spiritual ecstasy; a place where intoxicating herbs and liquor are served. मधुशाला

Madhuvidya /Madhu-vidyaa/ process of meditation on Brahman taking the sun (honey) as a symbol of Brahman. मधुविद्या

Madhya intermediate; interior; middle of the body; into the midst of, into; central; impartial. मध्य

Madhya Lakshya intermediate stage; intermediate aim. मध्य लक्ष्य

Madhyama /Madhyamaa/ middle, intermediate; intermediate sound, the second stage of nada yoga in which the meditator perceives nada and electromagnetic pulsation within the entire body, also called whispering sound (upanshu); see Nada Yoga. मध्यम

Madhyama Vairagya /Madhyama Vairaagya/ mediocre renunciation; not intense vairagya. मध्यम वैराग्य

Madri /Maadree/ the second wife of Pandu, who, with the help of Kunti, invoked the Ashwinau twins and bore Pandu two sons, Nakula and Sahadeva. मात्री

Madya wine; one of the five makara of tantra; see Panchamakara. मद्य

Magadha a place in south Bihar and the name of its people. मगध

Magha /Maagha/ 11th lunar month according to the Hindu almanac, corresponding to January/February; see Shishira; see Masa; see Ritu. माघ

Maha /Mahaa/ great; noble. महा

Maha Akasha great space; third intermediate space of the five subtle spaces of vyoma panchaka, which is described as being bright like the middle of the sun; see Vyoma Panchaka Dharana. महा आकाश

Maha Bandha /Mahaa Bandha/ the great lock, a combination of jalandhara bandha, uddiyana bandha and moolabandha, practised with external kumbhaka; see Bandha. महा बन्ध

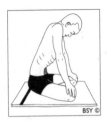

Mahabharata /Mahaa-bhaarata/ epic of ancient India said to be composed by Vyasa, involving the history and consequences of the great battle between the Kaurava and Pandava princes. It describes the rivalries and contests of the five sons of Pandu (the Pandava) and the 100 sons of Dhritarashtra (the Kaurava). It consists of 18 sections and the *Bhagavad Gita* is a part of it; see Krishna. महाभारत

Maha Bhashya /Mahaa Bhaashya/ a great commentary; particularly the great commentary of Patanjali on the sutras of Panini, which explain Sanskrit grammar. महा भाष्य

Maha Bhava /Mahaa Bhaava/ the highest type of self-dedication to the divine (as represented by Shri Radha in Vaishnava symbolism); see Radha. महा भाव

Maha Bheda Mudra /Mahaa Bheda Mudraa/ great piercing attitude; in kriya yoga it includes jalandhara bandha, uddiyana bandha and moolabandha with concentration on the breath and rotation of awareness through specific nadis and energy centres; see Mudra. महा भेद मुद्रा

Mahabhuta /Mahaa-bhoota/ the elements (space, air, fire, water and earth); see Pancha Mahabhuta. महाभूत

Mahabodhi /Mahaa-bodhi/ Buddha, literally 'the great awakening'. महाबोधि

Mahadeva /Mahaa-deva/ name of Shiva. महादेव

Mahah Loka; one of the seven higher dimensions of consciousness; plane of saints and siddhas; see Loka. मह:.लोक

Mahakala /Mahaa-kaala/ literally 'great or endless time'; cosmic time; timelessness; Shiva in his aspect of the destroyer. महाकाल

Mahakaleshvara /Mahaa-kaala-eeshvara/ one of the 12 jyotirlinga worshipped in India; see Jyotirlinga. महाकालेश्वर

Maha Kalpa /Mahaa Kalpa/ the great cycle, 100 years of Brahma, when the whole universe is dissolved in the unmanifested state. महा कल्प

Mahakalpitajagat /Mahaa-kalpita-jagat/ the world created by the mind or imagination. महाकल्पितजगत्

Mahakasha see Maha Akasha. महाकाश

Maha Moha /Mahaa Moha/ great infatuation (of mind); epithet of Durga. महा मोह

Mahamrityunjaya /Mahaa-mrityunjaya/ literally 'the great one who is victorious over death'; a form of Shiva. महामृत्युञ्जय

Mahamrityunjaya Mantra
/Mahaa-mrityunjaya Mantra/
the 'great victory over death'
mantra, used to avoid calamities. महामृत्युञ्जय मन्त्र

Maha Mudra /Mahaa Mudraa/
'great attitude', in this sitting posture the apertures at the top and
bottom of the trunk are held fast
and sealed. In kriya yoga it com-
bines moolabandha, akashi
mudra, khechari mudra and
shambhavi mudra along with rotation of awareness through specific nadis and energy centres
(chakras); see Mudra. महा मुद्रा

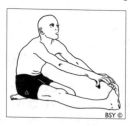

Mahan /Mahaan/ 'the great', according to Sankhya philosophy
the first evolute from prakriti
which reflects the consciousness
of purusha into the inert material world, also known as mahat,
Brahma and Hiranyagarbha; see
Mahat. महान्

Maha Nidra /Mahaa Nidraa/ literally 'the great sleep', the real
sleep: death. महा निद्रा

Maha Nirvana /Mahaa Nirvaana/
total extinction of individuality
according to Buddhist philosophy; see Nirvana. महा निर्वाण

Maha Prana /Mahaa Praana/
prana in its cosmic unmanifest
aspect. महा प्राण

Maharshi /Mahaa-rishi/ literally
'great seer'; a great sage or saint;
singer of vedic hymns. महर्षि

Mahas /Mahaas/ greatness; nu-
merousness; infiniteness; sacred
knowledge. महास्

Maha Samadhi /Mahaa
Samaadhi/ final liberation experienced on the departure of the
spirit from the body; death; see
Samadhi. महा समाधि

Mahatala /Mahaa-tala/ the sixth
centre of the instinctive or animal body below mooladhara
chakra; see Patalam. महातल

Maha Tattwa /Mahaa Tattva/ literally 'the great element', the
third of 25 principles of Sankhya;
of great essence; see Mahat. महा
तत्त्व

Mahatma /Mahaa-aatmaa/ literally 'great soul'; used with reference to a person who has destroyed the ego and realized the
self as one with all; high-souled,
high-minded, magnanimous, noble; supreme consciousness, supreme spirit. महात्मा

Maha Vakya /Mahaa Vaakya/ four
great statements of the Upanishads, viz. 1. Prajnanam Brahma:
Consciousness is Brahman, 2.
Aham Brahmasmi: I am Brahman, 3. Tat Twam Asi: You are
That, 4. Ayam Atma Brahma:
The soul (atma) is Brahman.
Continuous meditation (nididhy-
asanam) on these mantras can
lead the qualified aspirant directly to realization; any continuous composition or literary work.
महा वाक्य

Maha Videha /Mahaa Videha/
name of a certain state or condi-

tion of the mind where one loses body consciousness, according to yoga philosophy. महा विदेह

Maha Vrata /Mahaa Vrata/ literally 'great vow'; great spiritual observance; Jaina monks and nuns are renowned for their very devotional observance of such vows. In the *Yoga Sutras*, Rishi Patanjali explains that observing the yamas universally without regard for circumstance, time or place transforms them into maha vrata. महा व्रत

Mahavyahriti /Mahaa-vyaahriti/ the seven worlds: bhuh (or jiva), bhuvah, swahah (suvah), mahaloka, janah, tapah (or tapo) and satya (or Brahma) lokas; see Loka. महाव्याहृति

Maha Yatra /Mahaa Yaatraa/ the great pilgrimage, the pilgrimage to Varanasi (Benares). महा यात्रा

Mahayogin /Mahaa-yogin/ 'great yogi', epithet of Shiva and Vishnu. महायोगिन्

Mahendra (Mahaa-indra); literally 'the great Indra'; great leader; name of a mountain. महेन्द्र

Maheshvara (Mahaa-eeshvara); great lord, sovereign; name of Shiva; name of Vishnu; see Ishwara. महेश्वर

Mahodaya (Mahaa-udaya); literally 'great sunrise', the great dawning; birth of our consciousness. महोदय

Mahanta head of a matha; see Matha. महन्त

Mahat great; greater mind; the great principle; the total mind which includes manas, buddhi, chitta and ahamkara; universal intellect (also called buddhi); in Sankhya philosophy mahat is the first product from prakriti's process of manifestation and reflects the consciousness of purusha into the material realm of prakriti's evolutes; big, large, vast; ample, abundant; long, extended, extensive; epithet of Shiva. महत्

Mahatah Parah beyond the great, greater than the great; above the reach of the intellect. महत: पर:

Mahima /Mahimaa/ greatness; glory, majesty, dignity; might, power; high or exalted rank or position; one of the eight major siddhis, the power of increasing size at will; see Siddhi. महिमा

Maithuna physical union; fusion of male and female energies; one of the five makara of tantra; the first basic instinct; copulation; see Panchamakara; see Pravritih. मैथुन

Maitra a high state of existence; Brahman; intimate connection or association, union, contact; belonging to or given by a friend; friendly, well-disposed, amicable, kind. मैत्र

Maitraka friendship. मैत्रक

Maitri /Maitree/ friendliness. मैत्री

Majja /Majjaa/ bone marrow; the pith in plants. मज्जा

Makara /Makaara/ the letter 'M'; the mystic syllable 'M', the third letter that concludes Aum or the pranava nada (original sound); indicator of sushupti avastha (the unconscious state of mind close to samadhi); the first letter of the panchamakara (five M's) of tantra. मकार

Makara dolphin or crocodile, the

symbolic animal associated with swadishthana chakra; emblem of the god Kama. मकर

Mala, Malika /Maalaa, Maalikaa/ wreath, garland, necklace; rosary; in yoga a mala may be made of beads of various substances such as tulsi, rudraksha, sandalwood, sphatika (crystal). One function is to aid mantra repetition; series. माला, मालिका

Malya /Maalya/ wreath, garland. माल्य

Malam dirt; impurity of mind such as lust, greed, anger, etc. मलम्

Malinasattwa /Malinasattva/ impure sattwa; nescience or ignorance (avidya) in the individual. मलिनसत्त्व

Mamakara /Mamakaara/ mineness; the thought 'this is mine' in relation to the body and the things connected with it, such as spouse, children, relations, friends, house, wealth, etc. ममकार

Mamata /Mamataa/ feeling of mineness, sense of ownership, self-interest and selfishness; pride, arrogance; self-sufficiency; individuality. ममता

Mamsa /Maamsa/ flesh; one of the five makara of tantra; see Panchamakara. मांस

Man, Manati /Maan, Maanati/ to be proud; to worship. मान्, मानति

Manana thinking, cognition, reflection, intelligence, understanding; inference arrived at by reasoning; meditation on the eternal verities; second of the three steps on the path of knowledge in vedantic sadhana, the other two being shravana and nididhy-asana; see Maha Vakya. मनन

Mananashakti power of reflection and concentration. मननशक्ति

Mananat /Mananaat/ from reflection or introspection; pondering repeatedly. मननात्

Manas finite mind, rational mind; the mind concerned with senses, thought and counter-thought; perception, intelligence; the internal organ of perception and cognition; the individual mind having the creative power and faculty of attention, selection and rejection; mind classified in five stages, viz. 1. dull (mudha), 2. scattered (kshipta), 3. oscillating (vikshipta), 4. one-pointed (ekagrata), 5. cessation (nirodha); heart, understanding. मनस्

Manasah Manah 'mind of mind', the inner ruler or the self, Brahman. मनस: मन:

Manasaputra /Maanasa-putra/ 'mental son', mentally conceived. मानसपुत्र

Manasashakti /Maanasa-shakti/ mental or lunar energy. मानसशक्ति

Manasa Snana /Maanasa Snaana/ mental bath; a service or rite of worship. मानस-स्नान

Manas Chakram /Maanasa Chakram/ nervous plexus situated between the navel and the heart. मानस चक्रम्

Manasi /Maanasee/ mental. मानसी

Manasika Japa mental repetition of a mantra. मानसिक जप

Manasika Kriya /Maanasika Kriyaa/ mental action. मानसिक क्रिया

Manasika Puja /Maanasika Pooja/ mental worship. मानसिक पूजा

Manasika Shakti /Maanasika Shakti/ power of the mind; intelligence, understanding. मानसिक शक्ति

Manobhava mind-born; god of love, love. मनोभाव

Manodharma natural attributes or properties of the mind. मनोधर्म

Manogata existing in the mind. मनोगत

Manojavitvam speed of the mind. मनोजवित्वं

Manolaya involution and dissolution of the mind unto its cause. मनोलय

Manomaya Kosha mental sheath or body; one of the five sheaths (kosha) covering the self. It is investigated with the aid of pratyahara and dharana techniques and manifests in the dream state and during meditation. One realizes it through various manifestations of mental power and original thinking; mental body, mental sphere of life and awareness; see Pancha Kosha; see Lingasharira. मनोमय कोष

Manomurcha Kumbhaka /Manomoorchhaa Kumbhaka/ retention of breath wherein the mind lapses into unconsciousness; a variety of pralaya. मनोमूर्छा कुम्भक

Manonasha /Mano-naasha/ dissolution of the conditioned mind, destruction of the mind (enabling one to see beyond it); see Pancha Kosha. मनोनाश

Manorajya /Manoraajya/ building castles in the air; mental kingdom; the realm of fancy. मनोराज्य

Manoratha desire of the mind. मनोरथ

Mandala area, zone; circular or round pictorial representation; orb, globe, wheel, ring, disc; troop, group, a collection; a division of the *Rigveda*; diagram within a circumference symbolizing the deeper aspects of the human psyche and capable of invoking cosmic power; complex geometric symbol merging macrocosmic and microcosmic realities. मण्डल

Mandana Mishra also known as Vishvarupa, a famous scholar and champion of Purva Mimamsa and vedic rituals and the husband of Ubhaya Bharati (who was regarded as an incarnation of the goddess Saraswati due to her wisdom). He was defeated in debate by Adi Shankaracharya and became one of his foremost disciples with the name Sureshvaracharya and was the first pontiff of Shringeri Matha after his master. मण्डन मिश्र

Mandara name of a mountain used by the gods and demons as a churning rod when they churned the cosmic ocean. मन्दर

Manduka /Mandooka/ frog. मण्डूक

Manduki Mudra /Mandukee Mudraa/ 'frog attitude', a mudra by which youthfulness of body can be attained; in kriya yoga a technique which sensitizes one to the subtle body; see Mudra. माण्डुकी मुद्रा

Mandukya Upanishad
/Maanduukya Upanishad/ one of the major Upanishads which describes the three states of consciousness represented by the three sacred letters composing Aum and the fourth which unites yet transcends them; see Jagrat; see Swapna; see Sushupti; see Turiya; see Ayam Atma Brahma. माण्डूक्य उपनिषद्

Mangalasutra traditional mala or necklace of black pearl beads which the husband gives to the wife during the marriage ceremony. मङ्गलसूत्र

Mani globule; pearl, jewel, ornament, amulet. मणि

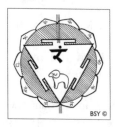

Manipura Chakra psychic/pranic centre situated behind the navel in the spinal column, corresponding to the solar plexus and associated with vitality and energy; centre of willpower; literally 'city of jewels'; see Chakra; see Ram; see Sankalpa. मणिपुर चक्र

Manisha /Maneeshaa/ independent power of thinking, reflection and wisdom; hymn, prayer. मनीषा

Mantra subtle sound vibration; tantric tool which liberates energy from the confines of mun-

dane awareness and expands the consciousness when repeated; a word or sentence propounded by liberated souls to help spiritual aspirants and ordinary people in gaining perfection, health or supernatural powers; vedic hymn; a sacred text; word of power; divine power transmitted through word; incantation; see Mananat. मन्त्र

Mantra Chaitanya the dormant potency of a mantra. मन्त्र चैतन्य

Mantra Diksha /Mantra Deekshaa/ initiation through mantra. मन्त्र दीक्षा

Mantrakara /Mantrakaara/ the author of vedic hymns. मन्त्रकार

Mantra Shakti the potency of any mantra; one of the three shaktis or powers of a ruler (the other two being prabhava and utsaha). मन्त्र शक्ति

Mantra Siddhi the accomplishment, knowledge or power achieved through mantra sadhana. मन्त्र सिद्धि

Mantravan /Mantravaan/ mastering the vedic texts; knowing spells. मन्त्रवान्

Mantra Yoga path of yoga which liberates the mind through sound vibration. मन्त्र योग

Manu the first law-giver; name of a celebrated personage regarded as being the representative and father of the human race (sometimes regarded as one of the divine beings); name of the 14 successive progenitors or sovereigns of the earth, the third Manu is supposed to be a type of secondary creator who produced the

10 Prajapatis or Maharishis and to whom the code of laws known as *Manu Smriti* is ascribed. मनु

Manushya human being; mortal; a male. मनुष्य

> **Manushya Jati** /Manushya Jaati/ humankind, human race. मनुष्य जाति

> **Manushya Yajna** 'sacrifice to be offered to men', hospitality or hospitable reception of guests is one of the five prescribed daily acts of a householder, also called nriyajna and atithi yajna; see Pancha Mahayajna. मनुष्य यज्ञ

Manu Smriti a highly respected book on dharma shastra (code of conduct), indicating one's duty to self and society and defining the purushartha. It was compiled by Bhrigu, believed to be a disciple of Manu; literally 'a text based on memories of the teachings of Manu'. मनु स्मृति

Manyu anger, wrath, resentment, indignation, rage; grief, sorrow, affliction; wretched or miserable state. मन्यु

Mara /Maara/ killing, slaughter, slaying; obstacle, hindrance, opposition; god of love; spiritual death (ignorance), state of being bound to the chain of karma. मार

Mara death; Valmiki's initial 'mantra' which through continued unbroken repetition became Rama and bestowed enlightenment; see Shadurmi. मरा

Mardava /Maardava/ mildness, tenderness, smoothness. मार्दव

Marga /Maarga/ track, path or way to the intended goal; search, inquiry, investigation; a means. मार्ग

Margashirsha /Maargasheersha/ ninth lunar month according to the Hindu almanac, corresponding to November/December; see Hemanta; see Masa; see Ritu. मार्गशीर्ष

Marichi /Mareechi/ name of one of the sons of Brahma, who was a sage and the father of Kashyapa; name of the sun. मरीचि

Marjara Nyaya /Maarjaara Nyaaya/ literally 'kitten theory', which holds that the devotee is picked up and carried effortlessly by the Lord, like a mother cat carries her kitten. मार्जार न्याय

Markata Nyaya /Markata Nyaaya/ literally 'monkey theory', which holds that the devotee must cling to the Lord with effort, like a baby monkey clings to its mother. मर्कट न्याय

Martanda /Maartanda/ the sun god. मार्तण्ड

Martya Loka the mortal world, earth plane. मर्त्य लोक

Marut god of wind. मरुत्

Maryada /Maryaadaa/ the spontaneous correct response to any situation, an attribute particularly notable in Shri Rama. मर्यादा

Masa /Maasa/ month; the 12 lunar months of the Hindu almanac are Chaitra, Vaishakha, Jyeshtha, Ashada, Shravana, Bhadrapada, Ashwina, Kartika, Margashirsha, Pausha, Magha and Phalguna; see Ritu; see Samvatsara. मास

Mata opinion; considered, thought out, understood; honoured. मत

Mati intellect, understanding, sense, knowledge, judgement; thought, idea; belief, opinion, supposition, impression; intention, design, purpose; resolution, determination; wish, desire, inclination; mind; heart. मति

Matha monastery; the four major matha said to be established by Adi Shankaracharya in the four geographical quarters of India are 1. Shringeri Matha, located at Shringeri in the south, 2. Sharada Matha, located at Dwarka in the west, 3. Govardhan Matha, located at Puri in the east, and 4. Jyotirmatha, located at Badrinath in the north, originally headed by Sureshvaracharya, Hastamalakacharya, Padmapadacharya and Trotakacharya respectively. He is also said to have founded the Kanchi Matha in honour of the Devi, and to have originally installed Ubhaya Bharati as its head. Numerous smaller mathas also claim him as founder. मठ

Mathura /Mathuraa/ name of an ancient town which is the birthplace of Lord Krishna, situated on the right bank of the river Yamuna; see Vasudeva. मथुरा

Matra /Maatraa/ unit of time; time interval in pronouncing a vowel; standard measure, rule; unit; moment; particle, atom, element; alone. मात्रा

Matramanameya /Matra-maanameya/ knower, knowing and the known; measurer, measuring and the measured. मात्रमानमेय

Matri /Maatri/ mother; mother as a term of respect or endearment; epithet of Lakshmi; epithet of Durga; epithet of the divine

mother; ether or space; sky; the earth. मातृ

Matrika /Maatrikaa/ little mother; inheritance passed down the female line; Sanskrit syllable with intense creative potential; creative energy concealed in mantra; letters of the Sanskrit alphabet. मातृका

Matsara jealousy, envy; see Shadvairi. मत्सर

Matsarya /Maatsarya/ jealousy; being jealous. मात्सर्य

Matsya fish; particular variety of fish; the king of Matsyas (name of a people and a country); an incarnation of Vishnu, who is the source and maintainance of the universe and of all things; one of the five makara of tantra; see Avatara; see Panchamakara. मत्स्य

Matsyendra, Matsyendranath /Matsyendra, Matsyendranaath/ one of the founders of hatha yoga; a great yogi and guru of Goraksha; though a Shaivite, he is also recognized as a Buddhist saint and a guardian deity of Nepal. मत्स्येन्द्र, मत्स्येन्द्रनाथ

Matta drunk; in a rut; furious; delighted; amorous; mad; shouting with joy. मत्त

Maya /Maayaa/ cause of the phenomenal world; in Vedanta philosophy, the two powers of maya are: 1. the power of veiling (avarana shakti), and 2. the power of projection (vikshepa shakti); partial understanding; wrong or false notions about self-identity; in Sankhya philosophy, pradhana or prakriti (nature); power of creation; illusive power. माया

Maya Mohajala /Maayaa Mohajaala/ the jugglery or deception set up by the infatuation of maya. माया मोहजाल

Maya Shabala Brahma /Maayaa Shabala Brahma/ another name for Saguna Brahman or Ishwara (the Brahman conjoined with attributes, enwrapped in and coloured with maya). माया शबल ब्रह्म

Mayavada /Mayaa-vaada/ theory of illusion, doctrine of the phenomenal character of the universe; also known as mithyavada. मायावाद

Mayavi /Maayaavee/ master magician, great juggler; Brahman. मायावी

Mayopadhi /Maayopaadhi/ (Maayaa-upaadhi); the upadhi or the apparently limiting conditions produced by maya. मायोपाधि

Mayate to think, believe, suppose, imagine, fancy, conceive; to consider, regard, look upon; to honour, respect; to set the heart or mind on. मयते

Medha /Medhaa/ power of retaining the import of studies; intelligence or intellect; power of understanding; wisdom; sacrifice. मेधा

Medhra /Medhraa/ plexus of the pranic body, nadi plexus located just a few centimetres below the navel. मेध्रा

Megha cloud; multitude. मेघ

Meghakasha /Meghaakaasha/ (Megha-aakaasha); cloud-environed ether or space. मेघाकाश

Megha Nada /Megha Naada/ the roll of thunder at a distance which may be meditated upon. मेघ नाद

Mekhala Traya / Mekhalaa Traya/ refers to the three concentric circles surrounding the lotuses yet within the protective wall of Sri Yantra which represent various triads such as rajas, tamas and sattva; see Sri Yantra. मेखला त्रय

Menaka /Menakaa/ a nymph who was the mother of Shakuntala and wife of Vishvamitra. मेनका

Meru name of a fabulous mountain consisting of gold; also known as Sumeru. मेरु

Merudanda spinal column. मेरुदण्ड

Mimamsa /Meemaamsaa/ deep reflection, inquiry; name of one of the six systems (darshana) of vedic philosophy. It was originally divided into two systems: 1. the Purva or Karma Mimamsa founded by Jaimini concerning itself chiefly with the correct interpretation of the ritual of the Veda and the settlement of dubious points in regard to vedic texts, 2. the Uttara or Brahma Mimamsa ascribed to Badarayana, dealing chiefly with the nature of Brahman or the supreme spirit. Today only Purva Mimamsa is usually called Mimamsa and Uttara Mimamsa is ranked separately and called Vedanta; see Purva Mimamsa; see Vedanta; see Shaddarshana. मीमांसा

Mitahara /Mitaahaara/ (Mita-aahaara); balanced, moderate diet; one of the chief disciplines in hatha yoga. मिताहार

Mithila /Mithilaa/ capital of the ancient kingdom of Videha, ruled by King Janaka (the father of Sita). मिथिला

Mithya /Mithyaa/ false; in vain. मिथ्या

Mithyabhimana /Mithyaa-abhimaana/ false egoism. मिथ्याभिमान

Mithyachara /Mithyaachaara/ (Mithyaa-aachaara); sinful conduct; hypocrisy. मिथ्याचार

Mithyadrishti /Mithyaa-drishti/ the vision that the world is unreal. मिथ्यादृष्टि

Mithyajnana /Mithyaa-jnaana/ false knowledge. मिथ्याज्ञान

Mithyasambandha /Mithyaa-sambandha/ false relationship. मिथ्यासम्बन्ध

Mithyavada /Mithyaa-vaada/ the doctrine of the phenomenal nature of this world, theory of illusion, also known as mayavada; see Maya. मिथ्यावाद

Mitra a friend; a name of Aditya or the sun god. मित्र

Moda the second type of bliss experienced in anandamaya kosha; see Anandamaya Kosha. मोद

Modita delighted, merry. मोदित

Modaka rice ball; a sweetmeat in the shape of a ball. मोदक

Moha swoon; confusion, delusion, error; infatuation; attachment; state of mind; see Shadvairi; see Shadurmi. मोह

Mohamudgara a song spontaneously composed by Adi Shankaracharya and his disciples urging dedication to the eternal reality rather than to the phenomenal reality; literally 'the rod or club to beat blind attachment'. मोहमुद्गर

Moksha liberation, freedom, release; state of existence; in yoga, final emancipation, liberation from the wheel of births and deaths, the aim of yogic practices. मोक्ष

Mokshasannyasayoga /Moksha-sannyaasa-yoga/ 'yoga of liberation by renunciation', the 18th and final chapter of the *Bhagavad Gita*, explaining the skilful yogic actions of sacrifice (yajna), giving (dana) and austerity (tapas) where there is no desire for reward and therefore no karma, no bondage. मोक्षसंन्यासयोग

Moodha see Mudha. मूढ

Moolabandha see Mulabandha. मूलबन्ध

Mooladhara see Muladhara. मूलाधार

Moorchha Pranayama see Murccha Pranayama. मूर्छा प्राणायाम

Mouna silence; measured silence, remaining silent for a specified span of time. मौन

Mridanga two-sided drum; a kind of drum or tabor; sound which may be meditated upon. मृदङ्ग

Mridula gentleness, tenderness. मृदुल

Mrigatrishna /Mrigatrishnaa/ mirage in the desert. मृगतृष्णा

Mrityu death; the god of death, Yama; epithet of Brahma, Vishnu, Kali and Maya; the god of love; see Shadurmi. मृत्यु

Mrityubandha fellow of death; a mortal. मृत्युबन्ध

Mrityunjaya 'conqueror of death', epithet of Shiva. मृत्युञ्जय

Mrityu Tattwa /Mrityu Tattva/ decayable element; manifest aspect of tattwa. मृत्यु तत्त्व

Mudha /Moodha/ perplexed, confounded; foolish, dull, stupid; a forgetful state of mind; lowest of the five states of the mind, state of ignorance or forgetfulness of one's real nature in which tamas predominates and the mind is in such a dull state that at times thinking also ceases to manifest; see Manas. मूढ

Mudita delighted, joyous, joyful. मुदित

Mudra /Mudraa/ literally means 'gesture'; physical, mental and psychic attitude which expresses and channels cosmic energy, (therefore technically bandhas are also a type of mudra); psycho-physiological posture, movement or attitude; a movement or position made or taken by the fingers or limbs in meditation as a result of the circulation of kundalini shakti; a seal, a sealing posture; also means 'grain' which is one of the five makara of tantra; see Bandha; see Panchamakara. मुद्रा

Mugdhata /Mugdhataa/ the state of very deluded forgetfulness of one's real divine nature through infatuation; innocence; the state of being a simpleton. मुग्धता

Muhurta /Muhoorta/ instant; while; hour; time period equal to 48 minutes; an auspicious time. मुहूर्त

Mukha mouth, face; entrance, forepart; surface, top, head. मुख

Mukhya chief, principal, foremost, prominent. मुख्य

Mukhya Samanyadhikarana /Mukhya Saamaanya-adhikarana/ literally 'the principal common ground'; the great vedantic statement 'Aham Brahmasmi' (I am Brahman) teaches the identity of the individual soul and the supreme being. Here the soul designated as 'I', the doer and the enjoyer, is not one with Brahman, rather it is the noumenal self who is the basis of that 'I' that is identical with Brahman, so this 'I', the doer, is to be deprived of its fictitious environments before establishing its identity with Brahman, the main common substratum; see Maha Vakya. मुख्य सामान्याधिकरण

Mukhyavritti primary sense; power or shakti of words. मुख्यवृत्ति

Mukta liberated. मुक्त

Mukta Purusha person liberated from all kinds of bondage; one freed from birth and death; see Kramamukti; see Videhamukti. मुक्त पुरुष

Mukti release, liberation; according to Vedanta, liberation is due to right knowledge, or intuition of truth (tattwa jnana); final absolution of the self from the chain of birth and death; see Kramamukti; see Videhamukti. मुक्ति

Mula /Moola/ root; basis. मूल

Mula Ajnanam /Moola Ajnaanam/ primal beginningless ignorance which contains all potentialities. मूल अज्ञानम्

Mulabandha /Moola-bandha/ contraction of the perineum in the male and the cervix in the female body; perineal lock; technique for locating and awakening mooladhara chakra; used to release Brahma granthi; see Bandha; see Granthi. मूलबन्ध

Muladhara /Moola-aadhaara/ base position, root foundation. मूलाधार

Muladhara Anusandhana
/Moola-aadhaara Anusandhaana/ discovery of mooladhara chakra. मूलाधार अनुसन्धान

Muladhara Chakra
/Moola-aadhaara Chakra/ the basic psychic and pranic centre in the human body situated in the perineum in men and the cervix in women and also connected to the coccygeal plexus, it is the seat of kundalini (the primal evolutionary energy in human beings); see Chakra; see Granthi; see Lam. मूलाधार चक्र

Muladhara Dhyana
/Moola-aadhaara Dhyaana/ practice involving visualization of mooladhara chakra and sensing the vortex of energy at this point. मूलाधार ध्यान

Mula Dhauti /Moola Dhauti/ cleaning of the anus through various techniques involving solid objects, water or air; see Shatkarma. मूल धौति

Mula Mantra /Moola Mantra/ root mantra; the most important and powerful of the mantras of any deity. मूल मन्त्र

Mula Mumukshu /Moola Mumukshu/ seeker after liberation. मूल मुमुक्षु

Mula Prakriti /Moola Prakriti/ the transcendental basis of physical nature; original source of all evolution. मूल प्रकृति

Mula Prakriti Avyakta /Moola Prakriti Avyakta/ the ultimate subtle cause of all matter. मूल प्रकृति अव्यक्त

Mula Shodhana /Moola Shodhana/ anal cleansing, a practice of dhauti; see Shatkarma. मूल शोधन

Mumukshu seeker of liberation; in Vedanta it is the term applied to a person in any of the first three stages of knowledge; see Jnana Bhumika. मुमुक्षु

Mumukshutva desire for liberation, intense longing for liberation; fourth kind of necessary spiritual effort; see Sadhana Chatushtaya. मुमुक्षुत्व

Mundaka Upanishad belongs to the *Atharva Veda* and teaches the difference between intellectual studies of the Vedas and their supplementary texts, and intuitive knowledge. मुण्डक उपनिषद्

Mundana Karana shaving (of the head). मुण्डन करण

Muni one who contemplates; one who has conquered the mind; one who maintains silence or stillness of mind; an ecstatic person; sage; ascetic; impulse. मुनि

Murchha /Moorchhaa/ literally 'fainting' or 'swooning'; spiritual ignorance or delusion. मूर्छा

Murchha Kumbhaka /Moorchhaa Kumbhaka/ technique where the breathing is stopped by holding the breath (kumbhaka) until it creates a feeling of senselessness or fainting. मूर्छा कुम्भक

Murchha Pranayama /Moorchhaa Praanaayaama/ a tranquillizing pranayama where, due to long inner retention of the breath, a condition of inertia is generated, resulting in a kind of fainting sensation. मूर्छा प्राणायाम

Murdha /Moorddha/ crown of the head. मूर्द्धा

Murtamurta /Moorta-amoorta/ personal and impersonal. मूर्तामूर्त

Murti /Moorti/ body, solid part of the body; form, shape, figure, statue, person; symbol; idol. मूर्ति

Murti Upasana /Moorti Upaasanaa/ meditation on an image or idol. मूर्ति उपासना

N

Pronunciation

न् *n – as in not*

Nabhi /Naabhi/ navel; centre; origin; affinity. नाभि

Nabhi Chakra /Naabhi Chakra/ naval centre or plexus, another name for manipura chakra. नाभि चक्र

Nabho Mudra /Nabho Mudraa/ another name for khechari mudra. नभो मुद्रा

Nachiketa /Nachiketaa/ name of the seeker who is a principal character in *Kathopanishad*. When his father, Uddalaka, decided to give away all his possessions to acquire religious merit, Nachiketa felt puzzled and kept on asking his father, "To whom will you give me?" His father answered, "I'll give you to Yama (the god of death)," so Nachiketa reached the realm of death. Yama, being quite impressed with the young seeker, offered him three boons, the last of which was the knowledge of the secret of life after death. नचिकेता

Nada /Naada/ subtle sound vibration created by the union of Shiva and Shakti tattwas; subtle sound vibration heard in the meditative state; voice, sound, cry, roaring; nasal sound represented by the semi-circle or half moon (ardha chandra) beneath the point (bindu) in the Sanskrit symbol for Aum or Om (ॐ); the prolongation of the sound in mantras such as Aum or mystic sounds (representing the eternal); the primal sound or first vibration from which all creation has emanated; the first manifestation of the unmanifested absolute; Aumkara (Omkara) or Shabda Brahman; the inner sound on which the yogi concentrates in meditation; flow. नाद

Nadabindukalatita /Naada-bindu-kalaa-ateeta/ 'beyond the states of nada, bindu and kala', according to tantric philosophy; the supreme state of Brahman. नादबिन्दुकलातीत

Nadanta /Naadaanta/ centre where difference between sound and experiencer dissolves. नादान्त

Nadanusandhana /Naada-anusandhaana/ enquiry or investigation into unstruck (anahata) sounds; concentration on inner sound. नादानुसन्धान

Nada Prakasha /Naada Prakaasha/ light which emanates from the primordial sound vibration. नाद प्रकाश

Nada Yoga /Naada Yoga/ flow of consciousness; nada yoga is the process of penetrating deeper and deeper into the nature of one's own reality via listening to subtle inner sound. There are four stages of nada yoga, viz. vaikhari, madhyama, pashyanti and para. *Hatha Yoga Pradipika* connects four states experienced by practitioners with the loosening of psychic blockages or knots (granthis); see Arambha Avastha; see Ghata Avastha; see Parichaya Avastha; see Nishpatti Avastha; see Laya Yoga. नाद योग

Nadin /Naadin/ sounding, resonant. नादिन्

> **Nadita** /Naadita/ made to resound, sounding. नादित

Nadi /Naadee/ a river or channel of energy, corresponding, though not identical, to the modern idea of nerves or the meridians of acupuncture; psychic current; flow of energy. *Hatha Yoga Pradipika* and *Shiva Swarodaya* posit 72,000 nadis in the human body of which three are most important; see Ida; see Pingala; see Sushumna. नाडी

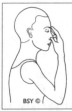

BSY ©

Nadi Shodhana Pranayama /Naadee Shodhana Praanaayaama/ a pranayama which purifies and balances ida and pingala nadis by alternate nostril breathing. It helps to eliminate toxins and other harmful elements and rhythmically stimulates alternate hemispheres of the brain. नाडी शोधन प्राणायाम

Nadi Shuddhi /Naadee Shuddhi/ ritual purification of the nadis performed by pranic healers in the early morning. नाडी शुद्धि

Naga /Naagaa/ militant sannyasa sect, an order of sadhus distinguishable by their nakedness. नागा

Naga /Naaga/ snake; fabulous serpent-demon or semi-divine being with the face of a man and the tail of a serpent; elephant. नाग

Naganatha /Naaga-naatha/ emanation of Shiva in the form of a serpent. नागनाथ

Naga Prana /Naaga Praana/ one of the five minor pranas (vital airs), it relieves abdominal pressure by causing one to belch, also responsible for hiccuping; see Uparana. नाग प्राण

Naimittika occasional; not daily or permanent. नैमित्तिक

> **Naimittikapralaya** occasional cosmic dissolution during Hiranyagarbha's sleep. नैमित्तिकप्रलय

Nairantarya continuously, without a break. नैरन्तर्य

Naishkarmya cessation of the workings of prakriti; state of being actionless (in salvation). नैष्कर्म्य

Naishtika Brahmachari /Naishthika Brahmachaaree/ one who has taken a vow of lifelong celibacy, residing in the house of his preceptor. नैष्ठिक ब्रह्मचारी

Naivedya edible offering to the deity offered in a temple or at the household altar; see Shodashopachara. नैवेद्य

Naiyayika /Naiyaayika/ follower of

the logic school (Nyaya) of Indian philosophy; a logician; see Shaddarshana. नैयायिक

Naka /Naaka/ vault of heaven; firmament. नाक

Nakshatra star, asterism, heavenly body; star of birth; collection of stars; lunar mansion (there are 27). नक्षत्र

Nakshatra Vidya /Nakshatra Vidyaa/ the science of stars, astronomy; see Jyotisha. नक्षत्र विद्या

Nakula mongoose; name of the fourth Pandava, one of the sons of Madri; see Madri. नकुल

Naman /Naaman/ name, appellation, personal name; the mere name; in grammar: noun, substantive; substance. नामन्

Namarupa /Naama-roopa/ name and form. नामरूप

Namarupajagat /Naama-roopa-jagat/ the world of name and form. नामरूपजगत्

Namarupavyakarana /Naama-roopa-vyaakarana/ evolution of names and forms. नामरूपव्याकरण

Namasmarana /Naama-smarana/ remembrance of the Lord through repetition of His name. नामस्मरण

Namas bow, pay obeisance to; to adore, reverence. नमस्

Nanabhava /Naanaa-bhaava/ feeling of plurality or multiplicity. नानाभाव

Nandi /Nandee/ the snow white sacred bull, attendant and favourite vehicle of Lord Shiva. नन्दी

Nandini /Nandinee/ the sacred cow of brahmarishi Vasishtha. Nandini could fulfil every wish of her owner and was therefore coveted by Vishvamitra. During the ensuing war, Vishvamitra became conscious that his prowess as a kshatriya (king and warrior) was useless and he must become a brahmin (priest). नन्दिनी

Nara decaying principle; matter; man, male, person, hero; supreme being, original or eternal man. नर

Narada /Naarada/ name of a celebrated devarishi; one of the 10 mentally conceived sons of Brahma, said to have sprung from his thigh. He is represented as a messenger from the gods, who is fond of promoting discord amongst gods and humankind. Supposedly the inventor of the lute or veena and also the author of the *Narada Bhakti Sutras*. नारद

Naraka underworld, hell; seven states of consciousness; seven lowest regions said to relate to demons or to beings with latent consciousness (e.g. plants); see Loka; see Chakra; see Patalam. नरक

Narasimha, Narahari Vishnu in his fourth incarnation, with the body of a man and the head of a lion; see Prahlada; see Avatara. नरसिंह, नरहरि

Narayana /Naaraayana/ 'companion of man', epithet of Vishnu, the supporter of life; the life forces of all lives; name of an ancient sage said to be a companion of Nara. नारायण

Narayana Bhava /Naaraayana Bhavaa/ seeing God in all; service of all beings. नारायण भाव

Nasa, Nasika /Naasaa, Naasikaa/ nose; trunk of an elephant; the subtle organ of smell, one of the five jnanendriyas; see Devata. नासा, नासिका

Nasikagra /Naasikaagra/ tip of the nose. नासिकाग्र

Nasikagra Drishti /Naasikaagra Drishti/ a mudra consisting of gazing and concentrating on the tip of the nose, which is a trigger point for mooladhara chakra; see Mudra. नासिकाग्र दृष्टि

Nasikagra Upachakra /Naasikaagra Upa-chakra/ minor chakra at the nose tip. नासिकाग्र उपचक्र

Nashwara /Nashvara/ the decaying principle described in Sankhya philosophy; manifest existence; becoming; changeable; see Ishwara. नश्वर

Nasti /Naasti/ (Na-asti); 'It is not', non-existence. नास्ति

Nastika /Naastika/ atheist, non-believer, one who denies the authority of the Vedas or the existence of a supreme ruler or creator of the universe. नास्तिक

Nataraja /Nataraaja/ name of Shiva during his cosmic dance, literally 'Lord of dance'; see Tandava. नटराज

Natha /Naatha/ lord, master. नाथ

Natyam /Naatyam/ dancing; dramatic representation, gesticulation, acting; the science or art of dancing and acting; scenic art. नाट्यम्

Natya Mudra /Naatya Mudraa/ mudras that express different attitudes or moods, such as love or anger, in the art of dance; see Mudra. नाट्य मुद्रा

Natya Priya /Naatya Priya/ literally 'lover of dance'; an epithet of Shiva. नाट्य प्रिय

Nauli practice of rotating the abdominal muscles; a kriya or process in which the abdominal muscles and organs are made to move laterally and vertically in a surging motion; a hatha yoga technique for awakening manipura chakra; see Shatkarma; see Lauliki. नौलि

Nava nine; new. नव

Navadha Bhakti /Navadhaa Bhakti/ nine stages of bhakti. नवधा भक्ति

Navadwarapuri /Nava-dvaarapuree/ 'the city of nine gates', the body with its nine apertures, viz. one mouth, two nostrils, two eyes, two ears, one anus and one genital organ. नवद्वारपुरी

Navagraha nine planets. नवग्रह

Navaratri Anushthana /Navaraatri Anushthaana/ literally 'nine night sadhana', a special sadhana done for nine days. It is celebrated twice a year, once during the month of Chaitra, which corresponds to March/ April and spring (vasanta ritu), and once during Ashwina, which corresponds to September/October and the autumn season (sharad ritu). During the sharad ritu, the three goddesses Durga, Lakshmi and Saraswati are worshipped for three days each and the tenth day (Vijaya Dashmi) celebrates two separate events: 1. The victory of Devi over the great demon Mahishasura, 2. Shri Rama's victory over Ravana. During vasanta ritu, Shri Rama's birth is celebrated with gaiety and fervour on the ninth day (Ramnaumi). नवरात्रि अनुष्ठान

Navarna Mantra /Navaarna Mantra/ the nine syllable mantra of Devi. नवार्ण मंत्र

Navatma /Navaatmaa/ nine states of consciousness or higher awareness; nine forms through which the atman can be realized. नवात्मा

Neti cleansing practice for the senses of sight, smell, taste and hearing, and for awakening ajna chakra. It is a process or kriya of cleaning the nasal passages with different liquids such as saline water, milk, oil, etc., or with thread; see Shatkarma; see Jala Neti; see Sutra Neti; see Usha Pan. नेति

Neti Neti (Na-iti Na-iti); literally 'Not this! Not this!'; as the experience of samadhi is not like any other experience which can be described in words, the sages thus declare that state of consciousness to be neti, neti. It also signifies one of the two processes of removing hindrances and clearing the path towards samadhi: one way is bhakti, saying 'This!', the other way is by saying 'Not this!' to all phenomenal manifestations. नेति नेति

Nidarshanam view, sight, vision; insight, looking into; proof, evidence. निदर्शनम्

Nididhyasana /Nididhyaasana/ profound, deep meditation; third step in vedantic sadhana, after hearing (shravana) and reflection (manana); see Maha Vakya. निदिध्यासन

Nidra /Nidraa/ fourth basic instinct; deep sleep; isolation from mind and senses; unconscious state; shutting off; sleepiness; sloth; one of the five vrittis listed in Patanjali's *Yoga Sutras*; see Vritti; see Pravritih. निद्रा

Nigama vedic knowledge; ritual procedures. निगम

Nigraha control. निग्रह

Nih prefix with many meanings according to context, including without; far; outside. निः

Nihshabda not expressed in words; inaudible. निःशब्द

Nihshreyas supreme bliss; unification with God; final emancipation; see Moksha. निःश्रेयस्

Nihshvasa /Nih-shvaasa/ breathing out, exhalation. निःश्वास

Nihspriha desireless; indifferent to, regardless of; content, not envious; free from any worldly ties. निःस्पृह

Nirabhimanata /Nirabhimaanataa/ (Nih-abhimaanataa); state of mindlessness; egolessness. निरभिमानता

Nirabhimani /Nirabhimaanee/ (Nih-abhimaanee); one devoid of pride (abhimana). निरभिमानी

Nirakara /Niraakaara/ (Nih-aakaara); without form, formless, devoid of form; unmanifest. निराकार

Nirakara Brahman /Niraakaara Brahman/ (Nih-aakaara Brahman); state of pure being without attributes or qualities. निराकार ब्रह्मन्

Niralambanam /Niraalambanam/ (Nih-aalambanam); not depending on another, independent, self-supported; having no proper support; friendless, alone. निरालम्बनम्

Niramaya /Niraamaya/ (Nih-aamaya); without disease. निरामय

Niranjana stainless, unstained, untainted; free from falsehood; pure, simple; an epithet of Brahman. निरञ्जन

Niranjanoham (Niranjanah-aham); 'I am unblemished, pure'. निरञ्जनोऽहम्

Niratishaya supreme, highest, greatest. निरतिशय

Niratishayaghaneebhutashakti /Niratishayaghanee-bhoota-shakti/ (Nih-atishaya-ghanee-bhoota-shakti); infinitely massive power or potency, concentrated power without limits. निरतिशयघनीभूतशक्ति

Niratishayananda /Niratishayaananda/ (Nih-atishaya-ananda); the highest bliss, above this bliss there is none other. निरतिशयानन्द

Niravarana /Niraavarana/ (Nih-aavarana); without veil. निरावरण

Niravayava without members or limbs. निरवयव

Nirbija /Nirbeeja/ (Nih-beeja); seedless, without any seeds. निर्बीज

Nirbija Samadhi /Nirbeeja Samaadhi/ (Nih-beeja Samaadhi); final state of samadhi in which there is absorption without seed; total disso-

lution (niruddha avastha); see Sabija Samadhi. निर्बीज समाधि

Nirdwandwa /Nirdvandva/ (Nih-dvandva); indifference towards opposite pairs of feelings, like pleasure and pain; not dependent upon another, independent. निर्द्वन्द्व

Nirgarbha Pranayama /Nirgarbha Praanaayaama/ (Nih-garbha Praanaayaama); pranayama without repetition of mantra. निर्गर्भ प्राणायाम

Nirguna without quality or attribute, formless; see Saguna. निर्गुण

Nirguna Brahman Brahman without attributes or form, powers or predicates; a state of pure being without qualities (gunas); the impersonal, attributeless absolute; see Saguna Brahman. निर्गुण ब्रह्मन्

Nirguna Dhyana /Nirguna Dhyaana/ (Nih-guna Dhyaana); meditation without qualities (gunas); see Saguna Dhyana. निर्गुण ध्यान

Nirguna Upasana /Nirguna Upaasanaa/ worship of God without form or attributes. निर्गुण उपासना

Nirlina /Nirleena/ (Nih-leena); undissolved. निर्लीन

Nirliptatva state of being unattached. निर्लिप्तत्व

Nirmana /Nirmaana/ (Nih-maana); creation, construction. निर्माण

Nirmana Chitta /Nirmaana Chitta/ (Nih-maana Chitta); manufactured mind, manufacturing mind. निर्माण चित्त

Nirmana Kaya /Nirmaana Kaaya/ (Nih-maana Kaaya); manufactured body. निर्माण काया

Nirmoha without attachment; without delusion. निर्मोह

Nirukta an account of the origin and history of vedic words, an auxiliary science of the Vedas; see Vedanga. निरुक्त

Nirupadhika /Nirupaadhika/ (Nih-upaadhika); without any limiting adjunct; see Upadhi. निरुपाधिक

Nirvana /Nirvaana/ (Nih-vaana); cessation of suffering, final liberation or emancipation in Buddhist thought (whereas Vedantins claim that not only absence of suffering but also the positive experience of bliss characterizes the ultimate state); higher state of existence or awareness. निर्वाण

Nirvichara /Nirvichaara/ (Nih-vichaara); thoughtlessness (in meditation); without argumentation; without logic, enquiry or investigation. निर्विचार

Nirvichara Samadhi /Nirvichaara Samaadhi/ (Nih-vichaara Samaadhi); transitional stage of samadhi; absorption without reflection; superconscious state where there is no intellectual enquiry; see Savichara Samadhi. निर्विचार समाधि

Nirvikalpa without any modifications or thoughts. निर्विकल्प

Nirvikalpa Kalpaka not admitting an alternative; being without determination or resolution; not capable of mutual relation; recognizing no such distinction as that of subject and object, or of the knower and the known. निर्विकल्प कल्पक

Nirvikalpa Samadhi /Nirvikalpa Samaadhi/ (Nih-vikalpa Samaadhi); state in which the mind ceases to function and only pure consciousness remains, revealing itself to itself and there is no object of the mind; superconscious state where mental modifications cease to exist, resulting in transcendence of the manifest world; see Savikalpa Samadhi. निर्विकल्प समाधि

Nirvikara /Nirvikaara/ (Nih-vikaara); unchanging, without modifications. निर्विकार

Nirvishaya without sense activity; without object. निर्विषय

Nirvishesha without any special characteristics. निर्विशेष

Nirvishesha Chinmatra /Nirvishesha Chinmaatra/ (Nih-vishesha Chinmaatra); undifferentiated consciousness alone. निर्विशेष चिन्मात्र

Nirvishesha Dhyana /Nirvishesha Dhyaana/ (Nih-vishesha Dhyaana); meditation without special attributes. निर्विशेष ध्यान

Nirvisheshatva absence of distinctive attributes. निर्विशेषत्व

Nirvitarka Samadhi /Nirvitarka Samaadhi/ (Nih-vitarka Samaadhi); transitional stage of samadhi involving purification of memory, which gives rise to true knowledge of the object of perception; superconscious state where there is no intellectual

argumentation or logic; see Savitarka Samadhi. निर्वितर्क समाधि
Nirvriti satisfaction, happiness,
fulfilment; accomplishment; emancipation. निर्वृति
Nishchaya ascertainment; reso-
luteness; resolution, conclusion.
निश्चय
Nishchayatmaka
/Nishchayaatmaka/ (Nih-chaya-
aatmaka); with firm conviction
or determination. निश्चयात्मक
Nishchaya Vritti the vritti or
state of mind where there is
determination. निश्चय वृत्ति
Nishchitatman /Nishchitaatman/
(Nih-chit-aatman); of resolute
mind. निश्चितात्मन्
Nishkama /Nishkaama/ (Nih-
kaama); selfless, unselfish; free
from wish or desire, desireless.
निष्काम
Nishkama Bhava /Nishkaama
Bhaava/ (Nih-kaama Bhaava);
motiveless spontaneous feeling;
attitude of non-expectation of
fruits of action. निष्काम भाव
Nishkama Karma /Nishkaama
Karma/ (Nih-kaama Karma);
action without expectation of
fruits and done without personal interest or egoism. This
type of action purifies the mind
and heart without creating new
bondage; see Karma Yoga.
निष्काम कर्म
Nishkama Sevaka
/Nishkaama Sevaka/
(Nih-kaama Sevaka); one who
does selfless service; see Karma
Yogi. निष्काम सेवक
Nishkami /Nishkaamee/
(Nih-kaamee); one who is be-

yond the influence of personal
desire. निष्कामी
Nishkampa motionless, steady;
immovable. निष्कम्प
Nishkarana /Nishkaarana/ (Nih-
kaarana); causeless; unnecessary;
disinterested, free from any motive. निष्कारण
Nishkriya without action, without movement. निष्क्रिय
Nishkriyarupa
/Nishkriya-roopa/ (Nih-kriya-
roopa); of the form of action-
lessness, a feature of the supreme state of Brahman.
निष्क्रियरूप
Nishpatti Avastha /Nishpatti
Avasthaa/ (Nih-patti Avasthaa);
state of consumation; fourth and
final state of hearing the inner
nada according to *Hatha Yoga
Pradipika*; stage of nada yoga attained after piercing Rudra
granthi. निष्पत्ति अवस्था
Nishshreyas see Nihshreyas.
नि:श्रेयस
Nijabodharupa /Nijabodha-roopa/
state of self-awareness; satchidananda Brahman; literally 'of the
form of real knowledge'. निजबोधरूप
Nilakantha /Neela-kantha/ literally
'blue-throated', an epithet of
Shiva referring to the blue colour of his throat which was caused
when he protected the world by
drinking the poison churned
from the ocean of milk by the
devas, who were seeking the
nectar of immortality (amrita).
नीलकण्ठ
Nimitta cause; instrument. निमित्त
Nimittakarana /Nimitta-kaarana/
instrumental cause, like the

potter who makes the pots; see Brahma. निमित्तकारण

Nirodha, Nirodhanam complete cessation of the patterns of consciousness when the mind is under perfect control; confinement, locking up, imprisonment; enclosing, covering up; suppression, control, restraint, check; hindrance, obstruction, opposition; state in which the mind is blocked or prevented from functioning; beyond the three qualities (gunas); fifth of the five states of mind, in which the awareness of consciousness alone prevails; see Gunatitha; see Manas; see Ritambhara Prajna. निरोध, निरोधनम्

Nirodha Bhumi /Nirodha Bhoomi/ the state of the mind when it is under control. निरोध भूमि

Nirodha Parinama /Nirodha Parinaama/ modification of control. निरोध परिणाम

Nirodhika /Nirodhikaa/ psychic centre where the experience of form is obstructed. निरोधिका

Niruddha obstructed, hindered, checked, restrained, curbed; confined, imprisoned; state of consciousness (chitta) where the mind becomes inactive, having realized its source. निरुद्ध

Nishedha the 'don'ts' of living; see Vidhi. निषेध

Nishiddha Karma forbidden action according to the Vedas or Smritis. निषिद्ध कर्म

Nishtha /Nishthaa/ steadfastness; being established in a certain state. निष्ठा

Nitya continual, perpetual, constant, uninterrupted; ever-lasting, eternal. नित्य

Nityabuddhi ideal; stability. नित्यबुद्धि

Nityakarma any daily and necessary rite; a constant act of duty; eternal actions. नित्यकर्म

Nityamukta eternally free; the supreme being, the supreme spirit. नित्यमुक्त

Nityanityavastuviveka /Nitya-anitya-vastu-viveka/ discrimination between the real and the unreal. नित्यानित्यवस्तुविवेक

Nityapralaya dissolution of everyday occurrences during sound sleep. नित्यप्रलय

Nityashuddha eternal purity. नित्यशुद्ध

Nityasiddhi eternal perfection. नित्यसिद्धि

Nityasukha eternal happiness. नित्यसुख

Nityata /Nityataa/ eternity. नित्यता

Nityatripti eternal satisfaction. नित्यतृप्ति

Nityayukta eternally united (with the absolute). नित्ययुक्त

Nityodaya (Nitya-udaya); daily creation; awakening of the individual in the morning. नित्योदय

Niveshanam entering; founding; a household, dwelling place, house; rest, bringing to rest. निवेशनम्

Nivritti no vritti. निवृत्ति

Nivritti Marga /Nivritti Maarga/ path of non-indulgence; path of introversion; literally 'path without vrittis'. निवृत्ति मार्ग

Niyama observances or rules of personal discipline to render the mind tranquil in preparation for meditation; the second step of ashtanga yoga mentioned by

Patanjali in the *Yoga Sutras*. He enumerates five rules of conduct that apply to individual discipline, viz. 1. purity (shaucha), 2. satisfaction or contentment (santosha), 3. austerity or penance (tapas), 4. self-study (swadhyaya), and 5. renunciation of the fruits of action or dedication to the Lord or to the highest principle (ishwara pranidhana; inner discipline; vedic text or explanation; doctrine; in yogic philosophy it means restraint of the mind or self-purification by discipline. नियम

Niyamaka /Niyaamaka/ 'he who controls', God or Ishwara. नियामक

Niyati destiny; that which is fixed. नियति

Niyata Karma bounden duty, obligatory duty; that which should not be renounced. नियति कर्म

Nritya dance; Lord Shiva's dance is known as Tandava Nritya. नृत्य

Nriyajna service and care of a guest; respect for every person; see Manushya Yajna. नृयज्ञ

Nyagrodha sami or Indian fig tree (*Ficus bengalensis*) whose wood is used to make the implements for sacrifice (yajna); another name for Vishnu. न्यग्रोध

Nyasa /Nyaasa/ renunciation; laying down; placing; planting; a pledge; entrusting; committing; giving up, resigning, abandoning, relinquishing; the practice of assigning the various parts of the body to different deities, which is usually accompanied with mantras and corresponding gestures or mudras. न्यास

Nyasin /Nyaasin/ one who has renounced all worldly ties, a sannyasin. न्यासिन्

Nyaya /Nyaaya/ one of the six darshanas or systems of Indian philosophy, logical realism founded by Gautama; recognition of real spiritual experience by the omniscient mind that is all encompassing and all pervading; the correct way; circumflex; see Shaddarshana. न्याय

Pronunciation
ओ o – as in omnipresent
ऊ oo – as in fool

Odana boiled rice; grain cooked with milk; food; cooked rice used as an oblation in some rites of shrauta yajna. ओदन

Oghah flood or stream; continuity; multitude; traditional instruction; a king of dance. ओघ:

Ojas vitality, subliminal sexual energy, bodily strength, vigour, energy; virility, the generative faculty; kundalini shakti; splendour, light; see Vajra Nadi. ओजस्

Ojas Shakti hormonal energy that may be developed by the practice of yoga, bringing increased health, longer life, mental power and control of the nervous system. ओजस् शक्ति

Ojasin strong person, powerful man. ओजसिन्

Okas house, residence; asylum or refuge. ओकस्

Okha to be able; to be sufficient; ward off, refuse; keep dry. ओख

Om, Aum bija mantra of ajna chakra; the universal cosmic mantra representing the four states of consciousness; the sound indicating the supreme sublime reality or Brahman; the sound representing the first formation from formless existence or the first acoustic expression of Brahman; word of power; like the Latin word omne it means 'all' and conveys concepts of omniscience, omnipresence and omnipotence; existence; see Mandukya Upanishad; see Aum. ॐ

Omkara /Omkaara/ the sound of Aum (Om); the symbol ॐ; the exclamation 'Aum' (Om) as respectful assent, to ward off something or to give affirmation. ॐकार

Om Tat Sat a designation of Brahman; a solemn invocation of divine blessing; tat sat means 'That exists'; remembrance of the almighty. ॐ तत् सत्

Oordhva top, high, above. ऊर्ध्व

Oordhvaretas one who sublimates and raises his/her energy to higher levels. ऊर्ध्वरेतस्

Oshadhi see Aushaddhi. ओषधी, औषधि

Oshadhipati see Aushadhi-pati. ओषधीपति

Oshadhi Yoga see Aushadhi Yoga. ओषधी योग

Oshtha lip (lower or upper). ओष्ठ

Oshthaputa the cavity made by opening the lips. ओष्ठपुट

P

Pronunciation
प् p – as in pink
फ् ph – as in photo

Pada /Paada/ foot, the organ of locomotion and one of the five organs of action (karmendriyas); a hill at the foot of a mountain; quarter of a stanza, i.e. a line; part or chapter of a book; ray of light; a tree; a column or pillar; see Devata. पाद

Pada Jala /Paada Jala/ water for washing the feet; water in which the feet of sacred and revered persons are washed and which is thus considered holy. पाद जल

Padangadam /Paada-angadam/ ornament for the foot or ankle. पादाङ्गदम्

Padangushtha /Paada-angushtha/ big toe. पादाङ्गुष्ठ

Padaseva, Padasevana /Paadasevaa, Paadasevana/ serving the feet (of the Lord). पादसेवा, पादसेवन

Padavasechana /Paada-avasechana/ washing the feet. पादावसेचन

Paduka /Paadukaa/ sandals. पादुका

Padya /Paadya/ water offered for washing the feet; see Shodashopachara. पाद्य

Padartha /Padaartha/ substance, material, matter. पदार्थ

Padarthabhavana /Padaartha-bhaavanaa/ the sixth of the seven states of knowledge (jnana bhumika) in Vedanta, where the jnani perceives the inner essence and not the outer physical form of things and experiences knowledge of truth. Described as a state similar to sushupti; see Brahma-vidvariya. पदार्थभावना

Padma lotus, the form or figure of a lotus, the root of a lotus. पद्म

Padmaksha /Padma-aksha/ lotus-eyed; epithet of Vishnu or the Sun. पद्माक्ष

Padmalaya /Padma-aalaya/ epithet of Brahma, the creator, 'whose home is the lotus'. पद्मालय

Padmanabha /Padma-naabha/ name of Vishnu from whose navel Brahma sprang forth on a lotus; see Anantapadmanabha. पद्मनाभ

Padmarekha /Padma-rekhaa/ a figure on the palm of the hand (of the form of a lotus flower) indicating the acquisition of great wealth. पद्मरेखा

Padma Sambhava epithet of Brahma, the lotus-born god (also

Padmaja, Padmajata, Padmabhu, Padmayoni); see Anantapadmanabha. पद्म सम्भव

Padma Vasa /Padma Vaasaa/ 'lotus dweller', epithet of Lakshmi, the goddess of wealth. पद्म वासा

Pakhanda /Paakhanda/ hypocrisy, false behaviour. पाखण्ड

Pakshin winged, furnished with wings; a bird. पक्षिन्

Pakshiraja /Pakshi-raaja/ epithet of Garuda, king of the birds; eagle. पक्षिराज

Pakti cooked; digested; sturdy; resolute. पक्ति

Palasha /Palaasha/ a tree (*Butea monosperma*) whose wood is used to make implements for sacrifice (yajna). पलाश

Panava a small drum, cymbal. पणव

Pancha five. पञ्च

Panchabhuta /Pancha-bhoota/ the five elements; see Pancha Mahabhuta. पञ्चभूत

Panchadashi /Panchadashee/ a highly respected book of Advaita Vedanta philosophy written by Swami Vidyaranya, who became Shankaracharya of Shringeri Matha. पञ्चदशी

Pancha Dharana /Pancha Dhaaranaa/ five kinds of concentration on five elements; see Pancha Mahabhuta; see Tanmatra; see Vyakta. पञ्च धारणा

Panchagni /Pancha-agni/ five fires. पञ्चाग्नि

Panchagni Vidya /Pancha-agni Vidyaa/ knowledge or science of the five fires; esoteric explanation of five processes of sacrifice; sadhana of sitting in the middle of four burning fires with

the summer sun of India acting as the fifth fire. पञ्चाग्नि विद्या

Pancha Klesha five afflictions or causes of suffering described in Patanjali's *Yoga Sutras*, viz. ignorance (avidya), ego or sense of doership (asmita), attraction (raga), aversion (dwesha) and fear of death (abhinivesha); see Klesha. पञ्च क्लेश

Pancha Kosha five sheaths, bodies or realms of experience and existence, viz. 1. physical dimension (annamaya kosha), 2. mental dimension (manomaya kosha), 3. energetic and emotional dimension (pranamaya kosha), 4. intuitive dimension (vijnanamaya kosha), 5. blissful dimension (anandamaya kosha). पञ्च कोष

Pancha Mahabhuta /Pancha Mahaa-bhoota/ the five gross or atomic states of nature, consisting of ether or space (akasha), gases or air (vayu), light or fire (agni), liquids or water (apas) and solids or earth (prithvi). They are an extension of the tanmatras into the physical world; see Vyakta. पञ्च महाभूत

Pancha Mahayajna literally 'the five great sacrifices', the acts of piety to be performed daily by every householder, viz. 1. bhuta yajna, 2. manushya yajna (also called atithi yajna and nriyajna), 3. pitri yajna, 4. deva yajna, 5. Brahma yajna. पञ्च महायज्ञ

Panchamakara /Pancha-makaara/ five elements used in tantric ritual sadhana, all of which begin with the letter 'm', viz. mudra (psychic attitude), mamsa (flesh), maithuna (physical union), matsya (fish) and madya (wine). The category of aspirant determines the symbolic interpretation. पञ्चमकार

Pancha Prana /Pancha Praana/ five major divisions of the pranic energy located in the physical body, viz. apana, prana, samana, udana, vyana; see Vayu. पञ्च प्राण

Pancha Tanmatra /Pancha Tanmaatraa/ five pre-nuclear states of nature, viz. sound (shabda), touch (sparsha), form (roopa), taste (rasa) and smell (gandha). They are the subtle states of the physical mahabhuta: space, air, fire, water and earth; see Shabda Tanmatra; see Sparsha Tanmatra; see Rupa Tanmatra; see Rasa Tanmatra; see Gandha Tanmatra. पञ्च तन्मात्र

Panchatantram collection of fables narrated by Pundit Vishnu Sharma to a group of princes. पञ्चतन्त्रम्

Pancha Tapas an ascetic practice in which the sadhaka is surrounded by five fires; see Panchagni Vidya. पञ्च तपस्

Pancha Tattwa, Pancha Tattwam /Pancha Tattva, Pancha Tattvam/ the five elements; fivefold state; collection of five; to be resolved into the five elements of which the body consists; to die, to perish; see Pancha Mahabhuta. पञ्च तत्त्व, पञ्च तत्त्वम्

Pancha Tattwa Dharana /Pancha Tattva Dhaaranaa/ concentration on the different qualities and symbols of the tattwas, part of daharakasha dharana. पञ्च तत्त्व धारणा

Panchaupasaka /Panchaupaasaka/ different groups worshipping five different deities, viz. Ganapathya, Saurya, Shakta, Vaishnava, Shaiva. पञ्चोपासक

Panchaupasana /Panchaupaasanaa/ (Panchaupaasanaa); five different kinds of worship related to worshipping five deities, viz. Ganapati, Surya, Shakti, Vishnu and Shiva. पञ्चोपासना

Pancha Vayu see Pancha Prana. पञ्च वायु

Panchikarana /Panchee-karana/ quintuplication; according to Vedanta, a particular process by which the five kinds of elementary constituents of the universe (the pancha mahabhutas) are compounded with one another to form grosser entities that serve as units in the composition of the physical universe. पञ्चीकरण

Panchikrita /Pancheekrita/ quintuplicated. पञ्चीकृत

Panchala /Panchaala/ name of Draupadi's country and its people. पञ्चाल

Panchali /Paanchaalee/ a woman or princess of the Panchalas; name of Draupadi, the wife of the Pandavas; one of the four styles of poetic composition. पाञ्चाली

Panchanga /Panchaanga/ current astrological calander (almanac) which gives daily astrological readings. पञ्चाङ्ग

Pandava /Paandava/ a son or descendant of Pandu; the five brothers: Yudhishthira, Bhima, Arjuna,

Nakula and Sahadeva, who held an inter-family feud against the Kauravas as recorded in the *Mahabharata* epic; see Pandu; see Kunti; see Madri. पाण्डव

Pandita priest; learned man; scholar; man of wisdom. पण्डित

Pandityam /Paandityam/ erudition, knowledge, intellectual mastery. पाण्डित्यम्

Pandu /Paandu/ pale-white or yellowish-white colour; white elephant; the name of the father of the Pandavas. Pandu was the son of Vyasa and Ambalika, and the warrior king of the Kuru dynasty. His blind half brother Dhritarashtra sired the 100 Kauravas. Due to a curse he was prevented from having progeny himself, so he permitted his first wife, Kunti, to make use of miraculous powers to bear sons: Yudhishthira, Bhima and Arjuna. She helped Pandu's second wife, Madri, to bear Nakula and Sahadeva by using the same powers. The battle between the Kauravas and the Pandavas is recorded in the *Mahabharata*. पाण्डु

Panini /Paanini/ celebrated author of the sutras on Sanskrit grammar known as *Ashtadhyayi*. पाणिनि

Pani /Paani/ hand. पाणि

Panitalam /Paani-talam/ palm of the hand. पाणितलम्

Papa /Paapa/ evil, sin, wickedness; viciousness; inauspiciousness; anything which takes one away from dharma. पाप

Papa Purusha /Paapa Purusha/ evil personified; personification of the sinful part of the individual;

a part of oneself that is purified and transformed in tattwa shuddhi sadhana. पाप पुरुष

Paparoga /Paapa-roga/ a disease as the penalty of a sin. पापरोग

Papatman /Paapa-aatman/ evil-minded, wicked. पापात्मन्

Para used in the *Bhagavad Gita* to indicate the supreme goal of life; other, different; distant, removed, remote; beyond; subsequent, following next to; higher, superior, highest, greatest; predominant, principal; but; opposite of apara. पर

Para Brahman absolute, supreme reality. पर ब्रह्मन्

Parakayapravesha /Para-kaayaa-pravesha/ entering into another body; the power by which the yogi can leave his/her own body and enter into another body. परकायाप्रवेश

Paramukha whose face is turned away; shunning; unfavourable. परमुख

Paratantra dependent on another; subservient. परतन्त्र

Paratantra Sattabhava /Paratantra Sattaa-bhaava/ possibility of dependent existence. परतन्त्र सत्ताभाव

Para Upakara /Para Upakaara/ working for the welfare and good of others, service to others. पर उपकार

Paravasha subject to someone else's will, dependent, subdued. परवश

Para /Paraa/ indicating the divine condition of Vak (sound, speech, word, the goddess of speech); the fourth or transcendental stage of nada yoga; opposite of 'aparaa'; feminine of 'para'; see Nada Yoga. परा

Para Bhakti /Paraa Bhakti/ supreme devotion (bhakti). It is said to accompany or follow the highest knowledge and be a state of consciousness which is self-contained; see Bhakti. परा भक्ति

Paragati /Paraa-gati/ highest state; see Moksha. परागति

Parajaya /Paraajaya/ a defeat. पराजय

Para Nada /Paraa Naada/ transcendental sound. The fourth stage of nada yoga, para nada is a quality of the psyche or soul. It is a sound without any vibration or a sound of infinite wave length and is heard only in samadhi, deep meditation or deeper states of nada yoga; see Nada Yoga. परा नाद

Parananda /Paraa-aananda/ celestial joy; higher state of awareness. परानन्द

Para Prakriti /Paraa Prakriti/ the higher cosmic energy through which the supreme Brahman appears as the individual soul. परा प्रकृति

Para Samvit /Paraa Samvit/ supreme knowledge or consciousness. परा संवित्

Para Shabda /Paraa Shabda/ supreme sound which is an undifferentiated state; the first, unmanifest (avyakta) state of sound. परा शब्द

Paratma /Paraa-aatmaa/ cosmic self. परात्मा

Para Vairagya /Paraa Vairaagya/ absence of attachment in any form; highest type or state of dispassion (vairagya); the mind turns away completely from worldly objects and cannot be brought back to them under any circumstances; renunciation of a liberated person in which no selfish motive can exert influence. परा वैराग्य

Paravak /Paraa-vaak/ transcendental sound; sound behind the normal sense perception. परावाक्

Paravastu /Paraa-vastu/ supreme substance: Brahman. परावस्तु

Para Vidya /Paraa Vidyaa/ higher knowledge, transcendental knowledge, direct knowledge of Brahman. परा विद्या

Paravritti, Paravarta /Paraa-vritti, Paraa-varta/ turning back, return, turn, retreat; exchange, barter; restoration; reversal of a sentence. परावृत्ति, परावर्त

Parak /Paraak/ one going upward; one going in the opposite direction; distant. पराक्

Parangmukha /Paraangmukha/ (Paraak-mukha); inverted order, backwards; having the face turned away or averted; turning the back upon. पराङ्मुख

Param, Parama the highest point or pitch, culminating point; the supreme being; final beatitude; extreme, farthest; last, worst; best, excellent; conspicuous. परम्, परम

Param Akasha /Parama Aakaasha/ 'supreme space'; second of the five mental spaces of vyoma panchaka; described as 'deep, dark space with a twinkling star-like light'; state of nothingness (shoonya); see Vyoma Panchaka Dharana. परम आकाश

Parama Dharma supreme duty; transcendental existence. परम धर्म

Parama Guru supreme guru. परम गुरु

Paramahamsa literally 'supreme swan', a swan is reputed to be able to separate milk from water, i.e. reality from unreality; one who controls or subdues their passions; a sage, an ascetic; title of a person in the fourth stage of consciousness; see Sannyasa. परमहंस

Paramahamsa Sannyasa /Parama-hamsa Sannyaasa/ a stage of sannyasa where, having completed their work, paramahamsa sannyasins approach the final goal of moksha or self-realization. परमहंस संन्यास

Paramakarana /Parama-kaarana/ the supreme cause of all causes. परमकारण

Paramakasha see Param Akasha. परमाकाश

Paramanu /Parama-anu/ the basic particle or energy unit (subatomic). परमाणु

Paramapada highest step or state of existence; supreme position. परमपद

Paramartha /Parama-artha/ highest truth, reality. परमार्थ

Paramartha Drishti /Parama-artha Drishti/ right vision; intuition. परमार्थ दृष्टि

Paramarthika /Paarama-arthika/ spiritual aspects; in an absolute sense (as opposed to relative or vyavaharika); related to reality (paramartha). पारमार्थिक

Paramarthikasatta /Paarama-arthika-sattaa/ absolute reality; transcendental truth; see Para Brahman. पारमार्थिकसत्ता

Paramashanti /Parama-shaanti/ supreme peace, absolute peace. परमशान्ति

Paramatma /Parama-aatmaa/ cosmic soul or consciousness, supreme self; the atma (self or soul) of the entire universe, of the individual as well as of the cosmos; liberated state of the inner self. परमात्मा

Paramavashyata /Paramaa-vashyataa/ supreme control over the mind and the senses. परमावश्यता

Paramadhama /Parama-dhaama/ supreme abode; Brahman; see Moksha. परमधाम

Parameshthi /Parameshthee/ (Parama-ishtee); the exalted one; a name generally applied to Brahma or Hiranyagarbha, sometimes to Lord Narayana or the supreme purusha. परमेष्ठी

Parameshwara /Parameshvara/ (Parama-eeshvara); supreme being. परमेश्वर

Parampara /Paramparaa/ tradition. परम्परा

Parashu an axe, a hatchet; a weapon in general; thunderbolt. परशु

Parashurama /Parashu-raama/ literally 'Rama with an axe'; name of a celebrated warrior, who was the son of Jamadagni and the sixth incarnation (avatara) of Vishnu; see Shasti; see Avatara. परशुराम

Parasparadhyasa /Paraspara-adhyaasa/ mutual superimposition: the body is mistaken for the self and the self is mistaken to be the body. परस्पराध्यास

Paratpara /Paraatpara/ greater than the great, higher than the high. परात्पर

Parayana /Paraayana/ final aim, last resort, the ultimate ground, the sole refuge; wholly intent upon, absorbed in. परायण

Pari a prefix often used in the Sanskrit language. परि

Paribhu /Pari-bhoo/ being around; protecting; existing everywhere. परिभू

Paricharya /Pari-charyaa/ service, attendance; adoration, worship. परिचर्या

Parichaya Avastha /Pari-chaya Avasthaa/ state of increase, the third state of nada yoga according to *Hatha Yoga Pradipika*, attained when Vishnu granthi is pierced. परिचय अवस्था

Parichchhinna finite, conditioned, limited. परिच्छिन्न

Paridrashta /Pari-drashtaa/ spectator, onlooker. परिद्रष्टा

Parigata surrounded, enclosed, encircled; diffused, spread, around; known, understood; obtained. परिगत

Parigraha collection; seizing, holding, grasping; encircling, surrounding, enclosing, fencing around; putting on, wrapping round; assuming, taking; marriage, wife; taking under protection, grace. परिग्रह

Parigrihita /Pari-griheeta/ seized; embraced; surrounded; received. परिगृहीत

Parihritasukha abandoning pleasures. परिहृतसुख

Parijnana /Pari-jnaana/ thorough knowledge, insight. परिज्ञान

Pariklesha hardship, vexation, pain. परिक्लेश

Parikrama /Pari-kramaa/ circumambulation. परिक्रमा

Pariksha /Pareeksha/ (Pari-eeksha); examination, investigation. परीक्षा

Parikshina /Pari-ksheena/ vanished, disappeared; wasted, decayed; emaciated, worn away, exhausted. परिक्षीण

Parikshipta scattered, diffused; encircled, surrounded; overspread, overlaid; left, abandoned. परिक्षिप्त

Parimala fragrance, fragrant substance. परिमल

Parimaladravya (Parimaladravya) aromatic, perfumed substances offered in worship to satisfy the deity and protect the place of worship. परिमलद्रव्य

Parimana /Pari-maana/ measuring, measure, size; compass. परिमाण

Parinama /Pari-naama/ transformation; according to Patanjali's

Yoga Sutras the transformation of mind consists of three stages: 1. transformation in the form of tranquillity (samadhi parinama), 2. transformation in the form of Aum (ekagrata parinama), 3. suppression of the inner object (nirodha parinama). परिणाम

Parinama Nitya /Pari-naama Nitya/ changing eternally; maya. परिणाम नित्य

Parinama Srishti /Pari-naama Srishti/ creation by evolution and actual change according to Sankhya. परिणाम सृष्टि

Parinama Upadana /Pari-naama Upaadaana/ the material cause which evolves out of itself an effect with which it is essentially one, e.g. the pradhana (prakriti) of Sankhya. परिणाम उपादान

Parinama Vada /Pari-naama Vaada/ doctrine of transformation (of the school of qualified non-dualism of Shri Ramanuja), upholding that God actually transforms a portion of His being into the universe. परिणाम वाद

Paripalana /Pari-paalana/ protection, care, nourishing. परिपालन

Paripurna /Pari-poorna/ full (moon); completely full, as in a river overflowing both its banks. परिपूर्ण

Pariraksha /Pari-rakshaa/ protection, good security. परिरक्षा

Parisarya Nadi, Parisarya Nadi Mandala /Pari-sarya Naadee, Pari-sarya Naadee Mandala/ yogic term for the peripheral nervous system which connects the central nervous system (related to sushumna) with bodily tissues. परिसर्य नाडी, परिसर्य नाडी मण्डल

Parityaga /Pari-tyaaga/ abandonment; repudiation; neglect. परित्याग

Pariveshin (the sun) surrounded by a halo. परिवेषिन्

Parivrajaka /Pari-vraajaka/ wandering mendicant; ascetic; stage of life lasting for 12 years in the traditional training of a sannyasin. परिव्राजक

Parivrajna wandering. परिव्रज्

Parivritta turned around, revolved. परिवृत्त

Parivritti revolution; return, turning back; barter, exchange. परिवृत्ति

Paryapta /Paryaapta/ (Pari-aapta); obtained, gained; completed, finished; full, whole, entire; able, competent, adequate. पर्याप्ति

Paryavarana /Paryaarvarana/ (Pari-aavarana); environment. पर्यावरण

Parikshit /Pareekshita/ name of a king who was cursed to die from a snakebite within seven days. During the seven days he listened to *Shrimad Bhagavata* as a discourse by Shuka Muni and reached the abode of Lord Vishnu. He was the son of Abhimanyu and grandson of Arjuna; see Abhimanyu. परीक्षित

Parna wing; feather; leaf. पर्ण

Paroksha out of sight, beyond the range of normal vision; invisible; escaping observation; secret, unknown; stronger. परोक्ष

Parokshajnana /Paroksha-jnaana/ indirect knowledge of Brahman through the study of the Vedas or other scriptures. परोक्षज्ञान

Paropakara see Para Upakara. परोपकार

Parshva /Paarshva/ region of the ribs, side, flank; nearness; lateral. पार्श्व

Parthiva /Paarthiva/ inhabitant of the earth; Lord of the earth, ruler. पार्थिव

Parvata mountain range, mountain, hill, rock, height; name of one of the 10 orders of sannyasins established by Adi Shankaracharya, which originally drew members from the mountainous areas; see Dashnami Sampradaya. पर्वत

Parvataraja /Parvata-raaja/ king of the mountains, epithet of the Himalayan mountains. पर्वतराज

Parvati /Paarvatee/ literally 'daughter of the mountain', goddess and consort of Shiva, mother of Ganesha and Kartikeya, and daughter of Himavanta, hence also called Haimavati; see Sati; see Uma. पार्वती

Pasha /Paasha/ noose, snare, net for catching birds; see Bhavapashavimukti. पाश

Pashchima /Pashchimaa/ west (direction); the back of the body. पश्चिम

Pashu animal, brute, beast; often added to words meaning 'man' to show contempt; in tantra it refers to a person living at the instinctive animal level of consciousness. पशु

Pashubhava /Pashu-bhaava/ instinctive personality. पशुभाव

Pashvachara /Pashvaachaara/ (Pashu-aachaara); 'conduct of brutes', a tantric course of spiritual discipline for the least advanced aspirants. पश्वाचार

Pashyanti /Pashyantee/ the third stage of nada yoga; meditation in which one perceives the entire universe as being sound (nada); see Nada Yoga. पश्यन्ती

Pashyanti Nada /Pashyantee Naada/ mental sound; sound made visible. पश्यन्ती नाद

Pataha a drum. पटह

Patala basket; a heap, lots; chapter of a book, section. पटल

Patalam /Paataalam/ abode of serpents and demons; instinctive or animal realm; hell; seven planes of consciousness or regions described as being below mooladhara chakra, viz. atala, vitala, sutala, rasatala, talatala, mahatala, patala; lowest of the seven patalam; see Chakra; see Loka; see Naraka. पातालम्

Patana fall, decline, setting (as of the sun). पतन

Patanjali author of the *Yoga Sutras*; an ancient rishi who codified the meditative stages and states of samadhi into the system of raja yoga and is famous as the propounder of ashtanga yoga. According to many authorities, the same person was also the author of *Mahabhashya* (a classical treatise on Sanskrit grammar), as well as a treatise on medicine. Some believe he was a contemporary of Lord Buddha. पतञ्जलि

Patati flies; falls down, drops down, sinks; forfeits one's position; throw oneself; happens. पतति

Patha /Paatha/ recitation of a sacred text. पाठ

Pathati reads aloud, recites, reads to oneself, teaches, studies. पठति

Patha, Pantha way, road, path, course; manner. पथ, पन्थ

Pathika traveller, wanderer. पथिक

Pati lord, ruler, husband. पति

Pativratadharma /Pati-vrataa-dharma/ woman's vows of devotion to her husband. पतिव्रताधर्म

Pativratya /Paati-vratya/ devotion of a wife to her husband. पातिव्रत्य

Patni wife. पत्नि

Patrika /Patrikaa/ a leaf for writing on; letter; document. पत्रिका

Pattana town; abode. पट्टन

Pausha 10th lunar month according to the Hindu almanac, corresponding to December/January; see Hemanta; see Masa; see Ritu. पौष

Pavaka /Paavaka/ fire; dynamism; motivation. पावक

Pavitra sanctified, pure. पवित्र

Payovrata an austere observance where one lives on milk alone. पयोव्रत

Payu /Paayu/ anus, the organ of excretion and one of the five organs of action (karmendriyas); see Devata. पायु

Peepal see Ashvattha. पीपल

Phala fruit; kernel; consequence, retribution, reward, punishment. फल

Phalahara /Phala-aahaara/ fruit diet (usually taken by yogis, spiritual aspirants and performers of austerities). फलाहार

Phalguna /Phaalguna/ 12th lunar month of the Hindu almanac, corresponding to February/March; see Shishira; see Masa; see Ritu. फाल्गुन

Pida /Peedaa/ pain, trouble, suffering, agony; annoyance, disturbance; injury, damage, harm; devastation, laying waste; violation. पीडा

Pinaka /Pinaaka/ the bow of Lord Shiva which Rama broke to win Sita. पिनाक

Pinda the foetus or embryo in an early stage of gestation; the body, corporeal frame. पिण्ड

Pindanda /Pindaanda/ the world of the body; microcosmos as opposed to the macrocosmos or cosmos (Brahmanda). पिण्डाण्ड

Pinda Prana /Pinda Praana/ the individual breath, as contrasted with the cosmic or universal breath. पिण्ड प्राण

Pingala Nadi /Pingalaa Naadee/ a major pranic channel in the body that flows from mooladhara chakra on the right, criss-crossing all the major chakras to ajna chakra. It conducts the dynamic pranic force manifesting as prana shakti, and governs the right side of the body and left side of the brain. It is associated with the mundane realm of experience and externalized awareness; also called surya nadi, as the solar energy flows through it; see Ida Nadi; see Sushumna Nadi. पिङ्गला नाडी

Pipal /Peepala/ holy fig tree; see Ashvattha. पीपल

Pipasa /Pipaasaa/ thirst; see Shadurmi. पिपासा

Pitri departing ancestor; a divine hierarchy consisting of deceased progenitors and ancestors; the manes; father. पितृ

Pitri Yajna oblations for gratifying the manes, libation to deceased ancestors; one of the daily sacrificial rites enjoined on all householders; see Pancha Mahayajna. पितृ यज्ञ

Pitriyana /Pitri-yaana/ the path of the forefathers or the manes. An individual soul, on doing good works or obtaining merit, ascends to the region of the moon by this path after death, enjoying there the effects of their work; also called the path of smoke (dhumamarga). पितृयान

Pitrya paternal, relating to a father, inherited from father, patrimonial. पित्र्य

Pitta bile, one of the three humours (doshas) described in ayurveda, related to fiery personality; see Dosha. पित्त

Pittamprahriti of a bilious or choleric temperament. पित्तम्प्रह्रति

Plavana float. प्लवन

Plavini Pranayama /Plaavinee Praanaayaama/ pranayama practice in which the abdomen is filled with swallowed air so one can float like a lotus leaf on water. प्लाविनी प्राणायाम

Pluta elongated accent with three

or more matras (time interval in pronouncing a vowel). प्लुत

Pooja see Puja. पूजा

Pooraka see Puraka. पूरक

Poornima see Purnima. पूर्णिमा

Poorva see Purva. पूर्व

Pra a prefix often used in the Sanskrit language. प्र

Prabhava /Pra-bhaava/ effect; lustre, splendour, brilliance; dignity, glory, majesty, grandeur; strength, valour, power, efficacy; superhuman power or faculty, miraculous power; regal power; one of the three powers (shaktis) of a ruler (the other two are mantra and utsaha). प्रभाव

Prabodhana awakening, arousing; understanding; instruction. प्रबोधन

Pracchanna /Prachchhanna/ covered, hidden. प्रच्छन्न

Prachela yellow sandalwood. प्रचेल

Prachetas epithet of Varuna, regent of the ocean; name of an ancient sage and law-giver. प्रचेतस्

Pradana /Pra-daana/ giving, granting, bestowing, offering; giving away in marriage; teaching, instructing. प्रदान

Pradhana /Pradhaana/ the chief; the root base for all elements; undifferentiated matter; a term used in Sankhya for prakriti, the material cause of the world. It corresponds to maya in Vedanta, but differs from maya on the following points: it is real while maya is unreal or phenomenal, and it is independent of purusha while maya is dependent on Brahman; see Prakriti. प्रधान

Pradhanya /Praadhaanya/ preeminence, superiority, predominance; ascendancy, supremacy; a chief or principal cause. प्रधान्य

Pragabhava /Praagabhaava/ (Praakabhaava); not existing previously, non-existence. प्रागभाव

Praharsha erection (of the hair), extreme joy, exultation. प्रहर्ष

Prahlada /Prahlaada/ great joy, pleasure, delight, happiness; name of a son of the demon Hiranyakashipu. According to the *Padma Purana*, Prahlada was a brahmana (priest) in his previous incarnation and retained his ardent devotion to Vishnu, believing that Vishnu fills all space and is omnipresent, omniscient and omnipotent. His father, annoyed that his son should be such a devout worshipper of his mortal enemies, the gods, subjected him to various cruelties with the object of getting rid of him, but Prahlada, by the grace of Vishnu, remained unscathed. Hiranyakashipu, in a fit of exasperation, asked him one day, "If Vishnu is omnipresent, then why don't I see him in the pillar of this hall?" Vishnu then appeared from the pillar as Narasimha, having the body of a man and the head of a lion, and tore Hiranyakashipu to pieces. Prahlada succeeded his father, reigned righteously and was the grandfather of Bali. प्रह्लाद

Praja /Prajaa/ procreation, generation, propagation, production, birth; offspring, progeny, issue; subjects, people, mankind. प्रजा

Praja Kama /Prajaa Kaama/ desirous of progeny. प्रजा काम

Prajapati /Prajaa-pati/ literally 'Lord of created beings'; the god presiding over creation; an epithet of Brahma; epithet of the 10 lords of created beings (Vishvakarma the architect of the gods, the Sun, Vishnu, etc.); a father; see Kashyapa. प्रजापति

Prajapatya /Praajaa-patya/ giving away the whole of one's property before entering upon the life of an ascetic; literally 'related to Prajapati'. प्राजापत्य

Prajati /Prajaati/ generation, generating power. प्रजाति

Prajna /Pra-jnaa/ knowledge with awareness; awareness of the one without a second; individual consciousness, intelligence, understanding, intellect, wisdom; discernment, discrimination, judgement; intention; device; see Ritambhara Prajna. प्रज्ञा

Prajna /Praajna/ a name according to Vedanta philosophy for an individual in the causal state (as in sound sleep), when the supreme reality is veiled by the causal body; the seer who observes the state of deep sleep (sushupti), the third state of consciousness expressed by the all knowing 'm' of Aum according to *Mandukya Upanishad*; see Avasthatraya. प्राज्ञ

Prajnanam Brahma /Prajnaanam Brahma/ 'Knowledge is Brahman', one of the four maha vakyas (great statements) of the Upanishads, the expression of the identity of the individual soul and the supreme consciousness found in *Aitareya Upanishad* of the *Rigveda*; see Maha Vakya. प्रज्ञानं ब्रह्म

Prajnatma /Prajna-aatmaa/ the intelligent self, the conscious internal self, the knower of oneself. प्रज्ञात्मा

Prakamya /Praa-kaamya/ psychic power by which yogis touch the higher sphere of existence; freedom of will; one of the eight major siddhis; see Siddhi. प्राकाम्य

Prakara /Prakaara/ sort, species; manner, way. प्रकार

Prakarana subject matter; section; preliminary text. प्रकरण

Prakasha /Prakaasha/ brightness, shining, brilliance; the essence of sattwa guna; spiritual brilliance, clarity, light; light of consciousness; the Shiva aspect in Kashmir Shaivism as the counterpart of vimarsha; see Vimarsha; see Kashmir Shaivmata. प्रकाश

Prakashaka /Prakaashaka/ revealer, illuminator. प्रकाशक

Prakasha Mandala /Prakaasha Mandala/ white light at the centre of ajna chakra; see Vidyut Mandala. प्रकाश मण्डल

Prakashya /Prakaashya/ object revealed or illumined. प्रकाश्य

Prakata manifest, revealed. प्रकट

Prakriti individual nature; manifest and unmanifest nature; cosmic energy; the active principle of manifest energy; nature or primordial matter (source of the universe); according to Sankhya philosophy, insentient prakriti consists of three aspects or qualities called gunas: sattwa, rajas and tamas. They remain unmanifest (avyakta) when in equilibrium, but when this equilibrium is disturbed by the proximity of the witnessing purusha consciousness, manifestation, creation and evolution set in; see Pradhana; see Pratibimbavada; see Purusha; see Samyavastha; see Vaishamyavastha; see Vikritti. प्रकृति

Prakrita /Praakrita/ original; natural; ordinary; vulgar; vernacular. प्राकृत

Prakritilaya one who is submerged in prakriti. प्रकृतिलय

Prakriya Grantha scripture that deals with categories of a subject. प्रक्रिय ग्रन्थ

Pralapa /Pralaapa/ talk, conversation, discourse; prating, prattling and incoherent conversation, nonsensical talk; lamentation. प्रलाप

Pralaya state of latency of the world or of periodic dematerialization; destruction, annihilation, dissolution; destruction of the whole universe at the end of a set period of time; death, dying; the mystic syllable Aum; complete merging; dissolution when the cosmos merges into the unseen immediate cause (the unmanifested cosmic energy); the ultimate substratum of absolute reality; see Kalpa; see Yuga. प्रलय

Pralaya Dahana the fire at the dissolution of the world. प्रलय दहन

Pralaya Jaladhara a cloud at the dissolution of the world. प्रलय जलधर

Pralayakala /Pralaya-kaala/ the time of universal destruction. प्रलयकाल

Pramada /Pramaada/ intoxication; negligence; inattention; indolence. प्रमाद

Pramadin /Pramaadin/ drunkard; negligent person; incautious person. प्रमादिन्

Pramada joy, pleasure. प्रमद

Pramana /Pramaana/ 'correct' knowledge; knowledge based on direct sensation or cognition; measure, standard, norm; authority; argument; proof, means of knowledge; one of the five modifications of mind (vrittis) described in Patanjali's *Yoga Sutras* as based on direct cognition (pratyaksha), inference (anumana) and/or reliable testimony (agama); see Vritti. प्रमाण

Pramana Chaitanya /Pramaana Chaitanya/ consciousness as knowing; the source of knowledge; proof. प्रमाण चैतन्य

Pramanika /Praamaanika/ established by proof; founded or resting on authority; founded on the authority of scriptures; authentic, credible, trustworthy. प्रामाणिक

Pramata /Pramaataa/ measurer; knower; the ego or jiva. प्रमाता

Pramatri Chaitanya /Pramaatri Chaitanya/ a subject who knows the objective consciousness which is determined by the fourfold mind or internal organ (antah karana); see Antahchatushtaya. प्रमातृ चैतन्य

Pramoda the pleasure one obtains through the actual enjoyment of an object; an attribute of the causal body (karanasharira) and the third type of bliss experienced in anandamaya kosha; see Anandamaya Kosha. प्रमोद

Prana /Praana/ vital energy force, essence of life permeating both the macrocosmos and microcosmos; the sum total of all energy residing within the universe, both in the unmanifest states and in manifest nuclear states; breath, respiration; principle of life; vital energy that functions in various ways for the preservation of the body and is closely associated with the mind; one of the five vital airs (pancha prana vayu), which operates in the region of the heart and lungs; see Prana Vayu; see Pancha Prana; see Vayu. प्राण

Pranabhrit /Praana-bhrit/ supporting life; creature, a being. प्राणभृत्

Pranachaitanya /Praana-chaitanya/ awareness of prana vayu. प्राणचैतन्य

Pranajaya /Praana-jaya/ mastery over the pranas (the vital airs); conquest of the life-force. प्राणजय

Pranakendra /Praana-kendra/ life centre. प्राणकेन्द्र

Pranamaya Kosha /Praana-maya Kosha/ energy sheath, or vital or pranic body; the sheath (kosha) covering the self which is composed of pranic vibration and the rhythm of pranic forces; see Pancha Kosha; see Lingasharira; see Prana. प्राणमय कोष

Prananada /Praana-naada/ a deep sound. प्राणनाद

Prananigraha /Praana-nigraha/ control of prana; practice to control the breathing pattern. प्राणनिग्रह

Prananirodha /Praana-nirodha/ control of the vital airs. प्राणनिरोध

Pranapratishtha /Praana-pratishthaa/ tantric ritual by

which an image or symbol of God or any deity is vitalized. प्राणप्रतिष्ठा

Prana Shakti /Praana Shakti/ dynamic solar force governing the dimension of matter; energy flow related to externalization of mind; the force of prana; see Pingala Nadi. प्राण शक्ति

Prana Tattwa /Praana Tattva/ element representing the vital or life-giving force. प्राण तत्त्व

Prana Vayu /Praana Vaayu/ one of the five vital airs which pervade different parts of the entire body, energy (prana) moving upwards between the diaphragm and the larynx. It controls the heart and the lungs; see Vayu; see Pancha Prana. प्राण वायु

Prana Vidya /Praana Vidyaa/ knowledge and control of prana; a healing technique involving awareness and movement of prana. प्राण विद्या

Pranayama /Praana-aayaama/ a series of techniques using the breath to control the flow of prana within the body; expansion of the range of vital energy; a systematic and scientific breathing technique by which one can control, conduct and conquer the flow of the life-force in the body; prana means life-force, ayama means expansion; in the Upanishads pranayama is said to have the ability to cut through mountains of karma. प्राणायाम

Pranopasana /Praanopaasanaa/ (Praana-upaasanaa); controlling prana (energy) through regulation of inhalation, exhalation and retention; sacrifice of prana. प्राणोपासना

Pranotthana /Praanotthaana/ (Praana-utthaana); awakening of the pranas in the different nadis and chakras. प्राणोत्थान

Pranama /Pranaama/ bending, bowing, reverential salutation, obeisance, prostration; stopping. प्रणाम

Pranava another word for the sacred syllable Aum (Om), the primal sound vibration; a kind of musical instrument; epithet of Vishnu. प्रणव

Pranavadhina /Pranava-adheena/ dependent on the pranava or Aum. प्रणवाधीन

Pranava Dhyana /Pranava Dhyaana/ meditation on the mantra Aum. प्रणव ध्यान

Pranava Japa repetition of the mantra Aum. प्रणव जप

Pranidhana /Pranidhaana/ to believe in. प्रणिधान

Prapancha Vishaya worldly objects. प्रपञ्च विषय

Prapanchika /Praapanchika/ worldly aspects. प्रापञ्चिक

Prapta /Praapta/ got, acquired; one who has attained; that which comes to us yet is not the result of present or recent effort. प्राप्त

Praptasya Prapti /Praaptasya Praapti/ attainment of whatever has been attained (although one is not aware of it until expansion of awareness happens). प्राप्तस्य प्राप्ति

Prapti /Praapti/ a power by which the yogi acquires everything; one of the eight major siddhis; see Siddhi. प्राप्ति

Prarabdha Karma /Praarabdha Karma/ actions already performed which, like arrows shot from the bow, cannot be retrieved; that portion of one's actions which is bound to fructify in the present life and cannot be averted; see Karma. प्रारब्ध कर्म

Prarambha /Praarambha/ beginning, commencement. प्रारम्भ

Prarthana /Praarthanaa/ worship through prayer. प्रार्थना

Prasada, Prasadam /Prasaada, Prasaadam/ clearness, purity, tranquillity; favour, grace, blessed gift or object, something full of grace; food dedicated to a god or the guru and thereafter eaten by faithful devotees as something holy. प्रसाद, प्रसादम्

Prasahya using force, forcibly. प्रसह्य

Prasanjana act of connection, combining, uniting; applying, bringing to bear upon, bringing into use. प्रसञ्जन

Prasanna pure, clear, bright, transparent; pleased, delighted, propitiated; kind, kindly disposed, gracious; true, correct. प्रसन्न

Prasarita /Prasaarita/ spread, stretched out (as a hand is); exposed. प्रसारित

Prashanta /Prashaanta/ calmed, quiet; tamed; intensified peace (shanti). प्रशान्त

Prashna question, query; inquiry, interrogation; judicial inquiry or investigation; point at issue, subject of controversy; problem for solution; inquiry into the future; lesson. प्रश्न

Prashnopanishad (Prashna-upanishad); name of an Upanishad consisting of six questions and the corresponding answers given by Sage Pippalada after the seekers had served in his ashram for one year. प्रश्नोपनिषद्

Prasiddha accomplished, arranged; well known, famous; usual. प्रसिद्ध

Prasthana, Prasthita /Prasthaana, Prasthita/ set out, departed, going. प्रस्थान, प्रस्थित

Prasthanatraya /Prasthaana-traya/ the three authoritative landmarks in spiritual literature: the Upanishads, the *Brahma Sutras* and the *Bhagavad Gita*, on which vedantic philosophy is based. प्रस्थानत्रय

Prasupta dormant; one of the four possible states of the kleshas according to Patanjali in the *Yoga Sutras*; see Klesha. प्रसुप्त

Prateek see Pratika. प्रतीक

Prathama first, eminent, earliest. प्रथम

Prathama Spandana first vibration. प्रथम स्पन्दन

Prati a prefix often used in Sanskrit with a wide range of meanings according to context, including opposite; inverted; other than; similarity. प्रति

Pratibandha an obstacle or hindrance on the spiritual path. प्रतिबन्ध

Pratibandhakabhava /Prati-bandhaka-abhaava/ power that removes the obstruction hindering realization of the self; absence of obstacles. प्रतिबन्धकाभाव

Pratibha /Prati-bhaa/ inner light; intelligence; intuition; splendour of knowledge. प्रतिभा

Pratibimba reflection as in a mirror. प्रतिबिम्ब

Pratibimbavada /Prati-bimba-vaada/ doctrine that the soul is a reflection of the self in the buddhi; in Sankhya philosophy, the doctrine that the consciousness of purusha is reflected into the insentient prakriti by her first evolute, mahat or buddhi; see Prakriti. प्रतिबिम्बवाद

Pratibimbita reflected, mirrored. प्रतिबिम्बित

Pratiksha /Prateekshaa/ (Prati-eekshaa); wait; anticipation. प्रतीक्षा

Pratipaksha the opposite side, party or function; hostility; adversary, enemy, foe, rival. प्रतिपक्ष

Pratipaksha Bhava,

Pratipaksha Bhavana /Prati-paksha Bhaava, Prati-paksha Bhaavanaa/ that principle of yoga which states that one may control a negative emotion by summoning its opposite, or a lower thought by countering it with a higher one; the method of substituting the opposite thought or emotion through imagination, e.g. fear is overcome by dwelling strongly upon its opposite of courage, or hate is overcome only by love. प्रतिपक्ष भाव, प्रतिपक्ष भावना

Pratishabda echo; reverberation; a roar. प्रतिशब्द

Pratishtha /Prati-shthaa/ reputa-

tion, fame; awareness of identity; standpoint, base, ground, support. प्रतिष्ठा

Pratispandanam throbbing. प्रतिस्पन्दनम्

Pratiyoginishakti /Prati-yoginee-shakti/ opposite power or force. प्रतियोगिनीशक्ति

Pratyabhijna /Pratyabhijnaa/ (Prati-abhijnaa); knowing; recognition or recovering consciousness; recollection. प्रत्यभिज्ञा

Pratyadishta /Pratyaadishta/ (Prati-aadishta); warned; prescribed; informed; rejected, repulsed; removed, set aside. प्रत्यादिष्ट

Pratyahara /Pratyaahaara/ (Prati-aahaara); drawing back, retreat; restraining the sensory and motor organs; withdrawal and emancipation of the mind from the domination of the senses and sensual objects; training the senses to follow the mind within; fifth stage of raja yoga; see Ashtanga Yoga. प्रत्याहार

Pratyaksha (Prati-aksha); direct evidence or sense evidence presented by Patanjali in the *Yoga Sutras* as one of the three sources for the vritti of right knowledge (pramana); present before the eyes, visible, perceptible, clear; immediate, real; corporeal. प्रत्यक्ष

Pratyavahara /Pratyavahaara/ (Prati-avahaara); withdrawal; universal destruction, dissolution (of the world). प्रत्यवहार

Pratyavasana /Pratyavasaana/ (Prati-avasaana); eating or drinking. प्रत्यवसान

Pratyaya (Prati-aya); seeds or impressions in the field of consciousness which do not disappear even in the first stages of samadhi; content of mind (in yoga philosophy). प्रत्यय

Pratibhasika /Praatibhaasika/ illusory, appearing. प्रातिभासिक

Pratibhasikasatta /Praatibhaasika-sattaa/ dream-reality; apparent or unreal as a dream. प्रातिभासिकसत्ता

Pratika /Prateeka/ symbol used in meditation or worship. प्रतीक

Pratikopasana /Prateekopaasanaa/ (Prateeka-upaasanaa); meditation in which Brahman is thought of with and through a symbol. प्रतीकोपासना

Pratyak in an opposite direction, backwards; in the interior, inwardly; against. प्रत्यक्

Pratyagatma /Pratyagaatmaa/ (Pratyak-aatmaa); inner self; Kutastha, Brahman; see Kutastha. प्रत्यगात्मा

Pravritih the four basic instincts, viz. 1. desire to procreate (maithuna), 2. fear (bhaya), 3. desire for food (ahara), 4. desire for sleep (nidra). प्रवृति:

Pravritta arisen, come forth, commenced; occupied with. प्रवृत्त

Pravritti rise; origin, source; flow; continued; advance, progress; tendency, inclination, predilection; conduct, behaviour; employment, occupation, activity; continued effort, perseverance. प्रवृत्ति

Pravritti Marga /Pra-vritti Maarga/ path of extroversion; path of action of life in worldly society or according to the nature of the world. प्रवृत्ति मार्ग

Pravrittivijnana /Pra-vritti-vijnaana/ quasi-external consciousness. प्रवृत्तिविज्ञान

Prayaga /Prayaaga/ name of a celebrated place of pilgrimage at the confluence of the Ganga and Yamuna rivers near the town of Allahabad; a sacrifice; name of India; horse; see Kumbhamela; see Triveni. प्रयाग

Prayana /Prayaana/ setting out, starting, departure; march, journey; progress, advance; death, departure (from the world). प्रयाण

Prayashchitta /Praayashchitta/ atonement for one's acts of unawareness during all births. प्रायश्चित्त

Prayashchitta Karma /Praayashchitta Karma/ expiatory action; bodily mortification; penance. प्रायश्चित्त कर्म

Prayatna effort, exertion, endeavour; perseverance or continued effort, labour; difficulty. प्रयत्न

Prayoga use; experiment. प्रयोग

Prayojana result, fruit, the final end. प्रयोजन

Prema love, affection; favour, kindness; tenderness; regard. प्रेम

Preyas pleasant; sensorial enjoyment; acts that lead to material happiness and are therefore preferred; worldly desires. प्रेयस्

Prithvi /Prithvee/ Earth, literally 'the broad one'; earth, the solid state of matter, in Sankhya philosophy it is the fifth mahabhuta with the special property of smell; see Pancha Mahabhuta. पृथ्वी

Prithvi Tattwa /Prithvee Tattwa/ earth element; see Pancha Mahabhuta. पृथ्वी तत्त्व

Priti /Preeti/ pleasure, happiness, gladness, favour, delight, friendliness; wife of Kama; love, affection. प्रीति

Priya the first type of bliss experienced in anandamaya kosha. प्रिय

Prokshana sprinkling water as purification of the place of worship. प्रोक्षण

Puja /Poojaa/ honour, respect; rites; worship; see Yajna. पूजा

Pujari /Pujaaree/ officiating priest at a religious ceremony. पुजारी

Punya merit. पुण्य

Punya Kshetram holy place. पुण्य क्षेत्रम्

Puraka /Pooraka/ filling up, completing; the first stage of pranayama i.e. inhalation; see Rechaka. पूरक

Purana the sea, ocean. पुरण

Puranam, Purana /Puraanam, Puraana/ past event; ancient, old; name of a class of sacred texts believed to be composed by Rishi Vyasa - 18 ancient texts containing the earliest mythology of the tantric and vedic traditions, viz. 1. *Brahma Purana*, 2. *Padma Purana*, 3. *Vishnu Purana*, 4. *Shiva Purana*, 5. *Bhagavata Purana*, 6. *Narada Purana*, 7. *Markandeya Purana*, 8. *Agni Purana*, 9. *Bhavishya Purana*, 10. *Brahmavaivarta Purana*, 11. *Linga Purana*, 12. *Varaha Purana*, 13. *Skanda Purana*, 14. *Vamana Purana*, 15. *Kurma Purana*, 16. *Matsya Purana*, 17. *Garuda Purana*, 18. *Brahmanda Purana*; see Upa Purana. पुराणम्, पुराण

Purascharana /Purashcharana/ observance consisting of the repetition of a mantra. पुरश्चरण

Puri /Puree/ town, city; name of one of the 10 orders of sannyasins founded by Adi Shankaracharya; see Dashnami Sampradaya. पुरी

Puri, Jagannath Puri /Puree, Jagannaatha Puree/ holy city in Orissa where Govardhan Matha is situated; see Govardhan Matha. पुरी, जगन्नाथ पुरी

Puritat Nadi /Pureetat Naadee/ one of the astral or subtle passages in the body. पुरीतत् नाडी

Purna /Poorna/ filled, full; whole, entire, complete; fulfilled, accomplished; strong, powerful. पूर्ण

Purnahuti /Poorna-aahuti/ total offering; final ceremonial offering in a sacrifice (yajna). पूर्णाहुति

Purnima /Poornimaa/ the day of the full moon. पूर्णिमा

Purnoham /Poornoham/ (Poornah-aham); literally "I am full"; "I am the absolute, the infinite", "I am Brahman". पूर्णोऽहम्

Purohita placed in front; appointed; house priest. पुरोहित

Purta /Poorta/ charitable construction of water tanks, etc. for the benefit of humanity; full, complete; concealed, covered; nourished; protected. पूर्त

Purusha literally 'who dwells in the city', the body being the dormant receptacle of consciousness, the soul; the totality of consciousness; male, man, mankind; the supreme being, God; in Sankhya philosophy purusha designates pure consciousness, undefiled and unlimited by contact with prakriti or matter; see Prakriti; see Pratibimbavada. पुरुष

Purushartha /Purusha-artha/ human attainment; the four goals to be fulfilled in life: 1. wealth (artha), 2. love (kama), 3. duty (dharma) and 4. liberation (moksha). पुरुषार्थ

Purusha Sukta /Purusha Sookta/ a hymn from the *Rigveda* composed by Narayana which praises creation and the creator who pervades it. पुरुष सूक्त

Purusha Vishesha a special purusha that is beyond modifications; see Ishwara. पुरुष विशेष

Purushottamayoga (Purusha-uttama-yoga); 'yoga of the highest purusha (supreme spirit)', the 15th chapter of the *Bhagavad Gita*, in which samsara (the manifest phenomenal world) is described as a pipal tree which must be felled with the strong axe of detachment so that the supreme can be known. पुरुषोत्तमयोग

Purva /Poorva/ being in front of, first, foremost; front of the body; eastern. पूर्व

Purva Mimamsa /Poorva Meemaamsaa/ often simply called Mimamsa, Purva Mimamsa is one of the six systems of Indian philosophy (darshana) in the form of questions and contains the theory of traditional rituals (karma kanda); the philosophy of the sage Jaimini regarding the portion of the Vedas on sacrificial works and other religious ceremonies; also called Karma Mimamsa; see Mimamsa; see Shaddarshana. पूर्व मीमांसा

Purvokta /Poorvokta/ (Poorva-ukta); as mentioned before. पूर्वोक्त

Pushpa a blossom, flower; see Shodashopachara. पुष्प

Pushpamaya made of flowers, full of flowers. पुष्पमय

Pushpadanta a celestial being (gandharva) devoted to Shiva who composed the *Shri Shiva-mahimnah Stotram* eulogizing Lord Shiva. पुष्पदन्त

Putra child, son. पुत्र

Putramoham blind affection for one's children. पुत्रमोहम्

Putreshana /Putreshanaa/ (Putra-eshanaa); desire for one's own children, desire for progeny; see Eshana Traya. पुत्रेषणा

R

Pronunciation

ऋ *ri* – *as in clarity*

र *r* – *as in red*

Rabhasa violence, force; haste, speed; rashness, precipitation; anger, passion, rage, fury; joy, pleasure, delight. रभस

Radha the milkmaid (gopi) most beloved of Gopala (young Lord Krishna) who is acknowledged as his counterpart. She is a symbol of bhakti; see Bhakti; see Gopala. राधा

Raga /Raaga/ love, affection; passion, amorous feeling; likes; attitude of mind towards the object of your love (the positive aspect); attachment, attraction; anything which colours the mind; colours, especially the colour red; one of the five causes of affliction (kleshas) described in Patanjali's *Yoga Sutras* as being attracted to (or being attached to) what gives pleasure; musical scale; see Raga-Dwesha; see Klesha. राग

Raga Bandha /Raaga Bandha/ manifestation of feeling; interest created by a proper representation (of various emotions). राग बन्ध

Raga Dravyam /Raaga Dravyam/ colouring substance; paint. राग द्रव्यम्

Raga-Dwesha /Raaga-Dvesha/ term used to evoke the concept of pairs of opposites or the positive and negative aspects; like and dislike; love and hatred; attraction and repulsion, constituting two of the kleshas as described in Patanjali's *Yoga Sutras*. राग-द्वेष

Ragini /Raaginee/ literally 'consort of raga', modification of a musical mode (raga). रागिनी

Rahasya secret, private, clandestine; mysterious; mystic spell or incantation; esoteric teaching; doctrine. रहस्य

Rahita without. रहित

Raja /Raajaa/ king, ruler, prince, chief; man of the military or ruling caste (kshatriya); name of Indra. राजा

Raja Marga /Raaja Maarga/ royal path of self-realization through control of the mind. राज मार्ग

Rajarshi /Raaja-rishi/ royal sage; philosopher king; a rishi who is a kshatriya; see Rishi; see Kshatriya; see Vishvamitra. राजर्षि

Rajasooya Yajna /Raaja-sooya Yajna/ sacrifice (yajna) of large dimensions to be performed by an emperor. Lord Krishna had it performed by King Yudhisthira in Dwapara yuga; see Yajna. राजसूय यज्ञ

Rajavidyarajaguhyayoga /Raaja-vidyaa-raaja-guhya-yoga/ 'yoga of sovereign knowledge and the sovereign secret', the ninth chapter of the *Bhagavad Gita*, which emphasizes the wisdom of identifying oneself with the highest. राजविद्याराजगुह्ययोग

Raja Yoga /Raaja Yoga/ the royal yoga; yoga of awakening the psychic awareness and faculties through meditation; the scientific method of union with the supreme universal being through control of the mental processes; enquiry into the inner awareness of samadhi; the most authoritative text is Patanjali's *Yoga Sutras*. The famous ashtanga yoga forms a small part of this work. राज योग

Raja Yogin /Raaja Yogin/ one who practises raja yoga. राज योगिन्

Rajas one of the three constituent qualities (gunas) of nature (prakriti), and all matter; dynamism; state of activity; creativity combined with full ego involvement; emotion; restlessness; oscillation; as a personality trait it is expressed by the desire to dominate; see Guna; see Viraja. रजस्

Rajasic /Raajasika/ pertaining to rajas. राजसिक

Rajoguna quality of rajas. रजोगुण

Rajogunasamudbhavah /Rajoguna-samudbhavaah/ that which comes forth from rajoguna. रजोगुणसमुद्भवा:

Raka /Raakaa/ the full moon day and particularly its night; the goddess presiding over the full moon day. राका

Rakini /Raakinee/ goddess of plants and swadhisthana chakra. राकिनी

Raksha /Rakshaa/ watch; protection; care. रक्षा

Rakshaka warder; protector. रक्षक

Rakshati to protect, to guard; to watch; to observe (a law); to rule (the Earth), to govern. रक्षति

Rakshasa /Raakshasa/ demon, evil spirit, goblin; one of the astronomical yogas. राक्षस

Rakta blood. रक्त

Ram bija mantra of fire and therefore of manipura chakra; see Mahabhuta. रं, (रम्)

Rama /Raama/ the hero of the epics *Ramayana* and *Ramacharitamanasa*, the seventh incarnation of Vishnu as the son of Dasharatha and Kaushalya and the most dutiful disciple of Vishvamitra. He married Sita after he performed the wonderful feat of bending Shiva's bow. On the eve of his coronation as king of Ayodhya, he was exiled for 14 years through the scheming of his father's favourite wife, Kaikeyi. During his exile he killed the demon Ravana, thus fulfilling the main purpose of his incarnation; pleasing, rejoicing, delighting; beautiful, lovely, charming; obscure, dark-coloured, black; white; see Avatara. राम

Ramacharitamanas /Raamacharitamaanasa/ a version of the *Ramayana* written in a Hindi dialect by Tulsidas. रामचरितमानस

Ramayana /Raamaayana/ literally 'the path of Rama', one of the most famous ancient Indian epics, composed by Valmiki, containing about 24,000 verses in seven chapters. रामायण

Ramanuja /Raamaanuja/ literally 'younger brother of Rama'; name of a celebrated reformer who founded a vedantic sect called Vishishta Advaita or conditioned non-dualism, and authored several treatises; see Vedanta; see Vishishta Advaita; see Vairagi. रामानुज

Rana battle, fight. रण

Ranatkara /Ranatkaara/ rattling, clanking or jingling sound; sound in general; humming (as of bees). रणत्कार

Ranga colour; theatre, stage. रङ्ग

Rasa serum found in the body tissues; taste; see Pancha Tanmatra. रस

Rasana /Rasanaa/ tongue; the organ of taste. रसना

Rasashastra /Rasa-shaastra/ the science of alchemy. रसशास्त्र

Rasasiddhi skill in alchemy. रससिद्धि

Rasendra (Rasa-indra); literally 'Lord of liquids'; mercury; philosopher's stone, the touch of which is said to turn iron/metal into gold. रसेन्द्र

Rasasvada /Rasa-aasvaada/ tasting the essence of the bliss of savikalpa samadhi. This is an obstacle to the higher advaitic realization as it prevents the meditator from attempting to reach the higher states of samadhi. रसास्वाद

Rasa Tanmatra /Rasa Tanmaatra/ the subtle essence of taste or flavour, the tanmatra associated with swadhisthana chakra; see Pancha Tanmatra. रस तन्मात्र

Rasatmaka /Rasa-aatmaka/ sentient; fluid, consisting of juice, liquid. रसात्मक

Rasakrida /Raasakreedaa/ transcendental sport that Lord Krishna played with the gopis of Vrindavana. रासक्रीडा

Rasatala /Rasaatala/ fourth centre of the instinctive or animal body below mooladhara chakra; see Patalam. रसातल

Rashtra /Raashtra/ kingdom, empire, country, people, subjects. राष्ट्र

Ratha carriage, chariot, car, vehicle; hero (especially one having a war chariot); body. रथ

Rati intense attachment. रति

Ratipriti /Rati-preeti/ intense attachment and love; joy derived from physical love. रतिप्रीति

Ratna gift; riches, treasure; precious stone, jewel, pearl. रत्न

Ravana /Raavana/ the 10-headed demon king of Lanka, who kidnapped Sita and was subsequently slain by Rama. His 10 heads symbolize attachment to phenomenal reality via the five jnanendriyas and the five karmendriyas. रावण

Rechaka the process of exhalation in pranayama; emptying of the lungs; see Puraka. रेचक

Richa /Richaa/ collection of mantras; single verse or stanza from the Vedas expressing shades of universal truth. ऋचा

Riddhi highest sensual delight;

wealth; nine varieties of extraordinary exaltation and grandeur that come as a yogi advances and progresses in yoga. Like supernatural powers (siddhis), riddhis are great obstacles on the path of yoga; see Siddhi. ऋद्धि

Rigveda (Rik-veda); oldest of the four Vedas (vedic texts) and the most ancient sacred book of the Hindus. It contains hymns to the deities or guardians of the law, such as Agni, Varuna, Indra and Mitra, and presents nature as an eternal force working in the interests of humanity; see Veda; see Vasishtha; see Angiras. ऋग्वेद

Rigveda Samhita /Rikveda Samhitaa/ (Rik-veda Samhitaa); part of the *Rigveda* containing mantras and suktas (hymns) in adoration of devatas; see Mantra; see Devata. ऋग्वेद संहिता

Rik hymn of the *Rigveda* composed by a rishi to express an inner experience. ऋक्

Rina debt (karmic debt); see Karma. ऋण

Rishi inspired poet, ascetic, anchorite, seer; realized sage; one who contemplates or meditates on the self; one who experiences other dimensions; see Loka. ऋषि

Rishi Patni /Rishi Patnee/ wife of a rishi. ऋषि पत्नी

Rishi Rin /Rishi Rina/ debt owed to the sages for their teachings. ऋषि ऋण

Rishi Yajna /Rishi Yajnaa/ study of the scriptures for gratifying the seers of truth; one of the five sacrificial rites enjoined on all householders for daily performance, also known as Brahma yajna; see Pancha Mahayajna. ऋषि यज्ञ

Rita, Ritam proper, right; honest, true; worshipped, respected; fixed or settled rule, law; sacred custom; eternal laws of the universe; divine higher truth; the absolute or cosmic aspect of creation beyond matter and energy; base of all creation. ऋत, ऋतम्

Ritambhara /Ritambharaa/ full of experience; cosmic harmony. ऋतम्भरा

Ritambhara Prajna /Ritam-bharaa Prajnaa/ that power or truth obtained in the super-reflective state of samadhi; cosmic experience; according to the raja yoga of Patanjali's *Yoga Sutras*, the repeated experience of nirodha in samadhi eventually itself becomes the dynamic truth-bearing samskara called ritambhara prajna, which blocks other samskaras, vrittis etc., giving birth to seedless samadhi (nirbija samadhi); see Nirodha; see Samskara; see Vritti. ऋतम्भरा प्रज्ञा

Ritu season; one of six periods of the (Indian) year, viz. 1. spring (vasanta), 2. summer (grishma), 3. rainy season or monsoon (varsha), 4. autumn (sharad), 5. winter (hemanta), 6. cold (shishira); epoch, period, any fixed or appointed time; see Masa. ऋतु

Rityam the changing principle. ऋत्यम्

Rochaka pleasure inducing; interesting. रोचक

Roopa see Rupa. रूप

Ru light; dispeller; the second syllable in the word guru. रु

Ruchi taste or liking. रुचि
Ruchi Upasana /Ruchi Upaasanaa/ the form of worship which one likes. रुचि उपासना

Rud to cry. रुद्
Rudana the cry. रुदन
Rudanti crying, wailing or howling. रुदन्ति

Rudra howling energy; deity of manipura chakra; name of Lord Shiva in the *Rigveda* meaning 'He who proclaims himself aloud'; signifies transformation through dissolution. रुद्र

Rudra Granthi literally 'knot of Rudra (Shiva)'; psychic knot within ajna chakra which symbolizes attachment to siddhis or higher mental attributes. As the psychic block is overcome, the sense of personal identity ceases to block one's identification with the cosmic consciousness; psychic knot or block between ajna and sahasrara chakras; see Granthi. रुद्र ग्रन्थि

Rudraksha (Rudra-aksha); literally 'eye of Rudra'; a large tree, the seeds of which are used for rosaries, particlularly by Shaivites. They are mentioned in the *Akshamalik Upanishad* as the best material for malas. The *Devi Bhagavatam* recommends large seeds for Devi worship. Each seed has from 1 to 21 faces, and each type of seed has different energies and powers; see Mala. रुद्राक्ष

Rudravasa /Rudra-vaasa/ the abode of Rudra; the mountain Kailasa; name for Varanasi (Benares or Kashi). रुद्रवास

Rudrayamala /Rudrayaamala/ intimate union of Rudra and his counterpart Yamala. रुद्रयामल
Rudrayamala Tantra /Rudrayaamala Tantra/ text of Kashmir Shaivism in which *Vijnana Bhairava Tantra* is found (it is devoted entirely to esoteric sadhana); see Kashmir Shaivmata. रुद्रयामल तंत्र

Rukmini /Rukminee/ consort of Krishna. रुक्मिणी

Rupa /Roopa/ form, figure; handsome form or figure; appearance; the quality of colour; any visible object or thing; natural state or condition; nature, characteristic; kind, sort, species; essence; the number one; arithmetical unit; see Pancha Tanmatra. रूप
Rupa Chaitanya /Roopa Chaitanya/ form or state of consciousness. रूप चैतन्य
Rupa Shakti /Roopa Shakti/ the power that creates forms. रूप शक्ति
Rupa Tanmatra /Roopa Tanmaatra/ subtle principle of colour and form, connected with manipura chakra; see Pancha Tanmatra. रूप तन्मात्र

Ruta speech. रुत

S

Pronunciation

श् sh – as in shun; ष् sh – as in assure

स् s – as in sun

Sa a prefix often used in Sanskrit meaning 'along with'. स

Sabija Samadhi /Sa-beeja Samaadhi/ absorption (samadhi) with seed (sabija), the state of samadhi in which the seeds of desire remain in the mind, thus the seed of actions (karma) is not destroyed; see Nirbija Samadhi; see Samadhi. सबीज समाधि

Sachetana (Sa-chetana); with consciousness. सचेतन

Sachetanata /Sa-chetanataa/ possessed of consciousness. सचेतनता

Saguna with form or attribute; with qualities; see Nirguna. सगुण

Saguna Brahman Brahman with attributes, forms, powers and predicates; reality conditioned by qualities such as bliss, and perhaps even form (sakara), as distinguished from the ultimate reality which is beyond all attributes whatsoever; see Nirguna Brahman. सगुण ब्रह्मन्

Saguna Dhyana /Sa-guna Dhyaana/ meditation to develop awareness of transcendental qualities; see Nirguna Dhyana. सगुण ध्यान

Sachchidananda /Sachchidaananda/ (Sat-chit-aananda); the supreme reality as self-existent existence-consciousness-bliss; see Sat; see Chit; see Ananda. सच्चिदानन्द

Sachchidananda Sagara /Sachchidaananda Saagara/ (Sat-chit-aananda Saagara); the ocean of existence-consciousness-bliss, a metaphorical expression suggesting the indescribable absolute reality. सच्चिदानन्द सागर

Sad see Sat. सद्

Sadbhashana see Sat Bhashana. सद्भाषण

Sadguna see Sat Guna. सद्गुण

Sadguru see Sat Guru. सद्गुरु

Sada /Sadaa/ always, ever, perpetually, at all times. सदा

Sadagati /Sadaa-gati/ wind; sun; everlasting happiness, final beatitude. सदागति

Sadaikarasa (Sadaa-eka-rasa); eternal homogeneous essence; see Rasa. सदैकरस

Sadashiva /Sadaa-shiva/ always auspicious; the presiding deity of the thousand-petalled lotus in the crown of the head; see Shiva; see Sahasrara Chakra. सदाशिव

Sadhaka /Saadhaka/ one who practises sadhana; spiritual aspirant, seeker; efficient, effective, skilful; adapting; assisting, helping. साधक

Sadhana /Saadhanaa/ fulfilment, accomplishment, complete attainment of an object; expedient tool, implement, means of accomplishing anything; worship, adoration; conciliation, propitiation; spiritual practice or discipline performed regularly for the attainment of inner experience and self-realization. साधना

Sadhana Chatushtaya /Saadhana Chatushtaya/ the four kinds of necessary spiritual effort, viz. 1. discrimination (viveka), 2. dispassion (vairagya), 3. the sixfold virtues (shadsampatti), 4. intense desire for liberation (mumukshutva); necessary qualifications for a student of Advaita Vedanta. साधन चतुष्टय

Sadhana Pada /Saadhanaa Paada/ second of the four chapters comprising Patanjali's *Yoga Sutras*, dealing with the five sources of suffering and how to overcome them, and the eight means to samadhi (ashtanga yoga); see Klesha; see Raja Yoga. साधना पाद

Sadhu /Saadhu/ good, excellent, perfect; fit, proper, right; enough; virtuous, righteous, honourable; kind, well disposed; good or virtuous or holy person; sage, saint; Jaina saint. साधु

Sadhusiddhi /Saadhu-siddhi/ accomplishment; conclusion. साधुसिद्धि

Sadharana /Saadhaarana/ ordinary, common. साधारण

Sadharana Karana /Saadhaarana Kaarana/ common cause. साधारण कारण

Sadharmya /Saadharmya/ becom-

ing one with the law of being and action (with the divine). साधर्म्य

Sadyomukti immediate liberation; see Mukti. सद्योमुक्ति

Sagara /Saagara/ sea, ocean; one of the 10 orders of sannyasins founded by Adi Shankaracharya, originally inhabiting coastal regions; see Dashnami Sampradaya. सागर

Saguna with qualities (guna). सगुण

Saguna Upasana /Saguna Upaasanaa/ worship of God with a form, attributes or qualities (guna). सगुण उपासना

Sah he; the nominative forms of this pronoun are: sa (masculine), saa (feminine), and tat (neuter) meaning he, she, it or that respectively. स:

Saha prefix meaning with, provided with, accompanied by, possessing. सह

Sahakarimatra /Saha-kaari-maatra/ a helping factor only, e.g. maya is a sahakarimatra of Brahman's projection. सहकारिमात्र

Sahasthita /Saha-sthita/ co-existence. सहस्थित

Sahadeva name of the youngest of the five Pandava brothers and a son of Madri, he is regarded as an epitome of manly beauty; see Madri. सहदेव

Sahaja spontaneous, easy, natural; true; native. सहज

Sahaja Dharma natural tendency. सहज धर्म

Sahaja Karma that to which one is born or naturally inclined; a particular action. सहज कर्म

Sahaja Kumbhaka effortless or natural retention of breath

(kumbhaka). सहज कुम्भक

Sahaja Nirvikalpa Samadhi
/Sahaja Nirvikalpa Samaadhi/
natural, non-dual state of brahmic consciousness. सहज निर्विकल्प समाधि

Sahaja Nishtha /Sahaja Nishthaa/
natural and normal establishment in one's own essential nature of sachchidananda; see Sachchidananda. स्सहज निष्ठा

Sahaja Samadhi /Sahaja Samaadhi/ spontaneous meditative experience where the mind is totally withdrawn from the external world; see Samadhi. सहज समाधि

Sahajavastha /Sahaja-avasthaa/
superconscious state that has become natural and continuous; the state of consciousness in samadhi. सहजावस्था

Sahajoli Mudra /Sahajolee Mudraa/
also called vajroli mudra in some traditions; contraction and release of the urinary passage to stimulate swadhisthana chakra and promote brahmacharya; smearing specific parts of the body with a specially prepared paste of ashes after practising vajroli mudra, according to *Hatha Yoga Pradipika*; see Vajroli Mudra. सहजोली मुद्रा

Saham /Saa-aham/ literally 'I am She', the mantra of the sects revering female energy or shakti; see Shakta. साहम्

Sahasa /Sahasaa/ forcibly; inconsiderately; rashly, precipitately; suddenly, all at once. सहसा

Sahasrara Chakra /Sahasraara Chakra/ the thousand-petalled lotus; abode of Shiva or superconsciousness; highest chakra or psychic centre, which symbolizes the threshold between the psychic and spiritual realms and is located at the crown of the head; see Chakra; see Samarasatva. सहस्रार चक्र

Sahita combined with something; accompanied, attended by, together with. सहित

Sahita Kumbhaka pranayama in which inhalation, retention and exhalation can be practised with or without bija mantra, according to the *Gherand Samhita*. सहित कुम्भक

Sahita Kumbhaka Pranayama
/Sahita Kumbhaka Praanaayaama/ when pranayama practices are observed with the intentional and deliberate accompaniment of outer (bahya) and inner (antara) breath retention (kumbhaka). सहित कुम्भक प्राणायाम

Sajatiyabheda /Sajaateeya-bheda/
the difference by which one individual of a species is distinguished from another, e.g. the difference between one man and another; see Jatyantaraparinama; see Vijatyabheda. सजातीयभेद

Sajjana see Sat Jana. सज्जन

Sajyotsna /Sajyotsnaa/ during a moonlit night. सज्योत्सना

Sakala together with the parts, all, whole, entire. सकल

Sakama /Sakaama/ desire-oriented attitude, motivated by selfish desire; see Kama. सकाम

Sakama Bhakti /Sakaama Bhakti/ devotion with expectations of the fruits and selfish motives. सकाम भक्ति

Sakama Bhava /Sakaama Bhaava/ attitude or feeling which has selfish desire as the motive force. सकाम भाव

Sakama Karma /Sakaama Karma/ actions motivated by selfish desire. सकाम कर्म

Sakara /Saakaara/ with form; manifest. साकार

Sakara Ishta /Saakaara Ishta/ the preferred deity (Ishta) with form; the form of the beloved. साकार इष्ट

Sakhya /Saakhya/ related to friendship. साख्य

Sakhya Upasana /Saakhya Upaasanaa/ friendship with God and all beings. साख्य उपासना

Sakini /Saakinee/ goddess of vishuddhi chakra. साकिनी

Sakshatkara /Saakshaat-kaara/ anything which is experienced personally; direct realization; experience of the absolute; knowledge of Brahman; see Brahma Jnana. साक्षात्कार

Sakshi /Saakshee/ eternal witness; witnessing principle; seer; that which passively observes the actions of the body, emotions, mind and the senses without being affected at all; see Drashta; see Kutastha. साक्षी

Sakshi Bhava /Saakshee Bhaava/ awareness; attitude of remaining the witness; seer. साक्षी भाव

Sakshi Chaitanya /Saakshee Chaitanya/ witnessing intelligence or consciousness. साक्षी चैतन्य

Sakshi Drashta /Saakshee Drashtaa/ witnessing subject; witnessing seer. साक्षी द्रष्टा

Salokya /Saalokya/ being on the same plane as one's object of contemplation; see Kramamukti; see Loka. सालोक्य

Sam perfect; balanced. सम्

Sama same, equal; similar, like; even; parallel; unchanged. सम

Samabhavana /Samabhaavanaa/ possibility; feeling of equality. सम्भावना

Samadhana /Samaadhaana/ mental equilibrium; constant concentration on reality; putting together, uniting; fixing the mind in profound abstract contemplation on the true nature of the self; steadiness, peace (of mind); one of the sixfold virtues necessary in a serious aspirant for spiritual understanding; see Shadsampatti. समाधान

Samadhi /Samaadhi/ culmination of meditation; state of unity with the object of meditation and the universal consciousness; final step of raja yoga; self-realization; a state in which the mind is either completely concentrated on its object of contemplation (savikalpa samadhi), or ceases to function and only pure consciousness or pure awareness remains, revealing itself to itself (nirvikalpa samadhi); see Samprajnata Samadhi; see Asamprajnata Samadhi; see Sabija Samadhi; see Nirbija Samadhi; see Samapatti. समाधि

Samadhi Pada /Samaadhi Paada/ the first part of Patanjali's *Yoga Sutras*, dealing with definitions of yoga, mental modifications, samprajnata and asamprajnata samadhi, Ishwara, obstacles to samadhi and how to overcome them and concluding with a delineation of the difference between the states of sabija and nirbija samadhi; see Vritti; see Samprajnata Samadhi; see Asamprajnata Samadhi. समाधि पाद

Samadhi Prajna /Samaadhi Prajnaa/ higher knowledge attained through samadhi; see Ritambhara Prajna. समाधि प्रज्ञा

Samadrishti equal vision; seeing the one inner spirit in all. समदृष्टि

Samarasatva term which is ordinarily applied to sexual union, but is also used symbolically to describe the union of kundalini shakti with Shiva in sahasrara chakra; merging of 'becoming' into 'being'. समरसत्व

Samavastha /Sama-avasthaa/ state of equilibrium; fixed condition; similar condition or state. समावस्था

Samavatara /Sama-avataara/ descent; descent into a river or sacred bathing place. समावतार

Samavritti equal movement of inhalation, exhalation and suspension of breath in pranayama. समवृत्ति

Samagana /Saama-gaana/ hymns of the *Sama Veda*. सामगान

Samana /Samaana/ a friend; an equal; balancing force; see Samana Vayu. समान

Samana Chaitanya /Samaana Chaitanya/ awareness of samana vayu. समान चैतन्य

Samanadhikarana /Samaana-adhikarana/ coordination; the relation of abiding in a common substratum, viz. Brahman. A traditional illustration is that the ether in a pot (ghatakasha) and the ether in the cloud (meghakasha) have a common substance. समानाधिकरण

Samana Vayu /Samaana Vaayu/ one of the five prana vayus, it is essential for digestion; a sideways moving flow of energy situated between the navel and diaphragm, which augments the pranic force of manipura chakra; the balancing vayu or vital air with the function of uniting prana vayu and apana vayu, an essential step in the awakening of kundalini; see Vayu; see Pancha Prana. समान वायु

Samanas unanimous, concordant. समनस्

Samanta /Samaanta/ being the same on every side; all around; complete, entire; universal. समान्त

Samanvaya unification; the agreement of all Upanishads in proving the highest reality. समन्वय

Samanya /Saamaanya/ general, common, ordinary. सामान्य

Samanyaguna /Saamaanya-guna/ general quality; common nature or characteristic. सामान्यगुण

Samanyavastha /Saamaanya-avasthaa/ undifferentiated condition; unmanifested state. सामान्यावस्था

Samanyavijnana /Saamaanya-vijnaana/ pure consciousness; homogeneous intelligence; see Kutastha; see Brahman. सामान्यविज्ञान

Samapatti /Samaapatti/ complete absorption; samadhi; a state of mind where there is complete acceptance and equilibrium, like the ocean fully accepting the water of a river and not keeping it separated from itself; samapatti or samadhi includes a wide range of superconscious states in which absorption becomes deeper and deeper; see Samadhi. समापत्ति

Samartha having a suitable attitude and aim or force; very forcible, strong, powerful; competent, allowed, qualified, capable, fit, suitable, proper; having the same meaning. समर्थ

Samashti an integrated whole of the same class of entity, e.g. samashtibuddhi means cosmic intelligence. समष्टि

Samatva equanimity under all conditions; equanimity of outlook making no distinction between friend and foe, pleasure and pain etc. समत्व

Samatvam equipoise. समत्वम्

Samavasa /Samaavaasa/ residence, habitation, dwelling place. समावास

Samavaya /Samavaaya/ combination, union, conjunction, aggregate, collection; number, multitude; intimate union, constant and inseparable connection, inseparable inherence or existence of one thing in another; one of the seven categories of the Vaisheshikas. समवाय

Sama Veda /Saama Veda/ third of the vedic texts, the Veda of chants and hymns, it deals mainly with devotion, worship and contemplation; see Veda; see Chandogya Upanishad; see Samagana; see Stotra. साम वेद

Samaveta something that has met or come together; joined; intimately united, inherent, inseparably connected; comprised or contained in a larger number. समवेत

Samavishta /Samaavishta/ entered thoroughly, completely occupied, pervaded; seized, overcome; engrossed; well instructed. समाविष्ट

Samaya time in general; occasion, opportunity; fit time, proper time or season, right moment; an established rule of conduct, a ceremonial custom, a usual practice. समय

Sambhasha /Sam-bhaasha/ discourse, conversation; greeting; criminal connection; an agreement, a contract. सम्भाष

Sambhava birth, production, springing up, arising, coming into existence; cause, origin, motive. सम्भव

Sambhavopaya see Shambhavopaya. सम्भवोपाय

Sambheda breaking, splitting. सम्भेद

Sambhoga enjoyment; possession, use, occupation; copulation, carnal enjoyment, sexual union; subdivision of the sentiment of love. सम्भोग

Sambhrita brought together, collected, concentrated; made ready, prepared, provided; furnished or enclosed with, possessed of; placed, deposited. सम्भृत

Sambhuti /Sambhooti/ birth, origin, production; combination, union; fitness, suitability; power. सम्भूति

Sambuddhi perfect knowledge or perception; full consciousness; calling to, addressing. सम्बुद्धि

Samhara /Samhaara/ destruction. संहार

Samhita /Samhitaa/ collection of hymns, prayers and mantras, structured using rules of grammar and tone. They are called stotras, suktas, etc. and are chanted during sacrifice (yajna). They are the oldest part of the Vedas; see Veda. संहिता

Samidha /Samidhaa/ wood, fuel; especially fuel or sacrificial sticks from specific trees for the sacred fire, traditionally given as a symbolic offering when an aspirant approaches a guru asking for instruction. समिधा

Samipya /Saameepya/ being in close proximity to one's object of contemplation; see Kramamukti. सामीप्य

Samiti assembly, council, commitee. समिति

Samkhya see Sankhya. साङ्ख्य
Samkhya Yoga see Sankhya Yoga. साङ्ख्य योग

Sampad wealth, riches; prosperity, affluence, advancement; good fortune, happiness, luck; success, fulfilment, accomplishment of desired object. सम्पद्

Sampadana accomplishing the required effect; fulfilment; gaining, obtaining, acquiring; cleaning, clearing, preparing. सम्पदन

Sampanna prosperous, thriving, rich; fortunate, successful, happy; effected, brought about, accomplished; perfect, finished. सम्पन्न

Sampidana /Sampeedana/ squeezing together, compression; pain, torture; agitation, disturbance. सम्पीडन

Sampradaya /Sampradaaya/ tradition; sect; custom; conventional procedure or course of action. सम्प्रदाय

Samprajnata /Samprajnaata/ knowledge with awareness. सम्प्रज्ञात
Samprajnata Samadhi /Samprajnaata Samaadhi/ samadhi with prajna (intuitive awareness); transcendental state where the phases are vitarka, vichara, ananda and asmita. It alternates with asamprajnata samadhi and culminates in nirbija samadhi (samadhi with seed); see Asamprajnata Samadhi. सम्प्रज्ञात समाधि

Samprasada /Samprasaada/ peace, serenity, calmness, tranquillity. सम्प्रसाद

Samprayoga contact of the senses with the objects. सम्प्रयोग

Samriddhi success, wealth, abundance. समृद्धि

Samsara /Samsaara/ illusory world, the manifest gross world; cycle of birth, death and rebirth, trans-migration, metamorphosis, meta-psychosis; passage; the course or circuit of worldly life, secular life, mundane existence; curse. संसार

Samsara Chakra /Samsaara Chakra/ wheel of birth and death. संसार चक्र

Samsara Guru /Samsaara Guru/ epithet of the god of love. संसार गुरु

Samsara Marga /Samsaara Maarga/ the course of worldly affairs, worldly life; the vulva. संसार मार्ग

Samsara Moksha /Samsaara Moksha/ final liberation or emancipation from worldly life. संसार मोक्ष

Samsari /Samsaaree/ the transmigrating soul. संसारी

Samshaya doubt, uncertainty, irresolution, hesitation; danger. संशय

Samshlesha mutual embrace, intimate connection. संश्लेष

Samskara /Samskaara/ mental impression stored in the subtle body as an archetype; form, mold; operation, influence; idea, notion, concept; effect of work, merit of action; the faculty of recollection. Impression on the memory of all patterns and mental impressions of the past, which remain unnoticed in the mind, yet set up impulses and trains of thought; unconscious memories; impressions that do not fit into the known categories of our present personality; 16 traditional rituals marking different stages in life observed in Hindu culture in a process of purification under-

gone by the soul after arrival in the body of a human being; process of consecration performed on an item of oblation; see Sanskrita. संस्कार

Samskrita see Sanskrita. संस्कृत

Samsmriti remembrance, recollection. संस्मृति

Samsparsha contact, touch, conjunction, mixture; being touched or affected; perception, sense. संस्पर्श

Samsriti world process; see Samsara. संसृति

Samuchchayavada /Samuchchaya-vaada/ the doctrine that action (karma) and wisdom (jnana) are both necessary for self-realization. समुच्चयवाद

Samvara a Buddhist religious observance; restraint. संवर

Samvatsara almanac; 12 months of a year; a yajna (sacrificial ritual) lasting a year; one of the names of Shiva; see Ritu; see Masa. संवत्सर

Samvritti becoming, happening, occurrence; accomplishment; relative truth; covering, concealment, suppression. संवृत्ति

Samya /Saamya/ equilibrium; stillness. साम्य

Samyavastha /Saamya-avasthaa/ literally 'state of stillness'; the state before manifestation or creation when the gunas of prakriti are in perfect balance; state of equilibrium; see Prakriti; see Vaishamyavastha. साम्यावस्था

Samyagdarshana
(Samyak-darshana); proper perception; equal vision; highest advaitic realization; complete intimation; perfect knowledge; one

of the three jewels in Jaina philosophy. सम्यग्दर्शन

Samyama mastery, control, restraint, self-discipline over one's behaviour; perfection of concentration; harmonious control of concentration (dharana), meditation (dhyana) and samadhi fused into one process by which the yogi can know the inner cause of anything concentrated upon; concentration of mind; see Trayamekatra Samyama; see Vibhuti Pada; see Siddhi. संयम

Samyogasambandha relation by contact, e.g. the stick and the drum. संयोगसम्बन्ध

Sanatana /Sanaatana/ eternal, everlasting. सनातन

Sanatana Dharma /Sanaatana Dharma/ system of eternal values underlying the vedic civilization. सनातन धर्म

Sanatani /Sanaatanee/ follower of sanatana dharma. सनातनी

Sanchalana /Sanchaalana/ to cause movement; to control; agitation, trembling. सञ्चालन

Sanchara /Sanchaara/ flow, movement; travelling, going, roaming; passing through, passage, transit; course, way, road, pass; setting in motion; difficult progress or journey. सञ्चार

Sanchara passage, a way, path; transit from one zodiac sign to another; development; the body. सञ्चर

Sanchita stored, collected; enumerated; full of, furnished or provided with; dense, thick. सञ्चित

Sanchita Karma the sum total of all actions done by the living being (jiva) during countless previous births, out of which a portion is allotted for every new birth; see Karma. सञ्चित कर्म

Sandeha doubt, uncertainty; suspense; risk, danger, peril. सन्देह

Sandesha information, news, tidings, message; errand, commission; command. सन्देश

Sandhi union, junction, combination, connection; compact, agreement; joint, articulation (of the body); euphony, euphonic junction or coalition (in grammar); interval, pause. सन्धि

Sandhikala /Sandhee-kaala/ conjunction time; the period just before sunrise, after sunset and noon. संधिकाल

Sandhi Mukti dislocation of joints. सन्धि मुक्ति

Sandhya /Sandhyaa/ spiritual practice required to be practised by a student after the upanayana samskara at three conjunction times of dawn, noon and dusk; rite performed by rishis; early morning or evening twilight; union; division; the period of time between one yuga and the commencement of another; see Upanayanam. सन्ध्या

Sangatyaga /Sanga-tyaaga/ renunciation of company or association. सङ्गत्याग

Sangha assemblage, crowd, host, multitude, company, community; brood (of birds). सङ्घ

Sangita /Sangeeta/ song, music, sung together. सङ्गीत

Sangraha collection. सङ्ग्रह

Sangraha Buddhi intellect that

wants to accumulate and possess. सङ्ग्रह बुद्धि

Sangrama /Sangraama/ war, battle, fight. सङ्ग्राम

Sanjaya name of a charioteer of King Dhritarashtra, who tried to bring about a peaceful settlement of the dispute between the Kauravas and the Pandavas, but failed. He narrated the teachings and events of the *Bhagavad Gita* to the blind King Dhritarashtra. सञ्जय

Sanjna /Sanjnaa/ consciousness; knowledge, understanding; intellect, mind; noun, name. संज्ञा

Sanjnasuta /Sanjnaasuta/ epithet of Saturn. संज्ञासुत

Sanjnavat /Sanjnaa-vat/ having consciousness; becoming sensible, revived; having a name. संज्ञावत्

Sankalpa will, volition, positive resolve; purpose, aim, intention; determination, conviction; desire, wish; thought, idea, reflection, fancy, imagination. सङ्कल्प

Sankalpapurti / Sankalpa-poorti/ service or rite at the completion of worship where the devotee reconfirms her sankalpa; desire that the deity be pleased with the worship and surrender of the merit to God. सङ्कल्पपूर्ति

Sankalpa Sadhana /Sankalpa Saadhanaa/ determination in spiritual discipline. सङ्कल्प साधना

Sankalpa Shunya /Sankalpa Shoonya/ devoid of thought. सङ्कल्प शून्य

Sankalpa Vikalpa thought and doubt. सङ्कल्प विकल्प

Sankathana narration; conversation. सङ्कथन

Sankhya /Saankhya/ one of the six systems of Indian philosophy (shaddarshana), attributed to the sage Kapila. Sankhya is a spiritual science dealing with the 25 elements of creation; relating to number, calculating, enumerating; discriminative, deliberating, reasoning; a reasoner; the philosophical basis of the yoga system, continually reverified by yoga practices; the philosophy underlying the tantras; see Purusha; see Prakriti; see Guna; see Satkaryavada. साङ्ख्य

Sankhyayoga /Saankhya-yoga/ 'yoga of wisdom' or 'the path of knowledge', the second chapter of the *Bhagavad Gita* which describes a person of steady wisdom; see Sthitaprajna. साङ्ख्ययोग

Sankirtan /Sankeertana/ singing of God's name, often in call and response. सङ्कीर्तन

Sanklishta pressed together; afflicted, tormented. सङ्क्लिष्ट

Sankocha contraction; involution; hesitation. सङ्कोच

Sankranti /Sankraanti/ going together, union; passage from one point to another, transition; the passage of the sun or any planetary body from one zodiac sign into another. सङ्क्रान्ति

Sankruddha enraged, furious. सङ्क्रुद्ध

Sankshaya complete destruction, extirpation. संक्षय

Sannyasa /Sannyaasa/ dedication; complete renunciation of the world, its possessions and attachments; abandonment of the temporal; the six stages of sannyasa life are known as kutichaka, bahudaka, hamsa, paramahamsa, turiyatita and avadhuta; the fourth of four stations (ashramas) in the vedic concept of a full life. संन्यास

Sannyasa Ashrama /Sannyaasa Aashrama/ traditionally the fourth stage of life for everyone from 75 years onwards; total renunciation classified into various types, viz. vairagya sannyasa, jnana sannyasa, jnana-vairagya sannyasa, vividisha sannyasa, vidvat sannyasa, atura sannyasa; see Ashrama. संन्यास आश्रम

Sannyasa Diksha /Sannyaasa Deekshaa/ initiation into the order of sannyasa given by guru to disciple. संन्यास दीक्षा

Sannyasanam /Sannyaasanam/ resignation, laying down; complete renunciation of the world and its attachments. संन्यासनम्

Sannyasin, Sannyasi /Sannyaasin, Sannyasee/ one who has taken sannyasa initiation (sannyasa diksha); a yogi; one who is not dependent on the results of action. संन्यासिन्, संन्यासी

Sanskrita literally 'well done'; the original vedic language, which is the source of the vedic scriptures; one who has been purified by samskaras and becomes cultured; see Samskara. संस्कृत

Sanskriti culture; social environment conducive for total evolution of individuals and especially their spiritual development. संस्कृति

Santana /Santaana/ family; progeny, offspring; race. सन्तान

Santosha contentment, satisfaction; one of the five niyamas enumerated by the *Yoga Sutras* of Patanjali; also known as the 'sword of Rama' due to its ability to cut through illusion (maya); see Niyama; see Tushta. सन्तोष

Sanyam see Samyama. संयम

Saphala fruitful, bearing or yielding fruit, productive; accomplished, fulfilled, successful. सफल

Sapta seven. सप्त

Saptapadi /Sapta-padee/ literally 'seven steps', ritual of the marriage ceremony. सप्तपदी

Saptavadhana /Sapta-avadhaana/ being aware of seven things simultaneously. सप्तावधान

Saptodharini /Saptodhaarinee/ (Sapta-udhaarinee); 'seven stories' narrated by Dattatreya to Kartaveerya to explain yoga. सप्तोधारिणी

Sara /Saara/ essential; best, highest, most excellent; real, true. सार

Sara /Sara/ movement; pond. सर

Sarani /Saranee/ flow, course, way. सरणी

Sarasi /Sarasee/ pool, lake. सरसी

Saraswati /Saraswatee/ goddess of knowledge, speech and learning represented as the daughter of Brahma; speech, voice, words; name of a river (which is submerged beneath the sands of the

great desert); sushumna nadi; soma; the name of one of the 10 orders of sannyasins founded by Adi Shankaracharya, which is dedicated to preserving spiritual wisdom; see Dashnami Sampradaya; see Triveni; see Shakta; see Ubhaya Bharati. सरस्वती

Sarupa /Saroopa/ having the same form; like, resembling, similar. सरूप

Sarupya /Saroopya/ having the same form as the object of contemplation; see Kramamukti. सारूप्य

Sarva whole, entire; all, every. सर्व

Sarvabhokta /Sarva-bhoktaa/ all-enjoyer, epithet of the supreme lord. सर्वभोक्ता

Sarva Bhutantaratma /Sarva Bhoota-antaraatmaa/ (Sarva Bhoota-antah-aatmaa); the inner self of all beings. सर्व भूतान्तरात्मा

Sarva Deshika pertaining to all places; present everywhere. सर्व देशिक

Sarva Duhkhanivritti removal of all pains. सर्व दु:खनिवृत्ति

Sarvaga present in all (things), omnipresent, all-pervading. सर्वग

Sarva Himsavinirmukta /Sarva Himsaa-vinirmukta/ against injury of all kinds. सर्व हिंसाविनिर्मुक्त

Sarvajna omniscient, knowing everything. सर्वज्ञ

Sarvakarana /Sarva-kaarana/ cause of everything; causality of creation, preservation and destruction; see Avyaktam. सर्वकारण

Sarva Karanakarana /Sarva Kaarana-kaarana/ the cause of all other causes. सर्व कारणकारण

Sarvakarta /Sarva-kartaa/ all-doer, doer of everything. सर्वकर्ता

Sarvantaryami /Sarva-antaryaamee/ the inner ruler of everything; see Antaryamin. सर्वन्तर्यामी

Sarva Pindavyapi /Sarva Pindavyaapee/ the one who permeates all bodies and also who permeates the entire body. सर्व पिण्डव्यापी

Sarva Sakshin, Sarva Sakshi /Sarva Saakshin, Sarva Saakshee/ eternal witness; witness of everything. सर्व साक्षिन्, सर्व साक्षी

Sarva Sankalpavarjita devoid of all thoughts or resolves. सर्व सङ्कल्पवर्जित

Sarva Shaktisamanvita with all powers, omnipotent. सर्व शक्तिसमन्वित

Sarvatitavadi /Sarvaateetavaadee/ (Sarva-ateeta-vaadee); transcendentalist, one who argues that the truth is transcendental. सर्वातीतवादी

Sarvatmakatva /Sarva-aatmakatva/ universality; the state of being the soul of everything. सर्वात्मकत्व

Sarva Tyaga /Sarva Tyaaga/ renunciation of everything. सर्व त्याग

Sarva Upadanatva /Sarva Upaadaanatva/ the state of being the material cause of all. सर्व उपादानत्व

Sarvavid, Sarvavit knower of all, omniscient; a liberated sage. सर्वविद्, सर्ववित्

Sarvayantratma /Sarva-yantra-aatmaa/ the inner soul that controls everything. सर्वयन्त्रात्मा

Sarveshvaratva (Sarva-eeshvaratva); supreme rulership over all. सर्वेश्वरत्व

Sarvosmi (Sarvah-asmi); 'I am all', an ancient mantra. सर्वोऽस्मि

Sat true; that which really exists; entity; essence; in Vedanta, one of the three attributes of the ulti-mate existence or reality (Brah-man); see Sachchidananda. सत्

Sat Bhashana /Sat Bhaashana/ right speech. सत् भाषण

Satchidananda see Sachchid-ananda. सच्चिदानन्द

Sat Guna see Sattwa. सत् गुण

Sat Guru the guru who directs the disciple towards the truth (sat); the dispeller of darkness and ignorance (avidya); inner guru. सत् गुरु

Sat Jana (Sat-jana); a good man. सत् जन

Satkama /Sat-kaama/ pure desire (of a liberated sage); desire for moksha. सत्काम

Satkara /Sat-kaara/ with faith. सत्कार

Satkaryavada /Sat-kaarya-vaada/ the doctrine that the effect exists in the cause, the distinguishing feature of the Sankhya system; see Karma. सत्कार्यवाद

Satsanga gathering in which the ideals and principles of truth are discussed; spiritual association; association with the wise and the good, along with the resolve and effort to express this in life. सत्सङ्ग

Satsankalpa true resolve; pure desire; perfect will. सत्सङ्कल्प

Sat Chandi Maha Yajna see Shata Chandi Maha Yajna. शत चण्डी महा यज्ञ

Sati /Satee/ virtuous or good woman (or wife); female ascetic; a name of the goddess Durga; Sati, the daughter of Daksha Prajapati, immolated herself for her father's insult to her husband, Shiva, and was then reborn as Parvati, the daughter of Himalaya (or Hima-vanta). She married Shiva and became the mother of Kartikeya (the god of war) and Ganesha (the god of learning, wisdom and good luck). Sati's self-immolation was regarded as so virtuous that women sometimes immolated themselves upon the death of their husband as an alternative to life-long widowhood. Such a woman was called a sati. Gross abuse of this custom led to its being outlawed in the 19th cen-tury; see Shaktipitha. सती

Sattwa /Sattva/ in Sankhya, one of the three constituent qualities (gunas) of nature (prakriti) and all matter; state of luminosity, harmony, equilibrium, steadiness and purity; being, existence, re-ality, true essence; in yoga the natural quality of purity, balance or goodness, which binds one by attachment to goodness and learning; life, spirit, breath, prin-ciple of vitality; consciousness, mind, sense; see Guna; see Guna-tita. सत्त्व

Sattwaguna Pradhana /Sattva-guna Pradhaana/ the quality of sattwa prevailing or predominat-ing. सत्त्वगुण प्रधान

Sattwapatti /Sattvaapatti/ abun-dance of sattwa; in Vedanta, the fourth of the seven stages of wis-dom (jnana bhumika) where the mind fills with purity and light, tattwa jnana dawns, and the root of all vasanas is destroyed; see Brahmavit. सत्त्वापत्ति

Sattwa Samshuddhi /Sattva Samshuddhi/ purity of heart, purity of feeling; increase of purity and light. सत्त्व संशुद्धि

Sattwic /Saattvika/ pertaining to sattwa. सात्त्विक

Satya true, real, genuine; honest, sincere, truthful, faithful; virtuous, upright; absolute truth; reality; as one of the yamas described by Patanjali's *Yoga Sutras*, it leads to a state where actions are based on and culminate in the truth; in life it is a vow to follow truth and renounce untruth in thought, word and action; see Yama. सत्य

Satya Loka one of the seven higher dimensions of consciousness; also called Brahma loka; see Loka. सत्य लोक

Satyam the unchanging principle; the relative aspect of creation perceptible by the senses and understood by the mind; truth; sincerity; goodness, virtue, purity. सत्यम्

Satyameva Jayate 'the truth alone will prevail', a tenet from *Kathopanishad* and the slogan in today's national emblem of India. सत्यमेव जयते

Satya Yuga the age in which piety and righteousness predominated and the first of the four aeons (yugas) of the world, the 'golden' age lasting for 1,728,000 years according to *Suryasiddhanta*, the age of truth and purity; another name for krita yuga; see Yuga. सत्य युग

Saubhagya /Sau-bhaagya/ good fortune or luck; blessedness, auspiciousness; beauty. सौभाग्य

Saubhagya Chakra /Sau-bhaagya Chakra/ the 14 triangles of Shri Yantra. सौभाग्य चक्र

Saubham name of Harishchandra's city said to be suspended in the air; see Harishchandra. सौभम्

Saubhratram /Sau-bhraatram/ good brotherhood, fraternity. सौभ्रात्रम्

Saugandhika sweet-scented; the blue lotus; a kind of fragrant grass (also called kattrina); ruby. सौगन्धिक

Saugata a Buddhist, follower of Sugata or Buddha. सौगत

Saumya relating or sacred to the moon; having the properties of soma; handsome, pleasing, agreeable; auspicious; see Soma. सौम्य

Saundarya beauty, loveliness, elegance, gracefulness. सौन्दर्य

Saundarya Lahari /Saundarya Laharee/ ode to Shakti reputedly by Adi Shankaracharya; see Ananda Lahari. सौन्दर्य लहरी

Saurya worshipper of the sun (surya); relating to the sun, solar; sacred or dedicated to the sun; blessed, divine; the planet Saturn; see Panchaupasana; see Panchaupasaka. सौर्य

Sauri name of the planet Saturn. सौरि

Sauvirya /Sauveerya/ great heroism or prowess. सौवीर्य

Sava water; extraction of soma juice; an offering, libation; sacrifice; sun; moon; see Soma. सव

Savadhana /Saavadhaana/ attention, alertness. सावधान

Savichara Samadhi /Savichaara Samaadhi/ savichara means with reflection, a phase of samprajnata Samadhi according to Patanjali's *Yoga Sutras*, where reflection alternates between time, space and object, but there is no thinking in words; see Nirvichara Samadhi. सविचार समाधि

Savikalpa Samadhi /Savikalpa Samaadhi/ a kind of samadhi in which the mind still retains its material impressions (distinctions such as that between subject and object, or of the knower and the known); see Nirvikalpa Samadhi. सविकल्प समाधि

Savishesa with distinguishing features, distinguished by qualities, associated with attributes. सविशेष

Savishesa Dhyana /Savishesha Dhyaana/ meditation with special qualities; awareness of the concept of shakti as a powerful force equal to that of Brahman. सविशेष ध्यान

Savishesa Sattwa /Savishesha Sattva/ presence of distinctive attributes. सविशेष सत्त्व

Savitarka with logic and argumentation. सवितर्क

Savitarka Samadhi /Savitarka Samaadhi/ savitarka means with reason, a phase of samprajnata samadhi according to the *Yoga Sutras* of Patanjali where there is alternating association of the consciousness between word, knowledge and sensory perception; see Nirvitarka Samadhi. सवितर्क समाधि

Savitri the sun; name of Shiva; name of Indra. सवितृ

Savitri /Saavitree/ a voluminous philosophical treatise by Shri Aurobindo; name of a celebrated verse of the *Rigveda* addressed to the sun; Savitri is the wife (power) of the sun symbolizng the descent of the divine (rays), while Gayatri is the wife symbolizing the ascent of consciousness; the ceremony of investiture with the sacred thread; name of the wife of Satyavan who was destined to die in a year from the date of marriage. However, due to Savitri's steadfast and undaunted devotion, Yama, the god of death, relented and restored the spirit of Satyavan to her. सावित्री

Sayuj associated; united. सयुज्

Sayujya /Saayujya/ abiding in the absolute; see Kramamukti; see Kaivalya. सायुज्य

Seetkari Pranayama see Sheetkari Pranayama. शीतकारी प्राणायाम

Sesha see Shesha. सेष

Setu a bridge in general; a ridge of earth, mound, bank, causeway, dam; the sacred syllable Om. सेतु

Seva /Sevaa/ offering oneself wholly for His cause; doing work for the Lord; service. सेवा

Shabda sound; object of the sense of hearing and property of space (akasha); note (of birds, human voice, etc.); sound of musical instrument; word, significant word; see Mantra; see Pancha Tanmatra. शब्द

Shabdadhishthana /Shabda-adhi-shthaana/ the ear, literally 'shabda's dwelling place'. शब्दाधिष्ठान

Shabda Bheda difference in words (name) only. शब्द भेद

Shabda Brahman the Vedas; spiritual knowledge conveyed in words; knowledge of the supreme existence or the spirit; the eternal sound that is the first manifestation of reality and lies at the root of all subsequent creation; see Om; see Nada; see Veda. शब्द ब्रह्मन्

Shabdadi /Shabda-aadi/ literally 'sound etc.', viz. sound (shabda), touch (sparsha), form (rupa), taste (rasa) and smell (gandha) as the objects of the senses; see Pancha Tanmatra. शब्दादि

Shabdakosha lexicon, dictionary. शब्दकोष

Shabdantara /Shabda-antara/ difference between words or terms; another word. शब्दान्तर

Shabdapramana /Shabda-pramaana/ scriptural proof; see Pramana. शब्दप्रमाण

Shabdartha /Shabda-artha/ the meaning of a word. शब्दार्थ

Shabda Shakti the force or expressive power of a word; significance of a word. शब्द शक्ति

Shabda Tanmatra /Shabda Tanmaatra/ the subtle element of sound, the tanmatra associated with vishuddhi chakra; see Pancha Tanmatra. शब्द तन्मात्र

Shabdatita /Shabda-ateeta/ beyond the power or reach of words, indescribable. शब्दातीत

Shabdavedhin hitting an invisible mark, only the sound of which is heard; an epithet of Arjuna and Dasharatha; a kind of arrow. शब्दवेधिन्

Shabdavidya, Shabdashasana, Shabdashastra /Shabda-vidyaa, Shabda-shaasana, Shabda-shaastra/ the science of words, i.e. grammar; see Vyakarana. शब्दविद्या, शब्दशासन, शब्दशास्त्र

Shad, Shat six; see Shat. षड्, षट्

Shadava /Shaadava/ passion, sentiment; singing, music; a raga in which six of the seven primary notes are used. षाडव

Shadayatana /Shadaayatana/ (Shat-aayatana); literally 'abode of the six', i.e. the five senses and the mind; see Jnanendriya; see Manas. षडायतन

Shaddarshana (Shat-darshana); the six systems of Indian philosophy, viz. Nyaya, Vaisheshika, Sankhya, Yoga, Mimamsa (technically this is Purva Mimamsa) and Vedanta (also known as Uttara Mimamsa); see Darshana. षड्दर्शन

Shadsampatti (Shat-sampatti); one of the four necessary qualifications for a serious spiritual aspirant according to *Aparokshanubhuti* of Adi Shankacharya, literally it means 'sixfold virtues': 1. equanimity (shama), 2. self-control (dama), 3. sensory withdrawal (uparati), 4. endurance (titiksha), 5. faith (shraddha), 6. constant concentration on reality (samadhana); see Sadhana Chatushtaya. षड्सम्पत्ति

Shadurmi /Shadoormi/ (Shat-oormi); six evils, six waves: 1. grief (shoka), 2. delusion (moha),

3. hunger (ashanaya), 4. thirst (pipasa), 5. decay (jara), 6. death (mara). षड्मि

Shadvairi (Shat-vairi); six 'enemies' of man, viz. 1. lust (kama), 2. anger (krodha), 3. greed (lobha), 4. delusion (moha), 5. arrogance (mada), 6. jealousy (matsara). षड्वैरि

Shaiva those who worship Shiva as the supreme reality; see Panchaupasana; see Panchaupasaka; see Aghora. शैव

Shaiva Mata Shaivism; practice of worshipping Shiva; sect in which Shiva is worshipped as the supreme reality; see Shripancha. शैव मत

Shaka an alternate Hindu calendar which commenced 78 years after the Christian era. शक

Shakini /Shaakinee/ a type of female being who attends Durga. शाकिनी

Shakta /Shaakta/ one who worships the various manifestations of Shakti in the form of Kali, Durga, Lakshmi, Saraswati, etc.; a sect in which Shakti (Devi or Ma) is worshipped as the supreme reality; see Saham; see Panchaupasana; see Panchaupasaka; see Shripancha. शाक्त

Shakti primal energy; manifest consciousness; power, ability, capacity, strength, energy; the power of composition, poetic power or genius; in Sankhya, the power inherent in a cause to produce its necessary effects; the female aspect of creation and divinity worshipped by the Shakta sect; power that is eternal and supreme and of the nature of consciousness; counterpart of Shiva; the moving power of nature and consciousness; in Hindu mythology Shakti is often symbolized as a divine woman; see Shri Yantra; see Shiva. शक्ति

Shakti Chalini Kriya /Shakti Chaalinee Kriyaa/ a secret practice with different versions suitable for different aspirants and purposes, it should only be done when instructed by the guru. शक्ति चालिनी क्रिया

Shakti Chalini Pranayama /Shakti Chalinee Praanaayaama/ a practice in which the psychic or pranic force is rotated and controlled. शक्ति चालिनी प्राणायाम

Shaktiman /Shaktimaan/ holder of shakti. शक्तिमान्

Shaktipat /Shaktipaat/ higher energy or experience transmitted by the guru to a worthy disciple; descent of power through worship (upasana). शक्तिपात

Shaktipitha /Shakti-peetha/ place where Shakti is worshipped, there are 64 main shaktipitha in India; see Chandisthan; see Sati. शक्तिपीठ

Shakti Puja /Shakti Poojaa/ worship of the mother of the universe. शक्ति पूजा

Shaktisanchara
/Shakti-sanchaara/ transmission of power to the disciple by the guru. शक्तिसञ्चार

Shakti Tantra tantric practice for worship of the deities or the attainment/awakening of 'superhuman' power. शक्ति तन्त्र

Shaktopaya /Shaaktopaayaa/ (Shaakta-upaaya); means of approaching the divine (reality) through shakti; one of the four upaya sadhanas of tantra; see Upaya. शाक्तोपाय

Shakuni bird; vulture, kite or eagle; cock; name of a son of Sulaba, who was the king of Gandhara (today's Afghanistan) and brother of Gandhari (wife of Dhritarashtra). शकुनि

Shakuntala /Shakuntalaa/ name of the daughter of Vishvamitra and the nymph Menaka, she is the heroine of Kalidasa's play bearing her name; see Kalidasa. शकुन्तला

Shakyamuni /Shaakyamuni/ one of Lord Buddha's names. शाक्यमुनि

Shalagrama /Shaalagraama/ auspicious black oval-shaped stone containing the preserved shell of an aquatic animal hunted for the tracings of gold it collects. They are found only in Lake Muktinath and the Gandaki river of Nepal, where hunters search for them by throwing tulsi leaves in the water to attract them; symbol of Vishnu; see Tulsi. शालग्राम

Shama quiet, tranquillity, rest, calm, repose, cessation; absence or restraint of passions, mental quietness; final emancipation (from all worldly illusions and attachments); the mind is kept in the heart and not allowed to externalize; it is the constant eradication of the mental tendencies according to *Aparokshanubhuti* of Adi Shankaracharya; one of six necessary qualities in an aspirant for realization; see Shadsampatti. शम

Shambhu name for Shiva. शाम्भु

Shambhavi /Shaambhavee/ name for Parvati, consort of Shambhu (Shiva). शाम्भवी

Shambhavi Mudra
/Shambhavee Mudraa/ eyebrow-centre gazing; gazing internally without any distraction, whether the eyes are opened or closed; psychic attitude focused on Shiva (supreme consciousness); see Mudra. शाम्भवी मुद्रा

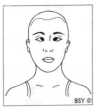

Shambhavopaya
/Shaambhavopaaya/
(Shaambhava-upaaya); direct approach to Shiva (Shambhu); sudden emergence of Shiva consciousness without any effort–just a mere hint that Shiva is one's essential self is enough; one of the four upayas of tantra; see Upaya. शाम्भवोपाय

Shamsati to praise, extol, approve of; to tell, relate, express, declare, communicate, announce, report; to indicate. शंसति

Shandilyavidya /Shaandilya-vidyaa/ the process of meditation on Brahman as the ideal effulgent indwelling spirit in its all-pervading aspect. शाण्डिल्यविद्या

Shankara name of Shiva, referring to his auspicious nature. शङ्कर

Shankaracharya /Shankaraachaarya/ originally the name of a celebrated teacher of the Advaita Vedanta philosophy, acclaimed as the author of the commentary (bhashya) on the *Brahma Sutras* and a large number of other works. He was the enlightened sage who is said to have established the Dashnami order of sannyasa and became the first or Adi 'Shankaracharya', which is an honorary title for pontiffs of the matha of that tradition. It is possible that two or more Shankaracharyas may have been amalgamated into the persona of the Adi Shankarcharya; see Adi Shankaracharya; see Matha; see Shadsampatti. शङ्कराचार्य

Shankari /Shankaree/ name of Parvati, wife of Shankara (Shiva); the sami tree. शङ्करी

Shankha the conch shell, which was traditionally blown in battle and worship. It is said to purify the physical and mental atmosphere and is also blown during worship (puja); the bone of the forehead; a military drum or other martial instrument; the stomach in yogic terminology. शङ्ख

Shankha Mudra /Shankha Mudraa/ conch mudra, gesture made with the hands which imitates the shape of a conch; gesture used while blowing the conch; see Mudra. शङ्ख मुद्रा

Shankha Nada /Shankha Naada/ the sound of the conch shell which may be used for meditation. शङ्ख नाद

Shankhaprakshalana /Shankhaprakshaalana/ literally 'cleaning the conch'; a cleansing technique (shatkarma) of hatha yoga that uses saline water to clean the stomach (which is shaped like a conch) and the small and large intestines; see Shatkarma. शङ्खप्रक्षालन

Shanmukha (Shat-mukha); literally 'with six mouths', another name of Kartikeya, the six-headed god of war and son of Shiva and Parvati. षण्मुख

Shanmukhi Mudra /Shanmukhee Mudraa/ an attitude where the apertures in the head are closed and the mind is directed inwards to train it for meditation. The senses are directed within to enable access to the source of one's being. A most important technique to awaken the latent powers of a human being, to free both the mind and body from their limitations. One may hear the anahata or unstruck sound in this mudra. Also known as shatmudra and yoni mudra in some texts; see Yoni Mudra; see Mudra. षण्मुखी मुद्रा

Shanti /Shaanti/ pacification, allayment, removal; peace, calmness, tranquillity, quiet, ease, rest; cessation, end; absence of passion, complete indifference to all worldly enjoyment. शान्ति
  Shanti Mudra /Shaanti Mudraa/ the posture of peace; see Mudra. शान्ति मुद्रा
  Shanti Rupa /Shaanti Roopa/ the form of peace. शान्ति रूप

Shara arrow or spear; weapon; Indra's thunderbolt. शर

Sharad Ritu autumn season comprised of the two months Ashwina and Kartika; see Ritu; see Masa. शरद् ऋतु

Sharada Matha /Shaaradaa Matha/ one of the four matha said to be established by Adi Shankaracharya, situated in Dwarka in the western quarter of India. It was assigned the *Sama Veda* with its maha vakya (great statement) 'Tat Twam Asi' (You are That). Its first head was Hastamalakacharya. The Tirtha and Ashrama orders of the Dashnami Sampradaya emanate from there. शारदा मठ

Sharanagati Yoga /Sharanaagati Yoga/ yoga of self-surrender. शरणागति योग

Sharira /Shareera/ the body (of animate or inanimate objects); the constituent element; bodily strength. शरीर

Shasana /Shaasana/ instruction, teaching, discipline; rule, government; order, command, direction; control of passion. शासन

Shashanka /Shashaanka/ the moon; an imaginary hare that can be seen on the moon when viewed from the Earth. शशाङ्क

Shashthi /Shashthee/ the sixth day of a lunar fortnight when Kartikeya is worshipped with devotion (especially in South India); epithet of Durga in the form of Katyayani, one of the 16 divine mothers. षष्ठी

Shashvata /Shaashvata/ forever, incessant, eternal; all. शाश्वत

Shasti /Shaasti/ to teach; to tame; to rule, to order; to punish; force behind Parashurama who is the sixth avatara of Vishnu. शास्ति

Shastra /Shaastra/ order; sacred book; any department of knowledge, science. शास्त्र
  Shastradhari /Shaastradhaaree/ knower or 'holder' of the scriptures. शास्त्रधारी

Shastra weapon, arms; iron. शस्त्र
  Shastradhari /Shastradhaaree/ a person who holds a weapon. शस्त्रधारी

Shat six; see Shad. षट्
  Shat Aayatana see Shadayatana. षट् आयतन
  Shatchakra Nirupana /Shat-chakra Niroopana/ ascertainment of the six chakras. षट्चक्र निरूपण

Shat Darshana see Shaddarshana. षट् दर्शन

Shatkarma, Shatkriya /Shatkarma, Shatkriyaa/ the original group of six purificatory techniques of hatha yoga. There are many variations of each of the six scientific yogic techniques using solid objects, water, heat and air as cleansing agents. When practised correctly, they are sufficient for perfect purification of the body and removal of disorders from different organs and from the metabolism, as they are based on deep yogic studies of the human body, viz. dhauti, basti, neti, nauli, trataka and kapalabhati. षट्कर्म, षट्क्रिया

Shat Mukha see Shanmukha. षट् मुख

Shat Sampatti see Shadsampatti. षट् सम्पत्ति

Shat Shastra /Shat Shaastra/ the six vedanga (adjuncts of the Vedas); see Vedanga. षट् शास्त्र

Shata hundred. शत

Shata Chandi Maha Yajna /Shata Chandee Mahaa Yajna/ a powerful fire sacrifice performed in honour of Chandi during which the *Durga Saptashati* is chanted 100 times over several days; see Chandi Yajna. शत चण्डी महा यज्ञ

Shatavadhana /Shata-avadhaana/ doing or paying attention to 100 things at a time. शतावधान

Shaucha cleanliness of the body and mind, purity (internal and external); one of the niyamas as described by Patanjali in the ashtanga yoga of the *Yoga Sutras*; see Niyama. शौच

Shava corpse, dead body. शव

Shayanam lying, sleeping. शयनम्

Shayaniyam /Shayaneeyam/ bed, couch. शयनीयम्

Sheetkari Pranayama /Sheetkaaree Praanaayaama/ literally 'hissing breath', the practice of drawing the breath in through clenched teeth, a variation of shitali pranayama in that it cools the system. शीतकारी प्राणायाम

Shesha result, effect; end, termination, conclusion; death, destruction. शेष

Sheshanaga /Shesha-naaga/ name of a celebrated multi-hooded serpent said to have 1000 heads, represented as forming the couch on which Vishnu reclines, or as supporting the entire universe on his head; other names are Ananta and Vasuki; see Naga. शेषनाग

Shikha /Shikhaa/ tuft of hair kept by Hindu brahmins on the top of the back of the head; peak; flame. शिखा

Shikha Sutra Sannyasa /Shikhaa Sootra Sannyaasa/ shaving the tuft of hair and removing the sacred thread which are the symbols of caste, showing readiness to go beyond all barriers towards unlimited and unconditioned consciousness. शिखा सूत्र संन्यास

Shiksha /Shikshaa/ the vedic science of the correct articulation and pronunciation of Sanskrit; education, teaching; see Vedanga. शिक्षा

Shila /Sheela/ dispassion; nature, tendency, inclination; habit, custom; character or moral perfection obtained through yoga; conduct, behaviour in general; good disposition or character. शील

Shilanam /Sheelanam/ repeated practice, exercise, study, cultivation; constant application; honouring, serving. शीलनम्

Shilavanta /Sheelavanta/ moral, ethical, virtuous; accustomed. शीलवन्त

Shila /Shilaa/ stone, rock. शिला

Shiras head, skull; peak, summit, top (of a mountain); head or top of anything. शिरस्

Shirobrahman the cerebral cortex completely developed by the practice of yoga. शिरोब्रह्मन्

Shirodbhava coming from the head. शिरोद्भव

Shirodhara /Shirodharaa/ literally 'head supporting', i.e. the neck. शिरोधार

Shirovrata literally 'vow of the head'; a vow in which fire is carried on the head or in which the head is shaven; sannyasa. शिरोव्रत

Shirsham /Sheersham/ the head. शीर्षम्

Shishira Ritu the cold season comprised of the two months Magha and Phalguna; see Ritu; see Masa. शिशिर ऋतु

Shishupala /Shishupaala/ name of a king from the *Mahabharata*, who used to abuse Lord Krishna un-necessarily. His family begged Krishna to show restraint, so he agreed not to avenge the insults as long as they numbered less than 100. Shishupala overstepped the mark and was killed. शिशुपाल

Shishya literally 'one who is under discipline'; pupil, disciple; scholar. शिष्य

Shita /Sheeta/ cold, frost. शीत

Shitali Pranayama /Sheetalee Praanaayaama/ literally 'cooling breath', a breathing technique where the breath is drawn in through the folded tongue to cool the whole system; see Seetkari Pranayama. शीतली प्राणायाम

Shitayati /Sheetayati/ to cool. शीतयति

Shithilayati relax, slacken, loosen; give up, abandon; lessen; allow to cool down. शिथिलयति

Shiva 'auspicious one' or 'good'; name of the god of the sacred Hindu trinity who is entrusted with the work of destruction, as Brahma and Vishnu are with the creation and preservation of the world; destroyer of ego and duality; the first or original yogi; cosmic consciousness, counterpart of Shakti; see Sadashiva; see Rudra; see Bhairava; see Nataraja; see Nilakantha;

see Prakasha; see Ardhanarishvara; see Tantra; see Trika; see Shaiva Matha. शिव

Shivalingam black oval-shaped stone (those occurring naturally in the Narmada river are especially revered); symbol of Lord Shiva; symbol of consciousness; see Jyotirlinga; see Itara Lingam; see Linga. शिवलिङ्गम्

Shivapada the state of Lord Shiva; blessedness. शिवपद

Shivapriya lover of Shiva, the auspicious. शिवप्रिय

Shiva Purana /Shiva Puraana/ collection of six ancient scriptures that tell the story of Shiva; see Puranam. शिव पुराण

Shivaratri /Shiva-raatri/ 14th night of the dark lunar fortnight in the month of Phalguna (which falls in February or March) on which a rigorous fast is observed in honour of the marriage of Shiva and Shakti. शिवरात्रि

Shiva Samhita /Shiva Samhitaa/ Sanskrit text enumerating the concepts and principles essential to the practice of yoga; classical textbook on hatha yoga. शिव संहिता

Shivoham (Shivah-aham); 'I am Shiva', an ancient mantra. शिवोऽहम्

Shloka verse of praise; verse generally consisting of 32 letters in Sanskrit (or 32 syllables of English); hymn; celebrity, fame, re-

nown, name; object of praise. श्लोक

Shmashana /Shmashaana/ cremation ground. श्मशान

Shmashana Bhumi /Shmashaana Bhoomi/ land used as a burial or cremation ground. श्मशान भूमि

Shmashana Sadhana /Shmashaana Saadhanaa/ a tantric practice performed in the graveyard. श्मशान साधना

Shobha /Shobhaa/ splendour, beauty. शोभा

Shobhita decorated. शोभित

Shodhasha sixteen. षोडश

Shodashi Puja /Shodashee Poojaa/ tantric ritual which consists of 16 steps of worship. षोडशी पूजा

Shodashopachara /Shodasho-upachaara/ traditional form of worship with 16 types of offering. 1. a seat (asana) 2. welcome (swagata) 3. water for washing the feet (padya) 4. water offered in a vessel (arghya) 5. water for sipping (achamana) 6. a mixture of honey, ghee, milk and yoghurt (madhuparka) 7. water for bathing (snana) 8. clothing (vastra) 9. jewels (abhushana) 10. perfume (gandha) 11. flowers (pushpa) 12. incense (dhupa) 13. lights (dipa) 14. food (naivedya) 15. betel nuts etc. (tambulam) 16. prayer (vandana). षोडशोपचार

Shodhana purification; to cleanse or purify; to search, to enquire. शोधन

Shoka sorrow, grief, distress, affliction, deep anguish; lamentation, wailing; see Shadurmi. शोक

Shoonya see Shunya. शून्य

Shraddha /Shraaddha/ commemorative religious rites; funeral rite or ceremony performed in honour of the departed souls of relatives. श्राद्ध

Shraddha /Shraddhaa/ trust, faith, belief, confidence; belief in divine revelation, religious faith; sedateness, composure of mind; respect, reverence; one of the sixfold virtues; see Shadsampatti. श्रद्धा

Shraddhatrayavibhagayoga /Shraddhaa-traya-vibhaaga-yoga/ 'yoga of the division of the threefold faith', the 17th chapter of the *Bhagavad Gita*, dealing with the three kinds of faith people have according to their nature. श्रद्धात्रयविभागयोग

Shrauta Yajna generic name for yajnas based on injuctions from shruti texts (Vedas). श्रौत यज्ञ

Shravana /Shraavana/ fifth lunar month according to the Hindu almanac, corresponding to July/August; see Varsha; see Masa; see Ritu. श्रावण

Shravana name of a Vaishya ascetic unwittingly shot dead by King Dasharatha, who was then cursed by Shravana's old, blind parents to die of a broken heart, separated from his sons; ear; the act of hearing; that which is heard or revealed, the Veda; hearing of the shrutis or scriptures; study; fame, glory; wealth; name of a lunar mansion containing three stars. श्रवण

Shravas the ear; fame, glory; wealth; hymn. श्रवस्

Shreyas more splendid, better, superior; the path of righteousness; inculcating divine virtues. श्रेयस्

Shri /Shree/ wealth, riches, affluence, prosperity; beauty, grace, splendour, lustre; the goddess of wealth, Lakshmi, the wife of Vishnu; the word Shri is often used as an honorific prefix to the names of scriptures, deities and eminent people. श्री

Shrikantha /Shreekantha/ name of Shiva; the four downward pointing triangles in Shri Yantra, so called because they belong to Shiva. श्रीकण्ठ

Shrimad Bhagavata /Shreemad Bhaagavata/ one of the 18 major Puranas. Dealing with the avataras of Vishnu, it speaks especially and in great detail about the life of Shri Krishna; see Puranam; see Parikshit. श्रीमद् भागवत

Shrimad Devi Bhagavatam /Shreemad Devee Bhaagavatam/ scriptural text containing myths and doctrines of Devi. श्रीमद् देवी भागवतम्

Shripancha governing body in the akhara system consisting of five persons representing Brahma, Vishnu, Shiva, Shakti and Ganesha. श्रीपञ्च

Shriya /Shriyaa/ happiness, prosperity; epithet of Lakshmi. श्रिया

Shri Yantra /Shree Yantra/ geometrical diagram representing the divine 'female' energy; highly respected esoteric vehicle for

meditation; see Tripura Sundari. श्री यन्त्र

Shringeri Matha, Shringeri Peetha one of the four matha said to be established by Adi Shankaracharya, situated in Shringeri in the southern quarter of India. It was assigned the *Yajurveda* with its maha vakya (great statement) 'Aham Brahmasmi' (I am Brahman), and its first head was Sureshvaracharya. It still functions actively today. Saraswati, Puri and Bharati orders of the Dashnami Sampradaya emanate from there. श्रृंगेरि मठ, श्रृंगेरि पीठ

Shrotra ear, one of the five jnanendriyas (organs of knowledge); proficiency in the Vedas; the Veda. श्रोत्र

Shrotrasiddhi clairaudience. श्रोत्रसिद्धि

Shrotriya one who guides the performance of a yajna. श्रोत्रिय

Shruta, Shruti the Vedas (created through revelation which was heard), literally 'what has been heard'; hearing; the musical notes; holy learning, sacred knowledge; reported, heard of, learnt, ascertained, understood; well-known, famous, celebrated; named, called; see Veda. श्रुत, श्रुति

Shrutipradhana /Shruti-pradhaana/ superiority or supremacy of the shrutis over all other proofs of knowledge. श्रुतिप्रधान

Shubha auspicous, blessed. शुभ

Shubhechcha /Shubhechchhaa/ (Shubha-ichchhaa); good desire; in Vedanta, the first of the seven stages of knowledge (jnana bhu-

mika), the right aspiration to cross samsara through satsanga and study of scriptures; see Mumukshu. शुभेच्छा

Shuchi radiant; white; pure, undefiled; virtuous, free from sin. शुचि

Shuddha pure in nature. शुद्ध

Shuddhabhavana /Shuddhabhaavana/ pure feeling or attitude. शुद्धभावना

Shuddhadvaita /Shuddha-advaita/ philosophy of pure monism. शुद्धाद्वैत

Shuddhamanas /Shuddha-maanasa/ pure mind. शुद्धमानस

Shuddhata /Shuddhataa/ virtue; purity. शुद्धता

Shuddha Vasana /Shuddha Vaasanaa/ pure desire or tendency; good impression from the past. शुद्ध वासना

Shuddhi purification; to purify; pure, clean, untainted; purity, cleanliness. शुद्धि

Shudra /Shoodra/ one of the four varnas or divisions of the caste system in India; one whose consciousness is least developed, due to which one remains in ignorance, causing one to weep and mourn; in the *Rigveda* it refers to the soul yet to be purified by samskaras; one with a services oriented tendency of mind or one engaged in such a profession; see Samskara; see Varna. शूद्र

Shuka Muni the exponent of *Shrimad Bhagavata* to King Parikshit; see Parikshit. शुक मुनि

Shukla Dhyana /Shukla Dhyaana/ meditation on pure white light. शुक्ल ध्यान

Shukra the planet Venus; name of the preceptor of the demons (asuras) who by means of his magical powers restored the lives of demons killed in battle; name of fire. शुक्र

Shunya /Shoonya/ void state of transcendental consciousness; state of darkness prior to enlightenment referred to as 'the dark night of the soul'; mental vacuum; empty-hearted; vacant glance; listless; absent; non-existent, empty, deserted, wholly destitute; solitary; state of nothingness, zero. शून्य

Shunyashunya /Shoonya-ashoonya/ the mind is in a state of void and yet in a state that is not void. शून्याशून्य

Shunyavada /Shoonya-vaada/ Buddhist doctrine of the non-existence of anything. शून्यवाद

Shunyavadi /Shoonya-vaadee/ Buddhist. शून्यवादी

Shvasa /Shvaasa/ breath. श्वास

Shveta white, bright. श्वेत

Shvetambara /Shvetaambara/ clad in white, an epithet applied particularly to Jaina monks and nuns who wear cloth, as distinct from those who do not; see Digambara. श्वेताम्बर

Shyama /Shyaama/ epithet of Lord Krishna; black, dark blue, dark coloured; cuckoo; name of a sacred fig tree at Allahabad on the banks of the river Yamuna. श्याम

Siddha perfected being; sage; seer; semi-divine being of great purity and holiness; accomplished soul particularly characterized by eight supernatural faculties called siddhis. सिद्ध

Siddhi paranormal or supernatural accomplishment; control of mind and prana; psychic abilities; eight supernatural powers obtained by yogis as a result of long practice. They are associated with opening of the chakras and the resultant power over the elements, viz. 1. anima, 2. laghima, 3. prapti, 4. prakamya, 5. mahima, 6. ishitvam, 7. vashitva, 8. garima; other siddhis include the power of entering other bodies, the ability to read another person's thoughts, clairvoyance, clairaudience, omniscience, effulgence, vanishing from sight, etc. They are considered to be obstacles on the path to realization because they maintain interest in samsara; see Vibhuti Pada. सिद्धि

Siddhanta the established end; the demonstrated conclusion of an argument, established view of any question, the true logical conclusion; an established text book resting on conclusive evidence; a proven fact. सिद्धान्त

Sita /Seetaa/ literally 'a furrow'; ploughed land, agriculture; the name of the daughter of Janaka and the wife of Rama. Sita is the heroine of the epic *Ramayana*, who remained faithful and undaunted though captured by terrorists (Ravana) and maligned by evil-thinking people. After being rescued by her Lord Rama and then exiled from his kingdom despite her purity being vouchsafed by an ordeal of fire, she brought up their twin sons in Valmiki's ashram. सीता

Skambha support; fulcrum; the supreme being. स्कम्भ

Skanda name of Kartikeya, the god of war; a Purana; see Puranam; see Kartikeya. स्कन्द

Skandha shoulder; body; trunk or stem of a tree; chapter, section, division (of a book); the five forms of mundane consciousness according to buddhist philosophy. स्कन्ध

Smara reflection, remembrance; love, god of love. स्मर

Smarta Yajna /Smaarta Yajna/ generic term for yajnas (sacrificial rituals) based on injunctions from Smriti texts (Puranas, tantra shastra, etc.) स्मार्त यज्ञ

Smrita remembered, mentioned, handed down, prescribed. स्मृत

Smriti memory; one of the five vrittis listed in Patanjali's *Yoga Sutras*; tradition, law, the body of traditional or memorial law; canon; vedic texts transmitted by memory; a class of works called dharma shastra handed down by tradition; remembrance, recollection, thinking of, calling to mind; see Vritti; see Dharma Shastra; see Manu Smriti. स्मृति

Smashana Bhoomi see Shmashana Bhumi. समशान भूमि

Snana /Water offered in worship for bathing of the deity; see Shodashopachara. स्नान

Sneha affection, love, kindness, tenderness; friendship, emotional adhesiveness. स्नेह

Soham (Sah-aham); literally 'That am I', 'so' representing cosmic consciousness and 'ham' representing individual consciousness; mantra used in ajapa japa, said to be the unconscious repetitive prayer produced by the breath itself, the inhalation sounding 'so' and the exhalation 'ham' (also the reverse according to some texts); see Hamsa Mantra. सोऽहम्

Soma name of a plant that was the most important ingredient in ancient sacrificial offerings; juice of a potent plant drunk during religious ceremonies to experience divine intoxication; the moon, which in mythology is represented as having sprung from the eye of the sage Atri, or as having been produced from the sea at the time of churning; nectar of the gods (amrita); see Amrita; see Saumya; see Sava. सोम

Soma Mandala yogic term for the pituitary gland. सोम मण्डल

Soumya see Saumya. सौम्य

Sourya see Saurya. सौर्य

Spanda movement, vibration; cosmic vibration, primordial pulsation; dynamic aspect of Shiva. स्पन्द

Spandabhasa /Spanda-aabhaasa/ reflection of vibration or movement. स्पन्दाभास

Spanda Karika /Spanda Kaarikaa/ treatise of Kashmir Shaivism; see Kashmir Shaivmata. स्पन्द कारिका

Sparsha the sense of touch; see Pancha Tanmatra. स्पर्श

Sparshadiksha /Sparsha-deekshaa/ initiation (diksha) through touch. स्पर्शदीक्षा

Sparsham touching, handling; affecting, influencing. स्पर्शम्

Sparshanaka a term used in

Sankhya philosophy for the skin. स्पर्शनक

Sparshanam touching, touch, contact; sensation, feeling; sense or organ of touch; gift, donation. स्पर्शनम्

Sparsha Tanmatra /Sparsha Tanmaatra/ the subtle element of touch, the tanmatra associated with anahata chakra; the essence of the sense of touch; see Pancha Tanmatra. स्पर्श तन्मात्र

Sparshayati to cause; to touch; to give, to present. स्पर्शयति

Sprishati to touch; to lay hands on, stroke gently; to adhere or cling to; to come into contact with; to attain to, obtain, reach a particular state; to act upon, influence. स्पृशति

Spashta distinctly visible, evident, clearly perceived, plain, manifest; real, true; one who sees clearly; full-blown, expanded. स्पष्ट

Sphatika a crystal; crystalline. स्फटिक

Sphota breaking forth, splitting open, bursting, blasting; the idea which bursts out or flashes on the mind when a sound is uttered; the impression produced in the mind on hearing the eternal sound Om; manifestor. स्फोट

Sphurana flashing on the mind, crossing the memory; throbbing, trembling; breaking forth, arising, starting into view. स्फुरण

Spriha /Sprihaa/ desire, covetousness, hankering. स्पृहा

Sri see Shri. श्री

Srikantha see Shrikantha. श्रीकण्ठ

Srishti creation, manifest universe; manifestation, emanation; letting go; see Unmesha. सृष्टि

Srishti Bheda difference in creation, i.e. one ego is the result of the predominance of sattwa, another of rajas, and the third of tamas, etc. सृष्टि भेद

Srishti Drishti the view that the outer objective world is real, which maintains a plurality of jivas and is the common sense view. सृष्टि दृष्टि

Srishti Sthiti Laya creation, preservation and destruction or absorption. सृष्टि स्थिति लय

Sthala place. स्थल

Sthana /Sthaana/ the act of standing; situation, position, state; place, locality, region; abode, house; domain, sphere. स्थान

Sthandila offering place for the Vedic sacrifices, to which the initial worship is dedicated. स्थण्डिल

Sthayi Bhava /Sthaayee Bhaava/ steadfastness. स्थायी भाव

Sthira firm, steady, fixed; immovable, still, motionless; permanent, eternal, everlasting; name of Shiva; name of Kartikeya; the planet Saturn. स्थिर

Sthairyam steadiness. स्थैर्यम्

Sthirata /Sthirataa/ steadiness or firmness, either of mind through concentration or of body through the practice of asanas, mudras etc. स्थिरता

Sthita standing, remaining, abiding, situated, existing, present; firm, constant, established; steadfast in conduct, upright, virtuous. स्थित

Sthitaprajna one whose wisdom is firmly established and does not waver (due to fluctuations of the gunas), who is unmoved by the dualities of pleasure and pain, gain and loss, joy and sorrow, victory and defeat and is unshakably established in super-consciousness. Such a person is described in the last 18 verses of the second chapter of the *Bhagavad Gita*; stabilized consciousness; see Gunatita; see Viraja. स्थितप्रज्ञ

Sthiti condition. स्थिति

Sthula /Sthoola/ gross; large, great, big, huge; strong, powerful; ignorant, foolish, doltish; relating to the waking state of consciousness (jagrata). स्थूल

Sthulabuddhi /Sthoola-buddhi/ gross intellect. स्थूलबुद्धि

Sthula Dhyana /Sthoola Dhyaana/ a meditation on concrete material forms, Rishi Gheranda has prescribed this method of meditation on the gross form of the deity as good for beginners. स्थूल ध्यान

Sthulakasha /Sthoola-akaasha/ space pervading the physical body, the whole body space. स्थूलाकाश

Sthula Sharira /Sthoola Shareera/ gross body, physical body; also called annamaya kosha; see Kosha. स्थूल शरीर

Stotra group of mantras sung in praise of a deity; the singing of mantras (hymns) from the *Sama Veda* during a shrauta yajna. स्तोत्र

Stuti singing the praises of God. स्तुति

Subrahmanyam epithet of Kartikeya, the son of Shiva and Parvati; a priest who chants mantras invoking Indra during a shrauta yajna. सुब्रह्मण्यम्

Suchayati /Soochayati/ point out, indicate, reveal. सूचयति

Sudarshan /Sudarshana/ literally 'auspicious vision' or 'correct understanding' (of reality); the name of the weapon (discus) of Lord Vishnu. सुदर्शन

Sugriva /Sugreeva/ a monkey chief who assisted Rama in his search for and recovery of Sita, he was the younger brother of Vali; see Vali. सुग्रीव

Sukha happiness, delight, joy, pleasure; prosperity; wellbeing, welfare, health; heaven, paradise; suitability, comfort. सुख

Sukhapurvaka Abhyasa /Sukhapoorvaka Abhyaasa/ simple preliminary practice; practised with ease. सुखपूर्वक अभ्यास

Sukshma /Sookshma/ subtle; subtle dimension; relating to the world of the psyche. सूक्ष्म

Sukshmabhuta /Sookshma-bhoota/ tanmatra, the subtle essence or state of elements; see Pancha Tanmatra. सूक्ष्मभूत

Sukshmadarshi /Sookshma-darshee/ seer of the subtle essence of things; one who has developed the subtle inner eye; a wise person; a sage. सूक्ष्मदर्शी

Sukshma Dhyana /Sookshma Dhyaana/ as prescribed by Rishi Gheranda in *Gheranda Samhita*, this meditation (dhyana) is linked with awakened kundalini shakti and is a subtle type of meditation beyond sensory perceptions or the lower mind. सूक्ष्म ध्यान

Sukshmasharira /Sookshma-shareera/ subtle body

or part of the subconscious which manifests in the dream state; the subtle body composed of prana-maya, manomaya and vijnana-maya koshas; see Kosha. सूक्ष्मशरीर

Sukta /Sookta/ set of hymns composed by rishis in adoration of deities as an expression of their perception in deep meditation. सूक्त

Sumeru the mountain used in the churning of the ocean; tassle on a rosary (mala); see Meru. सुमेरु

Sumitra /Sumitraa/ mother of Lakshmana and Satrughna and a wife of Dasharatha. सुमित्रा

Surati constant awareness of God. सुरति

Sureshvara Lord of the gods, Indra; according to tradition, the sannyasa name given to Mandana Mishra, husband of Ubhaya Bharati who was regarded as an incarnation of Saraswati. He was a highly respected scholar who became a disciple of Adi Shankaracharya on being defeated by him in debate and was later installed as the first pontiff of the Shringeri Matha. He is the author of *Naishkarmyasiddhi*, a treatise on Vedanta, and also wrote commentaries on Adi Shankaracharya's explanations of the *Taittiriya* and *Brihadaranyaka Upanishads*, also on his *Dakshinamoorti Stotram* and on the *Pancheekaranam*; see Matha; see Bharati. सुरेश्वर

Suruchira shining brightly; beautiful. सुरुचिर

Surya /Soorya/ sun; vital pranic energy; the sun god; symbol of the atma; see Saurya. सूर्य

Surya Akasha /Soorya-aakaasha/ literally 'space of the sun'; fifth of the five subtle spaces of vyoma panchaka; luminous space of the soul; see Vyoma Panchaka Dharana. सूर्य आकाश

Surya Chakra /Soorya Chakra/ psychic centre situated between the navel and the heart. सूर्य चक्र

Surya Mandala /Soorya Mandala/ image of the sun visualized at the eyebrow centre. सूर्य मण्डल

Surya Nadi /Soorya Naadee/ another name for pingala nadi, literally 'energy flow of the sun'; see Pingala Nadi. सूर्य नाडी

Surya Namaskara /Soorya Namaskaara/ literally 'salute to the sun', (which is a symbol of the atma or soul), a series of 12 asanas for revitalizing prana. While performing the series one can repeat the corresponding 12 surya mantras and concentrate on the chakra related to each asana. सूर्य नमस्कार

Surya Tantra /Soorya Tantra/ path of realization through visualizing and evoking the vital energy within the sun. सूर्य तन्त्र

Surya Vijnana /Soorya Vijnaana/ another name for surya tantra. सूर्य विज्ञान

Sushila /Susheela/ a person whose nature is purified, who has silenced the mind and is no longer subject to external or internal influences. सुशील

Sushumna Nadi /Sushumnaa Nadee/ central energy flow (nadi) in the spine which conducts the kundalini or spiritual force from mooladhara chakra to sahasrara chakra. It is the main energy flow related to transcendental awareness. It is 'situated' in the spinal cord of the human body, and opens when balance is achieved between ida and pingala nadis. Within it lie three more important subtle energy flows responsible for transcendental experience; see Vajra Nadi; see Chitra Nadi; see Brahma Nadi. सुषुम्ना नाडी

Sushumna Shirshakam / Sushumnaa Sheershakam/ the medulla oblongata in the brain where the centres controlling the breath and heartbeat are to be found. सुषुम्ना शीर्षकम्

Sushupti third dimension of consciousness, witnessed by Prajna according to *Mandukya Upanishad*; deep sleep or unconscious realm of mind; profound repose undisturbed by the senses. सुषुप्ति

Sushupti Avastha /Sushupti Avasthaa/ deep sleep; the third state of consciousness where there is no disturbance from inner or outer sources, related to the 'm' of Aum in *Mandukya Upanishad;* see Avasthatraya; see Prajna. सुषुप्ति अवस्था

Sutala /Sutala/ third centre of the instinctive or animal body below mooladhara chakra; see Patalam. सुतल

Sutra /Sootra/ a brief statement which explains the ancient spiritual texts; thread, string, line, cord, fibre; short rule or precept; aphorism or condensed statements strung together to give an outline of a philosophy, such as the *Yoga Sutras* of Patanjali. सूत्र

Sutradhara /Sootradhaara/ literally 'the holder of the string'; Hiranyagarbha or the Lord of the universe. सूत्रधार

Sutra Neti /Sootra Neti/ nasal cleansing using a catheter; one of the cleansing techniques in the shatkarmas; see Shatkarma. सूत्र नेति

Sutratman /Sootra-aatman/ the conscious energy which operates in the subtle universe or macrocosmos. सूत्रात्मन्

Suvarnam gold. सुवर्णम्

Suvarnamaya consisting of gold. सुवर्णमय

Suvichara /Suvichaara/ right enquiry; in Vedanta, the second of the seven stages of wisdom (jnana bhumika) which manifests as ceaseless enquiry into 'Who am I', what the world is, the nature of atma and Brahman; see Mumukshu. सुविचार

Swa /Sva/ one's own innate, real force; soul, self; see Swarupa. स्व

Swabhava /Sva-bhaava/ one's own nature. स्वभाव

Swachchanda /Sva-chchhanda/ the power of following one's own will or fancy; wilfulness; independence. स्वच्छन्द

Swadharma /Sva-dharma/ one's own duty in life; one's own real nature. स्वधर्म

Swadhisthana Chakra /Sva-adhishthaana Chakra/ literally 'one's own abode'; psychic/pranic centre situated at the base of the spinal column in the lumbar region (level of the generative organs), associated with the sacral plexus, and the storehouse of subconscious impressions; see Chakra; see Makara; see Vam. स्वाधिष्ठान चक्र

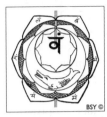

Swadhyaya /Sva-adhyaaya/ self-study; continuous conscious awareness of what one is doing; one of the niyamas recommended by Patanjali's *Yoga Sutras*; education of the self; study of the scriptures and texts of yoga and self-knowledge; see Niyama. स्वाध्याय

Swanubhuti /Sva-anubhooti/ direct experience of one's own self. स्वानुभूति

Swaprakasha /Sva-prakaasha/ self-luminous. स्वप्रकाश

Swarupa /Sva-roopa/ one's own form or shape, natural state or condition, essential nature; natural character or form, true constitution; nature; similar, like; handsome, pleasing, lovely; learned, wise. स्वरूप

> **Swarupadhyana** /Sva-roopa-dhyaana/ meditation on reality, i.e. on one's own essential nature. स्वरूपध्यान

> **Swarupajnana** /Sva-roopa-jnaana/ literally 'knowledge of one's own essential nature'; knowledge of pure consciousness, which is the highest aim in life. स्वरूपज्ञान

> **Swarupalakshana** /Sva-roopa-lakshana/ the characteristic of

one's own self defined as 'sachchidananda', or existence, consciousness, bliss, which is the essential nature of Brahman. स्वरूपलक्षण

Swarupapratishtha /Sva-roopa-pratishthaa/ being established in one's own self. स्वरूपप्रतिष्ठा

Swarupasambandha /Sva-roopa-sambandha/ connection with one's own essential nature. स्वरूपसम्बन्ध

Swarupashunyam /Sva-roopa-shoonyam/ a state of samadhi; see Shunya. स्वरूपशून्यम्

Swarupasthiti /Sva-roopa-sthiti/ becoming firmly established in one's own essential nature. स्वरूपस्थिति

Swarupavastha /Sva-roopa-avasthaa/ state of being one with Brahman, resting in the absolute reality or Brahman. स्वरूपावस्था

Swasamvedana /Sva-samvedanaa/ the feeling of one's own emotions. स्वसंवेदना

Swatantra /Sva-tantra/ independent. स्वतन्त्र

> **Swatantrasattabhava** /Sva-tantra-sattaa-bhava/ the possibility of independent existence. स्वतन्त्रसत्ताभाव

> **Swatantratva** /Sva-tantratva/ state of (absolute) independence. स्वतन्त्रत्व

Swagata /Svaagata/ (Su-aagata); welcome; see Shodashopachara. स्वागत

Swagatabheda /Svagata-bheda/ the difference between the different parts of the one being, e.g. the hands and feet of a person or the leaves, branches and trunk of a tree. स्वगतभेद

Swaha /Svaahaa/ mantra chanted to accompany the physical act of offering an oblation to the sacrificial fire; a name of the wife of Agni, who is also known as Gabhasti. स्वाहा

Swah Loka /Svah Loka/ one of the seven higher dimensions of consciousness; see Loka. स्व: लोक

Swami /Svaamee/ literally 'mastery over the mind'; master of the self; title of sannyasins; an honorific denoting respect; see Sannyasa. स्वामी

Swapna /Svapna/ second dimension of consciousness, witnessed by Taijasa according to the *Mandukya Upanishad*; subconscious realm of mind, state of dreaming. स्वप्न

Swapnakalpita /Svapna-kalpita/ imagined in a dream; dream creation. स्वप्नकल्पित

Swapnamayasvarupa /Svapna-maayaa-svaroopa/ of the form of a dream-illusion. स्वप्नमायास्वरूप

Swapnasiddhi /Svapna-siddhi/ contact with the cosmic mind through dream, revealing the truth about life, the world and the state of existence. स्वप्नसिद्धि

Swapnavastha /Svapna-avasthaa/ dream state of consciousness where external sensory disturbances are negligible but the mind is caught in its internal impressions (samskara); the second state of consciousness, related to the 'u' of Aum in the *Mandukya Upanishad*; see Taijasa; see Avasthatraya. स्वप्नावस्था

Swapnavat /Svapna-vat/ like a dream. स्वप्नवत्

Swar /Svar/ heaven, paradise; the sky; ether. स्वर

Swaraganga /Svara-gangaa/ the celestial river Ganges (Ganga); the galaxy or Milky Way. स्वरगङ्गा

Swarga /Svarga/ heaven, Indra's paradise. स्वर्ग

Swargadvaram /Svarga-dvaaram/ heaven's gate, the door of paradise, entrance into heaven. स्वर्गद्वारम्

Swargaloka /Svarga-loka/ the celestial region; paradise; the third region or state of existence beyond bhuvah loka, generally identified with heaven; also called swah loka; see Loka. स्वर्गलोक

Swara /Svara/ breathing cycle; flow of the breath in the nostrils; sound or tone, noise, voice; vowel; a note of the musical scale; accent (raised, low, circumflex); rules of pronunciation while chanting. स्वर

Swara Sadhaka /Svara Saadhaka/ one who practises swara yoga. स्वर साधक

Swara Sadhana /Svara Saadhanaa/ concentration on the seven notes of the musical scale; concentration on progressively subtler sounds leading back to the source; regulation of breath; a sadhana in which the flow of breath is continually watched and behaviour is regulated to be in harmony with cosmic rhythms; see Jyotisha. स्वर साधना

Swara Samyoga /Svara Samyoga/ the function of vowels; the union of notes or sounds. स्वर संयोग

Swara Shunya /Svara Shoonya/

without musical notes, unmelodious, unmusical. स्वर शून्य

Swara Yoga /Svara Yoga/ science of the breathing cycle. स्वर योग

Swarita the middle tone of the three tones for chanting vedic mantras aloud (the other two are udatta and anudatta). स्वरित

Swasti /Svasti/ a particle meaning 'may it be well with (one)'; farewell, adieu; wellbeing, fortune, good luck, success. स्वस्ति

Swastika /Svastika/ a kind of mystical mark on persons or things denoting good luck; lucky object; meeting of four roads; mansion or temple of a particular form. स्वस्तिक

Swatmarama /Svaatmaaraama/ (Sva-aatmaraama); literally 'one who revels within oneself'; the author of *Hatha Yoga Pradipika*, a classical text book on hatha yoga. स्वात्माराम

Swayam /Svayam/ self. स्वयम्

Swayambhu, Swabhu /Svayambhoo, Sva-bhoo/ self-existing, Brahman. स्वयम्भू, स्वभू

Swayamjyoti /Svayam-jyoti/ self-illumined, self-luminous. स्वयम्ज्योति

Swayamprabhasamvit /Svayamprabhaa-samvit/ self-luminous consciousness. स्वयम्प्रभासंवित्

Swayam Prakasha /Svayam Prakaasha/ self-illumined, an essential attribute of the supreme consciousness which does not require the aid of a mental or intellectual organ for its revelation. स्वयम् प्रकाश

Swayamvara /Svayamvara/ selection of a husband by a woman in a public ceremony. स्वयंवर

T

Tad that; That (Brahman); the beyond; other than 'this'; see Tat. तद्

Tadakara /Tadaakaara/ (Tataakaara); of that form, i.e. of the same form as That; see Brahman. तदाकार

Tadatmyasambandha /Taadaatmya-sambandha/ (Tataatmya-sambandha); identical relation, e.g. iron becomes fire at high temperatures, water becomes white when mixed with milk. तादात्म्यसम्बन्ध

Tadbodhi (Tat-bodhi); knowledge of the real nature of Brahman. तद्बोधि

Tadrigguna /Taadrigguna/ (Taadrik-guna); identifying with that quality. तादृग्गुण

Tadrish /Taadrish/ like that. तादृश

Tadrupa /Tadroopa/ (Tat-roopa); literally 'of that form'; thus formed. तद्रूप

Tadrupa Pratistha /Tadroopa Pratishthaa/ (Tatroopa Pratishthaa); knowledge of true identity; linking of name with form. तद्रूप प्रतिष्ठा

Tada /Taada/ blow, knock, thump; noise; sheaf; palm tree. ताड

Tadana /Taadana/ beating, whipping, flogging. ताडन

Tadani Mudra /Taadani Mudraa/ beating, a kriya in which one lightly beats the buttocks against the floor; see Mudra. ताडनी मुद्रा

Tadaga /Taadaaga/ pond, deep pool, tank. तडाग

Tadagi Mudra /Tadaagi Mudraa/ one of the mudras which removes old age and drives away death; see Mudra. तडागी मुद्रा

Tadaka /Taadakaa/ name of a female demon, daughter of Suketu, wife of Sunda and mother of Maricha. She was changed into a female demon by the sage Agastya whose devotion she had disturbed. Eventually she was killed by Rama when she began disturbing the sacrificial rites of Vishvamitra. At first Rama was unwilling to use his bow against a woman, but then overcame his scruples. ताडका

Taijasa a name used in Vedanta philosophy for an individual in a subtle state (as in a dream) when the supreme reality is veiled and coloured by an individual's subtle body; the seer of the dream state of consciousness (swapna), the second state of consciousness expressed by 'u' of Aum according to *Mandukya Upanishad*; see Avasthatraya. तैजस

Tailadhara /Taila-dhaara/ continuous flow of oil. This image is used to denote the continuous flow of one thought in meditation, as well as the unbroken current of love of the devotee to the beloved. तैलधारा

Taittiriya Upanishad an Upanishad in the form of a lesson to a student. The first chapter, *Shuksha Valli*, is on right education and the second, *Ananda Valli*, is on bliss. तैत्तिरीय उपनिषद्

Takshaka carpenter, woodcutter; chief actor in the prelude of a drama; name of the architect of the gods; name of one of the principal serpents of Patala, son of Kashyapa and his wife Kadru. तक्षक

Tala /Taala/ cymbals; rhythm, clapping the hands together. ताल

Talatala /Talaatala/ the fifth centre of the instinctive or animal body below mooladhara chakra; see Patalam. तलातल

Talumula /Taalu-moola/ root of the palate. तालुमूल

Tamas in Sankhya philosophy, one of the three constituent qualities (gunas) of nature (prakriti), and all matter; inertia, stability, stillness; ignorance, darkness; the gloom or darkness of hell; mental darkness; illusion, error; in yoga it is characterized by inertia, laziness, mental dullness, unwillingness to change; electrically

neutral; see Guna. तमस्

Tamasahamkara /Taamasahamkaara/ the lowest or grossest type of egoism, characterized by delusion, inertia and deep arrogation; that quality of ahamkara which leads to manifestation of the gross material world via the mahabhutas; see Pancha Mahabhuta. तामसाहङ्कार

Tamasic /Taamasic/ (Taamasika); pertaining to tamas. तामसिक

Tamasikotapas /Taamasikotapas/ extreme austerity of an unnecessary and dire type; self-torture practised by an ignorant person, mistaking this for real tapas; see Tapas. तामसिकोतपस्

Tamobhuta /Tamobhoota/ dark, covered with darkness. तमोभूत

Tamoguna quality of tamas; see Tamas. तमोगुण

Tambula /Taamboola/ areca-nut; the leaf of piper-betel, which, together with lime, areca-nut and catecu, is ritually offered to the deity during worship. It is also commonly chewed after meals as a digestive aid. ताम्बूल

Tandava /Taandava/ dancing in general; particularly the frantic or violent dance of Shiva, symbolizing the destruction of the universe; the art of dancing; see Nataraja; see Nritya. ताण्डव

Tandra /Tandraa/ lassitude, weariness, fatigue, exhaustion; sleepiness, sluggishness; half-sleepy state, an obstacle in meditation. तन्द्रा

Tankar /Tankaara/ twanging, making a hissing or twanging sound. टङ्कार

Tanmatra /Tanmaatraa/ subtle nature; quality or essence of the elements (mahabhutas) and the associated five senses (jnanendriyas), viz. 1. sound (shabda), 2. touch (sparsha), 3. form (rupa), 4. taste (rasa), 5. smell (gandha); see Pancha Tanmatra. तन्मात्रा

Tanmayata /Tanmayataa/ state of absorption into, or becoming one with, the object of contemplation. तन्मयता

Tanoti to expand, stretch, extend, spread, endure, perform. तनोति

Tantra most ancient universal science and culture which deals with the transition of human nature from the present level of evolution and understanding to a transcendental level of knowledge, experience and awareness; loom, thread, warps of thread extended lengthwise in a loom; main point, principle doctrine, rule; theory, science; scriptures devoted to spiritual techniques in the form of a dialogue between Shiva and Shakti, forming a set of rules for ritual worship, discipline, meditation and the attainment of supernatural powers; a particular path of sadhana laying great stress upon mantra japa and other esoteric upasanas; from the roots tanoti (to expand) and trayate (to liberate); see Upaya. तन्त्र

Tantraloka /Tantra-aaloka/ literally 'the illumination of the tantric way or path'; the text by Abhinava Gupta giving the supreme philosophical and practical teaching on trika, which subsumes the tantric stream of krama (steps), kula (family), and pratyabhijna (the doctrine of recollection); see Trika. तन्त्रलोक ः

Tantrasara /Tantrasaara/ literally 'the essence of tantra', name of a compilation. तन्त्रसार

Tantra Shastra /Tantra Shaastra/ specific scripture of the fourth or present age (Kali yuga) cast in the form of a dialogue between Shiva and his female consort, Shakti or Parvati; tantras were the encyclopaedias of knowledge of their time. The seven marks or topics of a tantra are: 1. creation (srishti), 2. destruction of the universe (pralaya), 3. worship of the gods (devatanam-archanam), 4. spiritual exercises (sadhana), 5. rituals (purascharana), 6. the six super- natural powers (siddhi), 7. meditation (dhyana); see Yamala. तन्त्र शास्त्र

Tantrik /Taantrika/ belonging to tantra which is a path of sadhana laying great stress upon repetition of mantras and other esoteric meditations; a Hindu sect worshipping God as the divine mother in a particular form. तान्त्रिक

Tantri /Tantree/ lute or veena; string, cord. तन्त्री

Tantrivina /Tantree-veenaa/ the harmonic sound of stringed instruments which may be meditated upon. तन्त्रीवीणा

Tanu body; thin, lean, emaciated; delicate, slender, slim; small, little, tiny, scanty, few, limited; one of the four possible states of the kleshas according to Patanjali in the *Yoga Sustras*; see Klesha. तनु

Tanu Avastha /Tanu Avasthaa/ thinned state of mind. तनु अवस्था

Tanumanasi /Tanu-maanasee/ thread-like state of mind; in Vedanta the third of the seven stages of wisdom (jnana bhumika) resulting from intense, continued spiritual desire and enquiry; see Mumukshu. तनुमानसी

Tapas austerity; process of burning the impurities; warmth, heat, fire; pain, suffering; penance, mortification; meditation connected with the practice of personal self-denial; tapas in yoga means a burning effort which involves purification, self-discipline and austerity, a process in which the inner impurities covering the inner personality are completely eliminated, but this austerity is not exaggerated into self-mortification; cleansing for the perfection of body and senses; one of the five niyama described by the *Yoga Sutras* of Patanjali; see Niyama; see Tamasikotapas. तपस्

Tapah Loka see Tapoloka. तप: लोक

Tapana the sun, sunshine; the hot season; name of a hell; epithet of Shiva. तपन

Tapanta penitent. तपन्त

Tapashcharya /Tapashcharyaa/ practice of austerity, penance. तपश्चर्या

Tapasvin ascetic, one who practises austerity or penance; devout; poor, miserable, helpless, pitiable. तपस्विन्

Tapasya /Tapasyaa/ practice of austerity. तपस्या

Tapati /Tapatee/ daughter of the sun. तपती

Tapati to make hot, burn; to be warm, to shine; to be affected; to repent, do penance; to distress. तपति

Tapodhana (Tapah-dhana); literally 'rich in penance'; an ascetic; a devotee. तपोधन

Tapoloka (Tapah-loka); one of the higher worlds just below satya loka; one of the seven higher dimensions of consciousness; see Loka. तपोलोक

Tapovana (Tapah-vana); forest suitable for tapas. तपोवन

Taptapinda heated ball. तप्तपिण्ड

Tara /Taaraa/ a star; a fixed star; pupil of the eye; a goddess; name of the wife of Sugriva. तारा

Taraka /Taarakaa/ a star; meteor, falling star; the pupil of the eye. तारका

Taraka /Taaraka/ ferrying, carrying over; rescuing, protecting, preserving; ferrying one across the ocean of samsara. तारक

Tarakajnana /Taaraka-jnaana/ the knowledge that leads to moksha. तारकज्ञान

Tarani boat, raft, ferry; heaven. तरणि

Tarakah /Taarakah/ name of a demon killed by Kartikeya. The son of Vajranga and Varangi, he propitiated the god Brahma through his penance on the Pariyatra mountain, requesting as a boon that he should not be killed by anyone except a child seven days old. On the strength of this boon he began to oppress the gods, who were obliged to go to Brahma asking for assistance. They were told that only the offspring of Shiva could vanquish the demon. Thus Shiva's son, Kartikeya, was born, killing the demon on the seventh day after his birth. तारक:

Taranga a wave, waving. तरङ्ग

Taranta the ocean; a hard shower; a frog; a demon. तरन्त

Taras speed, velocity; vigour, strength, energy; bank, place of crossing; float, raft. तरस्

Tarka, Tarkah logic; process of understanding through discussion and analysis; reasoning, supposition, conjecture, speculation, discussion, abstract reasoning; doubt. तर्क, तर्क:

Tarpana rite performed for ancestors. तर्पण

Tat that; That (Brahman); the beyond; other than 'this'; see Tad. तत्

Tat Twam Asi /Tat-tvam-asi/ literally 'That you are' or 'Thou art That', one of the four great vedic statements (maha vakya). Found in *Chandogya Upanishad* of the *Sama Veda*, it is the instruction given by the self-realized sage to the disciple (upadesha vakya) that the real nature of the human soul or the individual soul (jiva) is identical with the supreme spirit pervading the universe; see Maha Vakya. तत् त्वम् असि

Tatastha Vritti vritti of indifference, neutrality wherein there is neither attraction nor repulsion. तटस्थ वृत्ति

Tathabhuta /Tathaabhoota/ remaining as before. तथाभूत

Tathavritta /Tathaavritta/ of such behaviour; composed like. तथावृत्त

Tattwa /Tattva/ 'that-ness'; the truth about something, or the thing-in-itself; an element, a primary substance; essence, truth, reality; principle, category; in Sankhya 25 tattwas are mentioned, and in common parlance five of these, the pancha mahabhuta, are often referred to as the five tattwas; true state or condition, fact; true essential nature; the real nature of the human soul and the material world as being identical with the supreme spirit pervading the universe. तत्त्व

Tattwa Akasha /Tattva Aakassha/ literally 'elemental space'; fourth of the five mental spaces of vyoma panchaka, elemental space of perfect stillness; see Vyoma Panchaka Dharana. तत्त्व आकाश

Tattwadarshi /Tattva-darshee/ one who sees the subtle nature of things; a sage. तत्त्वदर्शी

Tattwa Dharana /Tattva Dhaaranaa/ technique of meditation involving awareness and experience of the elements (tattwas or mahabhutas). तत्त्व धारणा

Tattwa Jnana /Tattva Jnaana/ knowledge of the elements;

knowledge of the true principle or truth, insight into the true principles of philosophy; see Sattwapatti. तत्त्व ज्ञान

Tattwakasha see Tattwa Akasha. तत्त्वाकाश

Tattwa Shuddhi /Tattva Shuddhi/ 'purification of elements', the tantric science of inner purification. तत्त्व शुद्धि

Tattwatita /Tattva-ateeta/ beyond the elements. तत्त्वातीत

Tattwavit /Tattva-vit/ knower of the essence of things; sage or knower of Brahman (brahmajnani). तत्त्ववित्

Tattwika /Taattvika/ true; real; from the highest standpoint. तात्त्विक

Tejas 'golden light or flame'; luminosity; edge or tip of a flame; fire, heat; light, brilliance, splendour; might, majesty; fire as an element or mahabhuta; the light state of matter according to the Sankhya Yoga classification; see Taijasa. तेजस्

Tejomaya full of light; resplendent. तेजोमय

Tha, Ksha the second syllable of the word 'hatha', the first syllable 'ha' stands for the sun, the second syllable 'tha' stands for the moon, and the union of these two forces is hatha yoga; protection, preservation; terror, fear; auspiciousness; tha is a changed form (apabhramsha) of ksha. ठ, क्ष

Tikshna /Teekshna/ sharp (in all senses); pungent; hot, warm (as rays); fiery, passionate; hard, forcible, strong; intelligent, clever. तीक्ष्ण

Tilaka a species of tree with beautiful flowers; auspicious mark on the forehead made with sandal paste or vermilion kumkum. तिलक

Tiras disappearing. तिरस्

Tiraskara, Tiraskrita /Tiraskaara, Tiraskrita/ concealment, disappearance; abuse, censure, reproach; contempt, disdain. तिरस्कार, तिरस्कृत

Tiraskarini /Tiraskarinee/ curtain, veil; an outer tent, screen of cloth; science of disappearing. तिरस्करिणी

Tirobhava /Tiro-bhaava/ veiling. तिरोभाव

Tirodhana /Tiro-dhaana/ disappearance, removal; a covering, veil, sheath. तिरोधान

Tirtha /Teertha/ passage, road, way; fort; descent into a river, the stairs of a landing place (ghat); place of water; holy or sacred place, place of pilgrimage, a shrine dedicated to a holy object (especially on or near the bank of a sacred river), a sacred or holy personage, or object of veneration; name of one of the 10 orders of sannyasins founded by Adi Shankaracharya; see Dashnami Sampradaya. तीर्थ

Tirthasthana /Teertha-sthaana/ a holy place of India; a pilgrimage centre. तीर्थस्थान

Tirthagrahana /Teertha-grahana/ service or rite at the end of worship where the worshipper applies consecrated water to his head. तीर्थग्रहण

Tishthati to stand, stay, remain, continue to last; to be, to exist, to be present. तिष्ठति

Titha fire; love; time; the rainy season or autumn. तिथ

Tithi a lunar day; the number 15. तिथि

Tithikshaya the day of the new moon; the time at which a tithi ends (and therefore another begins); literally 'destruction of a tithi', referring to the absence of a tithi (i.e. its not being counted) when three lunar days fall between two sunrises. तिथिक्षय

Titiksha /Titikshaa/ endurance, bearing heat and cold and other pairs of opposites without complaint; one of the sixfold virtues; see Shadsampatti. तितिक्षा

Tivra /Teevra/ sharp, strong, violent, horrible. तीव्र

    Tivravairagya /Teevra-vairaagya/ intense dispassion. तीव्रवैराग्य

Torana an arched doorway, a portal; an outer door or gateway; any temporary and ornamental arch; the neck, throat. तोरण

Trataka /Traataka/ to gaze steadily; a concentration practice of gazing with unblinking eyes at one point to focus the mind; an important yogic practice for developing concentration and extrasensory perception, which consists of gazing at any external object with open eyes or at an internal object with the inner (third) eye for a relatively long period; a cleansing practice of hatha yoga; see Shatkarma; see Bhrumadhya Dristhi. त्राटक

Trayate /Traayate/ frees, liberates; to protect, rescue or save from. त्रायते

Tri three. त्रि

Traipada with three parts; the mantra Aum. त्रैपद

Traita one supreme reality manifesting as three. त्रैत

    Traitabhava /Traita-bhaava/ threefold awareness (of subject, object and process of practice). त्रैतभाव

Trayamekatra Samyama the last three internal stages of yoga practice, viz. concentration (dharana), meditation (dhyana) and samadhi, which taken together form samyama; alternating between dharana, dhyana and samadhi constitutes samyama. त्रयमेकत्र संयम

Trayi /Trayee/ the three Vedas taken collectively (the *Rigveda*, *Sama Veda* and *Yajurveda* are the three original, ancient and most revered vedas, with the *Atharva Veda* being a relatively later addition); a triad; a triplet; intellect, understanding; see Trivedi. त्रयी

Treta Yuga /Tretaa Yuga/ the second of the four aeons of the world, lasting for 1,296,000 years according to *Suryasiddhanta*; an aeon where goodness is on the increase leading up to Satya yuga; see Yuga. त्रेता युग

Trichakshus three eyes; epithet of Shiva, Lord of yoga. त्रिचक्षुस्

Tridandin a religious mendicant or sannyasin who has renounced all worldly attachments and who carries three long staffs tied together so as to form one in the right hand; one who has obtained command over mind, speech and body (or thought, word and deed). त्रिदण्डिन्

Triguna consisting of threads; three times repeated, threefold, triple; the three constituent qualities (gunas) of nature (prakriti) and all matter, namely sattwa, rajas and tamas; see Guna. त्रिगुण

Triguna Maya /Triguna Maaya/ the deluding force behind the expression of the gunas. त्रिगुण माया

Trigunamayi /Triguna-mayee/ a (connotative) name of the goddess as the divine mother suggesting that she possesses the three gunas. त्रिगुणमयी

Trigunatita /Triguna-ateeta/ beyond the three gunas; see Gunatita. त्रिगुणातीत

Trigunatmika /Triguna-aatmika/ characterized by the three qualities (gunas) sattwa, rajas and tamas; of cosmic energy or the divine power. त्रिगुणात्मिक

Trijagat the three worlds: the heaven, the atmosphere and the earth, or the heaven, the earth, and the lower world. त्रिजगत्

Trika triad; place where roads meet; lower part of the spine around the hips; the part of the spine between the shoulder blades; triple, threefold; three percent; another name for Kashmir Shaivism, a school of tantra which deals with the threefold principles. The literature of the system is called Trikashastra; system or philosophy of the triad: 1. Shiva, 2. Shakti, 3. the bound soul (nara), or 1. the highest, non-different from Shiva (para), 2. the intermediate state of identity in difference (parapara), 3. the state of difference (apara); see Kashmir Shaivmata; see Tantraloka. त्रिक

Trikala /Trikaala/ the three times, i.e. past, present and future, or morning, noon and evening; the three tenses (past, present and future) of a verb. त्रिकाल

Trikaladarshi /Trikaala-darshee/ seer of the three time periods; by the knowledge acquired through yoga, the yogi sees everything in the past, present and future. त्रिकालदर्शी

Trikona triangular, forming a triangle; a breathing practice where awareness of the breath in the nostrils leads to perception of prana, focusing at the eyebrow centre like two sides of a triangle; the vulva. त्रिकोण

Trikuti /Trikutee/ eyebrow centre; the space between the two eyebrows; meeting place of the three psychic channels of ida, pingala and sushumna. त्रिकुटी

Trimurti /Trimoorti/ the united form of Brahma, Vishnu and Shiva, representing the trinity of the concepts of creation, preservation and destruction. त्रिमूर्ति

Trimurti Dhyana /Trimoorti Dhyaana/ meditation on the three aspects of personality: sattwa, rajas and tamas. त्रिमूर्ति ध्यान

Triphala /Tri-phalaa/ an ayurvedic medicine combining three ingredients to balance the three doshas. त्रिफल

Tripitaka the collective name for the three groups of Buddhist scriptures. त्रिपिटिक

Tripura collection of three cities; the three cities of gold, silver and iron in the sky, air and earth built for demons by Maya; name of a demon or demons presiding over these cities. त्रिपुर

Tripura Rahasyam secrets of the three lokas or Tripura Sundari. त्रिपुर रहस्यम्

Tripura Sundari /Tripura Sundaree/ highest truth; the devi of the Shri Yantra; the divine mother. त्रिपुर सुन्दरी

Triputi the triple manifestation of the supreme unity of the one in time: as subject, object and the relation between the two, or as knower, knowledge and knowing, or seer, sight and seen. त्रिपुटि

Trishira Bhairava Tantra /Trishiraa Bhairava Tantra/ tri means 'three' and shira means 'that which carries'; text dealing with the three flows of energy known as ida, pingala and sushumna. त्रिशिरा भैरव तंत्र

Trishiropanishad Upanishad dealing with the three flows of energy known as ida, pingala and sushumna. त्रिशिरोपनिषद्

Trishula /Trishoola/ trident (often used as a symbol of the gunas or some other triad). त्रिशूल

Trishulin /Trishoolin/ one who holds the trident; epithet of Shiva. त्रिशूलिन्

Trivarga three objects of human pursuit: wealth (artha), pleasure (kama) and virtue (dharma); see Purushartha. त्रिवर्ग

Trivarnaka the first three of the four castes of Hindus taken collectively, viz. priestly (brahmana), warrior or ruling (kshatriya) and merchant (vaishya); see Varna. त्रिवर्णक

Trivedi /Trivedee/ a brahmana (person of the priestly caste) versed in the three Vedas; see Trayi. त्रिवेदी

Triveni /Trivenee/ the place near Prayaga (modern Allahabad) where the Ganges river joins the Yamuna and receives the underground Saraswati (often used as a symbol of the confluence of ida, pingala and sushumna nadis at the ajna chakra); see Atmic Triveni. त्रिवेणी

Trivikrama Vishnu in his fifth incarnation as the dwarf (Vamana), who with his three steps (krama) covered the earth, heaven and hell; see Bali; see Avatara. त्रिविक्रम

Trivritkarna triplication; intermixture of three visible elements: fire, water and earth, for the formation of bodies. त्रिवृत्कर्ण

Triyanuka, Trayanuka /Triya-anuka, Traya-anuka/ combination of three atoms; in Vaisheshika philosophy, a ternary or a form consisting of three variables associated in such a manner that they combine to form an integral whole operating and functioning as a single system. To produce this form, three lines must remain apart and relate themselves on different planes so as not to form a more extended line. In this manner, they produce an independent unit operating as a separate system with its own sphere of influence. Apart from the individual point (anu) from which it is made, this combination of lines gives thickness to the former unit having only length and breath, and thus produces all visible forms known to us in the objective world; see Vaisheshika. त्रियणुक, त्रयणुक

Tryakshara the mystic syllable Aum consisting of three letters; see Akshara. त्र्यक्षर

Trijata /Trijataa/ name of a female demon, one of the attendants kept by Ravana to watch over Sita during her captivity in the ashoka garden (ashoka vatika) in Lanka. She treated Sita very kindly and convinced her companions to do the same. त्रिजटा

Tripti satisfaction, contentment; satiety; pleasure, gratification; disgust. तृप्ति

Trishna /Trishnaa/ thirst; desire, strong desire, greed, avidity, desire for gain; craving for sense objects; internal craving; attachment. तृष्णा

Trishnakshayah /Trishnaa-kshayah/ cessation of desire, tranquillity of mind, contentment. तृष्णाक्षय:

Trishta thirsty; arid; rough, harsh. तृष्ट

Tulsi /Tulasee/ the holy basil plant of India, sacred to Lord Vishnu and venerated by the Vaishnavas as most divine, she is symboli-

cally married to Shalagrama (a symbol of Lord Vishnu); a herb with many healing capacities; the wood is considered to be very pure and is made into rosary beads (mala) used for mantra japa. तुलसी

Tulsidas /Tulaseedaas/ the author of one of the versions of the famous epic called the *Ramacharitamanasa*, which describes the life of Lord Rama. It is composed in poetic form and is chanted by devotees throughout India. तुलसीदास

Tulyabhava /Tulya-bhaava/ equality, equality of rights. तुल्यभाव

Turiya /Tureeya/ fourth dimension of consciousness, witnessed by atma according to *Mandukya Upanishad*; superconsciousness; simultaneous awareness of the conscious, subconscious and unconscious mind which links and transcends them; a quarter, a fourth part, fourth; in Vedanta, the seventh of the seven stages of wisdom (jnana bhumika), the final superconscious state of existence, a state of complete absorption of the mind in Brahman in which the individual self or soul becomes one with the universal spirit; a state of nirvana, or liberation; see Brahmavidvarishtha;

see Jivanmukta. तुरीय

Turiyatita /Tureeya-ateeta/ 'beyond the fetters of nature'; the fifth stage of sannyasa; see Sannyasa. तुरीयातीत

Turiyavastha /Tureeya-avasthaa/ the fourth state of existence, combining yet transcending the other three states of waking, dreaming and sleeping, and related to the full understanding or reverberation of the mantra Aum according to *Mandukya Upanishad*; the state of samadhi; see Atma; see Avasthatraya. तुरीयावस्था

Tushnim /Tooshneem/ silent; performance of a yajna (sacrifice) without mantra. तूष्णीम्

Tushnimbhutavastha /Tooshneem-bhoota-avasthaa/ a state of mind in which there is neither attraction nor repulsion; the state of being silent. तूष्णीम्भूतावस्था

Tushta pleased, satisfied, delighted, gratified, contented; state of mind contented with what one possesses and indifferent to anything else. तुष्ट

Tushti satisfaction, gratification, pleasure, contentment; a quality of Devi; in Sankhya: acquiescence, indifference to everything except that which is possessed. तुष्टि

Tushyati to become calm, be satisfied or contented. तुष्यति

Twacha /Tvachaa/ skin; the power to feel, one of the five abstract knowing senses (jnanendriyas); a cow's hide; see Jnanendriya; see Devata. त्वचा

Twak /Tvak/ skin. त्वक्

Twashtaa /Tvashtaa/ carpenter; creator; name of the artisan of the gods. त्वष्टा

Tyaga /Tyaaga/ renunciation or gradual dissociation of the mind from worldly objects and from the seed of desire; leaving, forsaking, abandoning, deserting, separation; giving up, resigning, renouncing; gift, donation, giving away as charity; liberality, generosity. त्याग

Tyagabhimana /Tyaaga-abhimaana/ pride of renunciation. त्यागाभिमान

Tyagadshantiranantaram /Tyaagaadshantiranantaram/ (Tyaagaat-shantih-anantaram); "renunciation of desire leads to endless peace", a famous quotation from the *Bhagavad Gita*. त्यागादशान्तिरनन्तरम्

Tyagi, Tyagin /Tyaagee, Tyaagin/ one who has renounced; leaving, abandoning, giving up; heroic, brave; one who does not look to any reward or result from the performance of ceremonial rites. त्यागी, त्यागिन्

Tyakta abandoned, forsaken, left, quitted; resigned, surrendered; shunned, avoided. त्यक्त

Tyakta Jivita /Tyakta Jeevita/ ready to abandon life; willing to run any risk. त्यक्त जीवित

Tyat /Tyata/ another name for prana; indirect knowledge of Brahman; see Prana. त्यत

U

Pronunciation

उ *u* – *as in* pull

Ubha both. उभ

Ubhaya both, of both kinds, in both manners. उभय

Ubhaya Bharati /Ubhaya Bharatee/ she was entitled Ubhaya because she had mastered both kinds of wisdom and was respected as an incarnation of the goddess of knowledge, Saraswati. When her husband, Mandana Mishra, was defeated in debate by Adi Shankaracharya, she insisted on her qualifications to challenge him herself. By asking questions concerning sexual relations, she forced the celibate teacher to plead for a break in the debate, during which time he occupied the body of a king and experienced sexual love in the harem. Although some say he broke the vows of sannyasa (thus disqualifying himself), his own body was not involved in his new acquisition of knowledge. It remains a moot point, but it is generally said he won the debate and that he installed Ubhaya Bharati as head of Kanchi Matha, which is still free from general prejudice against women; see Shankaracharya; see Bharati; see Matha. उभय भारती

Uchcha high (in all senses); tall, elevated; high-sounding; loud; intense; strong; violent. उच्च

Uchchakshus with the eyes directed upwards, looking upwards; with the eyes taken out, blind. उच्चक्षुस्

Uchchalam mind. उच्चलम्

Uchchalita on the point of going, setting out. उच्चलित

Uchcharanam /Uchchaaranam/ pronunciation, utterance; declaration, enumeration. उच्चारणम्

Uchchvasa /Uchchhvaasa/ outgoing breath, breathing out, exhalation. उच्छ्वास

Udaharana /Udaaharana/ saying, reciting; instance, example. उदाहरण

Udana Chaitanya /Udaana Chaitanya/ awareness of udana vayu. उदान चैतन्य

Udana Vayu /Udaana Vaayu/ one of the five pranas (energies) or vayus, which is located in the extremities of the body: arms, legs and head. It rises up the throat and enters into the head; breathing upwards; breathing, breath in general; see Vayu; see Pancha Prana. उदान वायु

Udara /Udaara/ exalted; generous; excellent; splendid; fully operational, one of the four possible states of the kleshas according to

Patanjali in the *Yoga Sutras*; see Klesha. उदार

Udarata /Udaarataa/ magnanimity; generosity; expansion. उदारता

Udaravastha /Udaara-avasthaa/ expanded state. उदारावस्था

Udaravritti /Udaara-vritti/ generous nature; expanded state of the psyche. उदारवृत्ति

Udara the belly. उदर

Udasina /Udaaseena/ indifferent, unconcerned, passive; (in law) not involved in any dispute; neutral. उदासीन

Udasin, Udasi /Udaasin, Udaasee/ a stoic, a philosopher; a witness; an indifferent or apathetic person. उदासिन्, उदासी

Udasinata /Udaaseenataa/ state of being indifferent. उदासीनता

Udatta /Udaatta/ the highest of the three tones used for chanting vedic mantras aloud (the other two are anudatta and swarita). उदात्त

Udbhuta /Udbhoota/ anything that can be comprehended by the senses; born (out of the elements). उद्भूत

Udbhijja /Udbheejja/ born from a seed; a plant. उद्भिज्ज

Udbodhaka stimulus, awakener. उद्बोधक

Uddalaka /Uddaalaka/ a great rishi of yore; the father of Nachiketa; see Nachiketa. उद्दालक

Uddayana raise up, fly up. उड्डयन

Uddiyana Bandha /Uddiyaana Bandha/ abdominal retraction lock whilst concentrating at manipura chakra. Drawing in the abdomen and stomach towards the backbone causes the diaphragm

to rise into the chest, manipura chakra is stimulated and Vishnu granthi is addressed. This helps direct prana to rise or fly up in sushumna; see Bandha; see Granthi. उड्डियान बन्ध

Uddesha a spot, place; specification; a brief statement or account; motive. उद्देश

Uddharana lifting up; taking out; tearing out; deliverance (from danger); destruction. उद्धरण

Uddharsha excessive joy, delight. उद्धर्ष

Uddhava devotee of Lord Krishna. He was a childhood friend of Lord Krishna and a philosopher who later learned bhakti from the gopis. उद्धव

Udgatri /Udgaatri/ the priest who recites the *Sama Veda*. उद्गातृ

Udgitha /Udgeetha/ chanting of the hymns of the *Sama Veda*; sonorous prayer prescribed in the *Sama Veda* to be sung aloud; the mantra Aum. उद्गीथ

Udghata /Udghaata/ awakening of the kundalini shakti that is lying dormant in mooladhara chakra. उद्घात

Udyanam /Udyaanam/ going out, strolling; a garden, a park. उद्यानम्

Udyoga effort, exertion, industry; work, duty, office; persevering, industrious. उद्योग

Ugra fierce, violent, ferocious, savage, cruel; terrific, frightful, fearful; formidable, powerful, strong; intense; sharp; hot. उग्र

Ujjayi Pranayama /Ujjaayee Praanaayaama/ ujjayi literally means 'victorious', but this pranayama is often referred to as 'psychic breathing' because it is so successful in internalizing the awareness and inducing meditative states. It is performed by concentrating at vishuddhi chakra while physically contracting the epiglottis and producing a light sonorous sound. उज्जायी प्राणायाम

Ukta said, spoken, uttered, told, addressed; described, related. उक्त

Uktam a speech; words that have been spoken; a sentence. उक्तम्

Ukti speech, expression, statement; sentence; power of expression, the expressive power of a word. उक्ति

Ullola violently moving; excessive, tremendous; a large wave or surge. उल्लोल

Uma /Umaa/ another name of Parvati, the consort of Shiva, born as the daughter of Himavanta and Maina; light, splendour; fame, reputation; tranquillity, calmness; night. उमा

Umapati /Umaa-pati/ literally 'Uma's husband'; a name of Shiva. उमापति

Umasuta /Umaa-suta/ literally 'Uma's son'; a name of Kartikeya and Ganesha. उमासुत

Unmada /Unmaada/ madness, insanity, intense passion. उन्माद

Unmadana /Unmaadana/ intoxication. उन्मादन

Unmanas excited or disturbed in mind, agitated; regretting, repining for a lost or departed friend; anxious, eager, impatient. उन्मनस्

Unmani /Unmanee/ literally 'no mind'; centre beyond mind and thought where the mind is turned completely inwards. उन्मनी

Unmani Avastha /Unmanee Avasthaa/ the state beyond mind. उन्मनी अवस्था

Unmani Mudra /Unmanee Mudràa/ psychic attitude in which the eyes are open, gazing outwards, but the awareness is fixed within; also known as bhairavi mudra; see Mudra. उन्मनी मुद्रा

Unmesha coming forth, becoming visible, appearing, unfoldment; another term for the manifestation of the universe (srishti); expansion; opening the eyes, blinking. उन्मेष

Unmukhi /Unmukhee/ the state in which prakriti is ready to create. उन्मुखी

Upachara /Upachaara/ materials or services offered in worship; medical treatment; see Shodashopachara. उपचार

Upadana /Upaadaana/ taking, receiving, obtaining; mentioning, enumerating; including, containing; withdrawing the organs of sense and perception from the external world and its objects; a cause, motive, natural or immediate cause; material. उपादान

Upadana Karana /Upaadaana Kaarana/ material cause, like the clay for making the pot; see Brahman. उपादान कारण

Upadesha instruction, teaching; advice, prescription, specification, mention; initiation, communication of an initiatory mantra or formula. उपदेश

Upadesha Vakya /Upadesha Vaakya/ instructive statement, i.e. 'Tat Twam Asi', one of the four maha vakyas (great statements) of the Upanishads; see Tat Twam Asi; see Maha Vakya. उपदेश वाक्य

Upadhi /Upaadhi/ superimposed thing or attribute that veils and gives a coloured view of the substance beneath it; limiting adjunct; instrument, vehicle, body; a technical term used in the philosophy of Vedanta for any superimposition that gives a limited view of the absolute and makes it appear as relative, e.g. a jiva's upadhi is avidya; Ishwara's upadhi is maya; a word which denotes respect. उपाधि

Upadhidharma /Upaadhi-dharma/ characteristic of the limiting adjunct. उपाधिधर्म

Upadhita Chaitanya /Upaadhita Chaitanya/ individual soul; intelligence associated with upadhi. उपाधित चैतन्य

Upadhi fraud, dishonesty, false inducement; (in law) suppression of the truth, a false suggestion; terror, threat, compulsion; obstruction. उपधि

Upadrashta /Upa-drashtaa/ supervisor. उपद्रष्टा

Upahara /Upahaara/ oblation, gift. उपहार

Upaharana /Upaaharana/ bringing near; fetching; taking, seizing. उपाहरण

Upajata /Upajaata/ born, arisen; see Jati. उपजात

Upakara /Upakaara/ service, help, assistance, favour, obligation; preparation; ornament, decoration. उपकार

Upakrama Upasamhara Ekovakyata /Upakrama Upasamhaara Ekovaakyataa/ the unity of thought in the beginning as well as in the end. उपक्रम उपसंहार एकोवाक्यता

Upala rock, stone. उपल

Upalabdhi perception; knowledge; attainment. उपलब्धि

Upalabdhri the perceiving or knowing subject. उपलब्ध्रृ

Upalakshana a mark or distinctive feature; looking; using a term elliptically. उपलक्षण

Upama /Upamaa/ resemblance, similarity; equality; comparison of two objects different from each other; simile; the standard of comparison. उपमा

Upamana /Upamaana/ comparison; a means of correct knowledge defined as knowledge of a thing derived from its similarity to another previously well known thing; simile. उपमान

Upanayanam literally 'to lead near (to the spiritual teacher)'; the sacred thread ritual, investiture with a sacred thread to initiate participants into sacred learning, one of the samskaras in the vedic tradition; see Sandhya; see Upavita; see Samskara. उपनयनम्

Upanishad literally 'to sit near and listen (to the spiritual teacher)'; derived from the prefixes 'upa', meaning near, and 'ni', meaning down, added to the root 'shad', meaning to sit, thus it means sitting down near a guru to receive spiritual instruction; ancient vedic text containing intimate dialogues and discussions between guru and disciple on the nature of the absolute and the path leading towards it; vedantic texts conveyed by ancient sages and seers containing their experiences and teachings on the ultimate reality; the Upanishads are the philosophical portion of the Vedas, the most ancient and sacred literature of the Hindus, dealing with the nature of human beings and the universe. The Upanishads are regarded as the source of the Vedanta, Yoga and Sankhya philosophies; see Advaita Vedanta. उपनिषद्

Upanshu /Upaanshu/ whispered sound; one of the stages of mantra japa; also called madhyama; see Nada Yoga. उपांशु

Upanshujapa /Upaanshu-japa/ japa done with a whispered or light humming sound, semi-verbal repetition of a mantra. उपांशुजप

Upaprana /Upa-praana/ five minor pranas, viz. krikara (or krikala), devadatta, dhananjaya, naga and kurma responsible for such actions as sneezing, yawning, decomposition, belching and blinking respectively. उपप्राण

Upa Purana /Upa Puraana/ group of 18 secondary Puranas that were later additions to the puranic literature; see Puranam. उप पुराण

Uparama withdrawal from sensual experiences; indifference; also called uparati; one of the sixfold virtues; see Shadsampatti. उपरम

Uparamata /Uparamataa/ calmness of mind; cessation of action. उपरमता

Uparati desisting from worldliness; ceasing, stopping; death; abstaining from sexual enjoyment; indifference; also called uparama; one of the sixfold virtues; see Shadsampatti. उपरति

Upasana /Upaasanaa/ personalized form of worship; sitting near, worshipping or contemplating on God or a deity; devout meditation; see Panchaupasana. उपासना

Upasaka /Upaasaka/ one who does worship; see Panchaupasaka. उपासक

Upasana Kanda /Upaasanaa Kaanda/ ritual of worship. उपासना काण्ड

Upasana Vakya /Upaasanaa Vaakya/ a sentence for meditation. उपासना वाक्य

Upastha genital organ; see Karmendriya; see Devata. उपस्थ

Upasthana /Upa-sthaana/ being close to. उपस्थान

Upasya /Upaasya/ that which is the object of upasana, namely God. उपास्य

Upavana a grove of trees, a small wood. उपवन

Upavasa /Upavaasa/ a fasting day; to reside in close proximity to the self. उपवास

Upaveda class of writings subordinate to the Vedas. There are four Upavedas, one attached to each Veda: *Ayurveda* belongs to *Rig-veda*, *Dhanurveda* to *Yajurveda*, *Gandharva Veda* to *Sama Veda* and *Sthapatya Shastra Veda* to *Atharva Veda*. उपवेद

Upavishta seated, sitting. उपविष्ट

Upavita /Upaveeta/ cloth or thread given to an initiate during up-anayanam. उपवीत

Upaya /Upaaya/ approach, means, plan, stratagem, an expedient remedy; beginning, commencement; effort, exertion; means of success against an enemy; there are four main upaya sadhanas in tantra, viz. anavopaya, shakto-paya, shambhavopaya, anupaya (although anupaya requires no means or effort). उपाय

Upaya Pratyaya /Upaaya Pratyaya/ the mastery of the individual mind by universal consciousness obtained through the highest practice of asamprajnata samadhi. उपाय प्रत्यय

Upeksha /Upekshaa/ overlooking, disregard, neglect; indifference; contempt, disdain; a self-examination to find out how one would have behaved in difficult circumstances, and how far one is responsible for the state of others and for keeping them on the right path. उपेक्षा

Urdhva /Oordhva/ erect, upright; rising or tending upwards; raised, elevated, above; high, superior, upper. ऊर्ध्व

Urdhvaretas /Oordhvaretas/ yogi whose seminal energy has been converted and turned upwards into spiritual energy. ऊर्ध्वरेतस्

Urmi /Oormi/ a wave; an evil; reference is often made to six evils, viz. 1. hunger (ashanaya), 2. thirst (pipasa), 3. old age (jara), 4. death (mara), 5. grief (shoka), 6. delusion or loss of consciousness (moha); see Shadurmi. ऊर्मि

Urvi /Urvee/ Earth; literally 'the wide one'. उर्वी

Usha /Ushaa/ dawn, daybreak, morning light; morning light personified as the goddess of dawn; wife of the grandson of Krishna, Anirudha. उषा

Usha Pan /Ushaa Paana/ drinking water through the nose, a traditional form of cold water neti; drinking water in the morning as soon as one gets up after cleaning the teeth, a hatha yogic treatment against constipation. उषा पान

Ushtra camel; buffalo; bull with a hump. उष्ट्र

Uta a particle expressing doubt, uncertainty or guesswork; association, connection; alternative; interrogation. उत

Utkantha literally 'having the neck uplifted', hence being prepared, ready, on the point of doing anything. उत्कण्ठ

Utkata large, spacious; powerful, mighty; abounding in, richly endowed with; drunk, mad, furious, fierce. उत्कट

Utpatti origin, creation. उत्पत्ति

Utpattinasha /Utpatti-naasha/ beginning and end, or creation and destruction. उत्पत्तिनाश

Utsaha /Utsaaha/ effort, exertion; energy; inclination, desire; perseverance; one of the three shaktis or powers of a ruler (the other two being mantra and prabhava); power, ability; firmness, fortitude, strength. उत्साह

Utsava festival, holiday; joy, pleasure. उत्सव

Uttama highest, best; principal; excellent. उत्तम

Uttama Kotyadhikari /Uttama Kotyaadhikaaree/ (Uttama Kotiadhikaaree); highest category of student; qualified person of the first degree. उत्तम कोट्याधिकारी

Uttama Rahasya highest secret. उत्तम रहस्य

Uttana /Uttaana/ stretched out, expanded, dilated; lying on the back with the face upwards; open, unreserved, candid, frankminded. उत्तान

Uttara future time, futurity; name of Vishnu; name of Shiva; name of a son of Virata; being or produced in the north, northern; upper, higher; left; superior, chief, excellent; later, latter, following; an answer, reply; (in law) defence, rejoinder; the last part

or following member of a compound; conclusion. उत्तर

Uttara /Uttaraa/ the north; a lunar mansion; name of the daughter of Virata and wife of Abhimanyu; see Abhimanyu. उत्तरा

Uttara Mimamsa /Uttara Meemaamsaa/ one of the six principal systems of Indian philosophy (darshanas), also called Vedanta; see Vedanta; see Mimamsa. उत्तर मीमांसा

Uttarayana /Uttaraayana/ summer solstice; 'northern path' of the sun which takes six months of the solar year. Departing then, people who know Brahman go to Brahman (and are freed from the cycle of life and death); one of the two prescribed paths of meditation; path of light; see Dakshinayana. उत्तरायण

Utthana /Utthaana/ the act of rising, standing or getting up; rising (as of luminaries); origin; effort, exertion, activity; joy, pleasure. उत्थान

Uvacha /Uvaacha/ to speak. उवाच

V

Pronunciation
व् v – as in svelte

Vach, Vak /Vaach, Vaak/ word, sound; talk, language, speech, voice; assertion, statement; phrase, proverb, expression, saying; name of Saraswati, the goddess of speech. वाच्, वाक्

Vachaka /Vaachaka/ speaking, declaring, explaining; expressing, signifying, denoting directly; verbal. वाचक

Vacharambhana /Vaachaarambhana/ ornament of speech; existing in speech only; not real; not the essence, e.g. with a mud-pot, the mud is the truth and the pot is only an ornate expression, or with golden jewellery, the gold is the reality and the ornament is only an expression. वाचारम्भण

Vahni fire; see Devata. वह्नि

Vahnisar Kriya /Vahnisaar Kriyaa/ practice which stimulates the digestive fire responsible for the assimilation of food; see Agnisara Kriya. वह्निसार क्रिया

Vaigunya absence of qualities or attributes; absence of good qualities; difference of properties, diversity, contrariety; inferiority, lowness; defect, fault, imperfection. वैगुण्य

Vaikarika /Vaikaarika/ relating to modification, modifying, modified. वैकारिक

Vaikriti modification. वैकृति

Vaikhari /Vaikharee/ audible speech or sound; one of the stages of nada yoga; one of the ways of practising mantra japa; that sound which is produced by the striking or friction of two things, e.g. speech or music produced by playing instruments; see Nada Yoga. वैखरी

Vaikhari Japa /Vaikharee Japa/ articulate or loud repetition of a mantra. वैखरी जप

Vaikuntha epithet of Vishnu; epithet of Indra; heaven. वैकुण्ठ

Vaira Bhava /Vaira Bhaava/ having the feeling of enmity towards the Lord. वैर भाव

Vairagi /Vairaagee/ sannyasins of the Vaishnava Ramanuja Sampradaya; those not attached to the sensory material world; sect of renunciates who have transcended matter; see Ramanuja. वैरागी

Vairagika /Vairaagika/ an ascetic who has subdued all the passions and desires. वैरागिक

Vairagya /Vairaagya/ non-attachment, dispassion, detachment from the world and its cause; it is spoken of as lower (apara), when it denotes detachment from the objects of pleasure, and higher (para), when referring to a cleansing detachment from the gunas or nature (prakriti) due to the attraction to purusha; see Sadhana Chatushtaya; see Para Vairagya; see Adhimatra Vairagya. वैराग्य

Vairagya Sannyasa /Vairaagya Sannyaasa/ one of the stages of sannyasa, where one is detached and indifferent to worldly pleasure from an early age; see Sannyasa Ashrama. वैराग्य संन्यास

Vaishakha /Vaishaakha/ churning stick; second lunar month according to the Hindu almanac, corresponding to April/May; see Vasanta; see Masa; see Ritu. वैशाख

Vaishamyavastha /Vaishamya-avasthaa/ the state wherein the equilibrium of the three gunas of prakriti is disturbed, leading to creation or manifestation; a state opposite to the state of equilibrium of the three gunas; see Samyavastha; see Vikritti; see Prakriti. वैशम्यावस्था

Vaisheshika /Vaisheshikaa/ a treatise by the sage Kanada on the subtle, causal and atomic principles in relation to the five elements; one of the six principal systems of Indian philosophy (darshanas); see Shaddarshana; see Samavaya; see Triyanuka. वैशेषिका

Vaishishtyam distinction, difference; peculiarity, speciality, particularity; excellence; possessing or endowed with some characteristic attribute. वैशिष्ट्यम्

Vaishnava those who worship Vishnu in the form of Rama, Krishna, Narayana etc.; the sect that reveres incarnations of Vishnu as the supreme reality, and who worship God in his supreme form; see Panchaupasana; see Panchaupasaka. वैष्णव

Vaishnavashastra /Vaishnavashaastra/ the scriptures concerned with Vishnu. वैष्णवशास्त्र

Vaishnavi /Vaishnavee/ the shakti or the divine power of Vishnu. वैष्णवी

Vaishvanara /Vaishvaanara/ the seer who observes the manifest universe or the external, waking consciousness (jagrat), the first state of consciousness discussed in *Mandukya Upanishad* as relating to the 'A' of Aum; a name according to Vedanta philosophy for an individual in the gross (waking) state, where reality appears through the veil of an individual gross body; epithet of fire, fire of digestion (in the stomach), the god of fire; general consciousness (in Vedanta philosophy); the sum total of created beings; Brahman in the form of the universe (Viratpurusha); the supreme being; see Jagrita. वैश्वानर

Vaishvanara Vidya /Vaishvaanara Vidyaa/ the process of meditation on Brahma, taking the digestive fire as the symbol; method of meditation on the manifest universe (virat) as a form of the divine. वैश्वानर विद्या

Vaishvasika /Vaishvaasika/ trusty, confidential. वैश्वासिक

Vaishya one of the four divisions of the caste system (varnas) in India, those who specialize in trade or undertake the responsibility of caring for society; see Varna. वैश्य

Vaiyaktika personality. वैयक्तिक

Vaiyaktika Sarvamedha total surrender of one's personality. वैयक्तिक सर्वमेध

Vajasaneyin /Vaajasaneyin/ name of sage Yajnavalkya, author and founder of the white (shukla) *Yajurveda*; follower of the *Shukla Yajurveda*; one belonging to the sect of the Vajasaneyins. वाजसनेयिन्

Vajra thunderbolt, Indra's weapon; diamond. वज्र

Vajra Nadi /Vajra Naadee/ subtle energy current which connects the flow of sexual energy with the brain and is concerned with the flow of ojas; the least subtle of the three major energy flows within sushumna nadi. वज्र नाडी

Vajroli Mudra /Vajrolee Mudraa/ contraction and release of the urinary passage to stimulate swadhisthana chakra and promote brahmacharya; controlling the emissions during sexual intercourse according to *Hatha Yoga Pradipika*; this mudra vitalizes the mind and the body, generating a lot of energy; see Sahajoli Mudra; see Mudra. वज्रोली मुद्रा

Vakra crooked, bent, curled; roundabout, indirect; dishonest; retrograde (as regards motion). वक्र

Vaktra mouth; face; point (of an arrow); spout of a vessel; name of a poetic metre. वक्त्र

Vali see Bali. वालि

Valmika /Valmeeka/ a heap of clay made by white ants (termites). वल्मीक

Valmiki /Vaalmeeki/ name of a celebrated sage who meditated for so long he became interred in a termite mound. He was also the author of the first *Ramayana*. वाल्मीकि

Vam bija mantra of the water element and therefore of swadhisthana chakra; see Varunabija; see Mahabhuta. वं (वम्)

Vama /Vaama/ left side; being or situated on the left side; reverse, contrary, opposite, adverse; lovely, beautiful, charming. वाम

Vamachara, Vamamarga /Vaamaachaara, Vaamamaarga/ the left hand ritual of the tantras. वामाचार, वाममार्ग

Vamana /Vaamana/ dwarf; pigmy; name of Lord Vishnu in his fifth incarnation when he was born as a dwarf to humble the demon Bali; name of the elephant that presides over the south; name of the author of the *Kashikavritti*, a commentary on Panini's *Ashtadhyayi* (sutras on Sanskrit grammar); see Avatara; see Bali; see Trivikrama. वामन

Vamana ejecting; vomiting; drawing out; taking or getting out. वमन

Vamana Dhauti a form of dhauti, one of the six cleansing techniques of hatha yoga, in which the stomach is cleaned by voluntary vomiting, includes kunjal kriya and vyaghra kriya; see Shatkarma. वमन धौति

Vanam forest; name of one of the 10 orders of sannyasins founded by Adi Shankaracharya, whose members originally came from forest regions; see Dashnami Sampradaya. वनम्

Vanaprastha /Vaanaprastha/ forester; one who retires to the forest. वानप्रस्थ

Vanaprastha Ashrama /Vaanaprastha Aashrama/ third stage of life, traditionally from 50 to 75 years of age, where one retires from worldly life in order to practise sadhana in relative seclusion; see Ashrama. वानप्रस्थ आश्रम

Vani /Vaanee/ speech. वाणी

Varaha /Varaaha/ third incarnation of Lord Vishnu when he came as a boar to rescue the earth which the demon Hiranyaksha had drowned under the ocean. Legend says he dived into the water and raised the earth on his tusks; see Avatara. वराह

Varenyam saffron; that which is eulogized. वरेण्यम्

Varenyavat like one who is revered. वरेण्यवत्

Varna colour of a mantra; colour, hue; paint; complexion, beauty; class of men, tribe, caste (especially applied to the four principal castes); race, kind, species; groups of letters in the Sanskrit alphabet. वर्ण

Varna Ashrama /Varna Aashrama/ the four principal castes (varnas) in India, viz. priest (brahmana), warrior or ruling (kingly) class (kshatriya), merchant (vaishya) and servant (shudra); the laws of the caste and stage of life; see Trivarnaka; see Ashrama. वर्ण आश्रम

Varsha /Varshaa/ raining, rain, a shower of rain; sprinkling, effusion, throwing down, a shower of anything; seminal effusion. वर्षा

Varsha Ritu /Varshaa Ritu/ the rainy season or monsoon comprised of the two months Shravana and Bhadrapada; see Ritu; see Masa. वर्षा ऋतु

Varuna name of an aditya (usually associated with Mitra); in later mythology, the regent of the ocean and of the western quarter, represented with a noose in hand; the ocean; firmament. वरुण

Varunabija /Varuna-beeja/ literally 'the seed mantra of Varuna', the syllable vam, which is also the bija mantra of the water element and hence swadhisthana chakra. वरुणबीज

Vasana /Vaasana/ dwelling, abiding; perfuming, fumigating; infusing; any receptacle, a basket, box, vessel; knowledge. वासन

Vasana /Vaasanaa/ knowledge derived from memory; fancy, imagination, idea; false idea, ignorance; wish, desire, inclination; subtle desire; mental disposition; a tendency created in a person by performing an action or by enjoyment, which then induces the person to repeat the action or to seek a repetition of the enjoyment; subtle impressions acting like seeds in the mind capable of germinating or developing into action; the cause of birth and experience in general; the impression of action that remains unconsciously in the mind; desires that are the driving force behind every thought and action in life; passion. वासना

Vasanakshaya /Vaasanaa-kshaya/ annihilation of subtle desire. वासनाक्षय

Vasanarahita /Vaasanaa-rahita/ without subtle desires. वासनारहित

Vasanatyaga /Vaasanaa-tyaaga/ renunciation of subtle desires. वासनात्याग

Vasanta Ritu the spring; vernal season comprised of the two months Chaitra and Vaishakha; spring personified as a deity and regarded as a companion of the god of erotic love (Kamadeva); see Ritu; see Masa. वसन्त ऋतु

Vasati dwelling, residing, abiding; house, residence, habitation; receptacle, reservoir; the time when one halts or stays to rest. वसति

Vasham wish, desire, will; power, influence, control, mastery, authority; independence. वशम्

Vashikara /Vasheekaara/ control; highest state of lower vairagya, where there is non-attachment to pleasures of the past, present or to those merely heard of, according to Patanjali's *Yoga Sutras*. वशीकार

Vashitva one of the eight siddhis by which the yogi gains control

over everything; see Siddhi. वशित्व

Vasishtha /Vashishtha/ a celebrated sage or seer (brahmarishi), the family priest of the solar race of kings and the author of *Yoga Vasishtha* and several vedic hymns, particularly the seventh mandala of the *Rigveda*. He was a typical representative of brahmanic dignity and power and is one of the seven sages who are identified with the stars of the Great Bear. The rivalry between him and the royal sage (rajarshi) Vishvamitra forms the subject of many legends; see Nandini. वशिष्ठ

Vastra cloth, garment. वस्त्र

Vastra Dhauti a technique of dhauti, one of the six cleansing practices of hatha yoga (shatkarma) in which the stomach and oesophagus are cleansed with a long strip of cloth; see Shatkarma. वस्त्र धौति

Vasu /Vaasu/ the soul; the soul of the universe; supreme being; name of Vishnu; the name of Narayana; etymologically the term means a god who abides in all things and in whom all things abide. वासु

Vasudeva /Vaasudeva/ any descendant of Vasudeva, particularly Krishna. वासुदेव

Vasudeva one of the royal family of Mathura, husband of Dewaki

and father of Lord Krishna. वसुदेव

Vasu group of eight devatas (divine beings) residing on earth: Ap, Dhruva, Soma, Dhar/ Dharma, Anil, Anal, Pratyusha and Abhasa/Prabhasa. वसु

Vasuki /Vaasuki/ name of a celebrated serpent (Sheshanaga), the king of snakes and said to be a son of Kashyapa. वासुकि

Vata /Vaata/ wind, gas; one of the three doshas described in ayurveda; see Dosha. वात

Vata Nadi /Vaata Naadee/ nadi running along the back of the neck and head into the brain, controlling gas formation and elimination. वात नाडी

Vatasara Dhauti /Vaatasaara Dhauti/ a technique of dhauti, one of the six cleansing practices of hatha yoga (shatkarma), in which air is swallowed into the stomach and belched out; a system of cleansing with the help of air; see Shatkarma. वातसार धौति

Vatavaran /Vaataavarana/ atmosphere. वातावरण

Vatsalya Bhava /Vaatsalya Bhaava/ the attitude of parent and child relationship with the Lord. वात्सल्य भाव

Vayu /Vaayu/ god of wind; wind, air; life breath or vital air, used as another name for prana, of which there are five main types, viz. prana, apana, samana, udana and vyana; in Sankhya philosophy vayu is the second mahabhuta, having the special property of touch; see Pancha Prana; see Pancha Mahabhuta; see Devata. वायु

Vayu Bhakshana /Vaayu Bhakshana/ literally 'eating air', a means of subsisting without food, a hatha yoga practice. वायु भक्षण

Vayu Dharana, Vayavi Dharana /Vaayu Dhaaranaa, Vaayavee Dhaaranaa/ concentration on a particular vayu (vital air or prana); one of the five modes of concentration in the hatha yoga of *Gheranda Samhita*, involving meditation on awareness of the vayu element, which bestows the siddhi of levitation; this mudra is one of the most important because it removes 'death' and old age; see Mudra; see Pancha Mahabhuta. वायु धारणा, वायवी धारणा

Vayu Shuddhi /Vaayu Shuddhi/ purification of air. वायु शुद्धि

Vayu Tattwa /Vaayu Tattwa/ air element; see Pancha Mahabhuta. वायु तत्त्व

Veda knowledge; sacred knowledge, holy learning; the most ancient and authentic scripture of the sanatana dharma composed before 5000 BC, revealed to sages and seers and expressing knowledge of the whole universe. The Vedas are not written by any human (apaurusheya), having been directly revealed by the supreme being, Brahman. They are what is heard or revealed (shruti), as distinguished from that which is remembered (smriti). The Veda is therefore free from the imperfections to which human productions are subject. As the sounds forming the text of the Veda occur in the same order and are pronounced in the same manner, it is said to be eternal. It teaches who and what Brahman is, and how Brahman should be worshipped. Smritis, Itihasas and Puranas only amplify its teachings; see Rigveda; see Yajurveda; see Sama Veda; see Atharva Veda; see Samhita; see Aranyaka; see Brahmana; see Trayi; see Upanishad; see Upaveda. वेद

Vedanga /Veda-anga/ an auxiliary to the Vedas. The vedangas number six: 1. the science of proper articulation and pronunciation (shiksha), 2. rituals and ceremonies (kalpa), 3. grammar (vyakarana), 4. etymological explanation of different vedic words (nirukta), 5. the science of prosody (chandas), 6. astronomy (jyotisha). वेदाङ्ग

Vedanta /Vedaanta/ literally 'the last part of the Vedas'; the Upanishads; Vedanta teaches the ultimate aim and scope of the Vedas. It states that there is one eternal principle (Brahman); philosophy of realization of Brahman; the end of perceivable knowledge, where the mind experiences its own limits and goes beyond them, gaining realization and understanding through that exploration; the school of Hindu thought based primarily on the Upanishads. It upholds the doctrine of either pure non-dualism (Advaita Vedanta) or conditional non-dualism (Vishishta Advaita). Vedanta is also called Uttara Mimamsa; one of the six principal systems of Hindu philosophy (darshanas); see Shaddarshana; see Prasthanatraya; see Yogavasishtha; see Maya; see Upadhi; see Turiya; see Jnana Bhumika. वेदान्त

Veda Vyasa see Vyasa. वेद व्यास

Vedana feeling, sensation; knowledge; precept in Buddhist terminology. वेदन

Vedanashakti power of cognition or sensation. वेदनशक्ति

Vedi /Vedee/ altar; platform; place near the fire pit in a yajna (sacrifice). वेदी

Vibandhah constipation; obstruction. विबन्ध:

Vibhu glorious; gracious. विभु

Vibhushana /Vibhooshana/ ornament, decoration. विभूषण

Vibhuti /Vibhooti/ sacred ash; psychic glory and power; manifestation of divine glory and divine power; pervasion; the special forms in which the Lord exhibits himself; the one supreme form revealed in all objects of the senses; might, power, greatness; outer expression of the inner reality; supernatural powers acquired by a yogi in the course of the journey towards perfection through purification of the mind; prosperity, welfare. विभूति

Vibhuti Pada /Vibhooti Paada/ the third part of Patanjali's *Yoga Sutras*, dealing with dharana (concentration), dhyana, (meditation) and samadhi, their effects and the powers a yogi comes across in the quest; see Samyama; see Siddhi. विभूति पाद

Vibhutiyoga /Vibhooti-yoga/ 'yoga of divine glories', the 10th chapter of the *Bhagavad Gita*, in which Arjuna asks to hear of the Lord's essential nature and is told of his glories. विभूतियोग

Vibodha awakening, becoming conscious, being awake; perceiving, discovering; intelligence. विबोध

Vibudha a wise or learned person, sage; a god, deity; the moon. विबुध

Vichakshu blind, sightless; perplexed; sad. विचक्षु

Vichalana moving; deviation; unsteadiness; fickleness; conceit. विचलन

Vichara /Vichaara/ reflection; enquiry into the nature of the self, Brahman or truth; ever-present reflection on the why and wherefore of things; enquiry into the real meaning of the maha vakya (great saying) 'Tat Twam Asi'; contemplation on the real and the unreal. विचार

Vichara Samadhi /Vichaara Samaadhi/ a form of samadhi with seed (sabija samadhi), which can be experienced in two phases: savichara (with reflection) or nirvichara (without reflection); see Samprajnata Samadhi. विचार समाधि

Vichara Samyama /Vichaara Samyama/ thought control. विचार संयम

Vichara Shakti /Vichaara Shakti/ power of enquiry. विचार शक्ति

Vichchhina scattered; one of the four possible states of the kleshas according to Patanjali in the *Yoga Sutras*; see Klesha. विच्छिन्न

Vichitra diversified; various, varied; variegated, spotted, speckled; painted; beautiful, lovely; peculiar. विचित्र

Videha unembodied. विदेह

Videhamukti 'freedom from body', a state of realization or liberation (mukti), which is not usually experienced by anyone with sufficient karma to warrant their still inhabiting a body. In exceptional cases videhamukti is a state possible even with a body; see Mukti; see Jivanmukti. विदेहमुक्ति

Vidhana /Vidhaana/ arranging, disposing; performing, making, doing, executing; creating; employment, use, application; ruler, precept, sacred injunction; creation. विधान

Vidhi doing; performance, practice, an act or action; method, manner, way, means, mode; rule, commandment, any precept which enjoins something for the first time; sacred precept or rule, ordinance, injunction, law, a sacred command, religious commandment; an explanatory statement coupled with legends and illustrations; any religious act or ceremony, a rite; the 'do's' of living; see Nishedha. विधि

Vidura a great devotee of Krishna who was a minister to the Kaurava king, Dhritarashtra. विदुर

Vidya /Vidyaa/ from the root 'vid' or inner knowledge; knowledge, learning, lore, science; higher knowledge, right knowledge, spiritual knowledge; a spell, an incantation; the goddess Durga; see Avidya. विद्या

Vidyut lightning; a thunderbolt. विद्युत्

Vidyotana illuminating, irradiating; illustrating, elucidating; splendour. विद्योतन

Vidyut Loka a region of lightning. विद्युत् लोक

Vidyut Mandala visualization of lightning within the white light at ajna chakra (prakash mandala). विद्युत् मण्डल

Vighna an obstacle, impediment, hindrance; interruption; difficulty, trouble. विघ्न

Vigraha literally 'to grasp firmly'; identification of oneself with the grasped object; an image which when concentrated upon through mantras or through the devotion and adoration of the worshipper becomes the being itself. विग्रह

Vihara /Vihaara/ monastic centre; relaxed state of awareness. विहार

Vijatiyabheda /Vijaateeya-bheda/ the difference between two different species, e.g. the difference between a man and an animal; see Jatyantaraparinama; see Sajatiyabheda. विजातीयभेद

Vijaya victory, conquest; overcoming, vanquishing, defeating; booty; the exclamation of respectful acclaim 'hail!'; a chariot of the gods; name of Arjuna; an epithet of Yama. विजय

Vijnana /Vijnaana/ intuitive ability of mind; essential knowledge, higher understanding; knowledge, wisdom; the principle of pure intelligence; understanding; discrimination, discernment; secular knowledge of the self; worldly or profane knowledge derived from worldly experience; science. विज्ञान

Vijnana Bhairava /Vijnaana Bhairava/ state of consciousness where one achieves union with the cosmic consciousness; state where special and sacred knowledge begins to flow freely and spontaneously into the individual consciousness. विज्ञान भैरव

Vijnanamatrika /Vijnaana-maatrika/ an epithet of Buddha. विज्ञानमातृक

Vijnanamaya Kosha /Vijnaanamaya Kosha/ astral or psychic (higher mental) sheath or body (kosha); one of the sheaths of the soul, consisting of the principle of intellect or buddhi, the subtler level of our own existence with its vision, intuition, wisdom and power of understanding; the covering of the self which is made of knowledge; see Pancha Kosha; see Lingasharira. विज्ञानमय कोष

Vijnana Pada /Vijnaana Paada/ the theory of knowledge, the doctrine taught by Buddha. विज्ञान पाद

Vijnana Siddhi /Vijnaana Siddhi/ knowledge of the future. विज्ञान सिद्धि

Vijnana Spandita /Vijnaana Spandita/ movement of consciousness. विज्ञान स्पन्दित

Vijnanatma /Vijnaana-aatmaa/ cognitional or intellectual self; soul. विज्ञानात्मा

Vijnana Yoga /Vijnaana Yoga/ yoga to realize the real nature of maya; scientific enquiry. विज्ञान योग

Vijnata /Vijnaata/ known, understood, perceived; well-known, celebrated, famous. विज्ञात

Vikalpa fancy, unfounded belief, imagination; oscillation of the mind; doubt, uncertainty, indecision, hesitation; contrivance, art; option, alternative (in grammar); error, mistake, ignorance; one of the five modifications of mind (vrittis) described by the *Yoga Sutras* of Patanjali; see Vritti; see Savikalpa Samadhi; see Nirvikalpa Samadhi. विकल्प

Vikara /Vikaara/ modification or change, generally with reference to the modifications of the mind; impurities (in Sankhya philosophy) which are evolved from a previous source or from prakriti. विकार

Vikarshana Shakti power of repulsion. विकर्षण शक्ति

Vikasa /Vikaasa/ state of expansion, as in the evolution of the world. विकास

Vikranta /Vikraanta/ stepped or passed beyond; powerful, heroic, valiant; victorious, overpowering. विक्रान्त

Vikrita manipulated; changed, modified; ready or prone to create; made impure. विकृत

Vikriti change; products derived from prakriti, viz. the universal intellect (mahat or buddhi), the ego principle (ahamkara), mind (manas), the five organs of perception (jnanendriyas), the five organs of action (karmendriyas), the five subtle elements (tanmatras) and the five elements (mahabhutas); modification (of mind, purpose, form, etc.); unnatural circumstance; see Prakriti. विकृति

Vikriya /Vikriyaa/ change, modification, alteration; agitation, perturbation, excitement; passion; anger, wrath, displeasure. विक्रिया

Vikshepa dissipation; throwing away, throwing asunder, scattering about, casting; discharging; waving, moving about, shaking; the tossing of the mind which obstructs concentration. विक्षेप

Vikshepa Shakti the power of maya that projects the universe and causes movement and superimposition; see Avarana Shakti; see Maya. विक्षेप शक्ति

Vikshipta an oscillating state of mind between one-pointedness and dissipation, the third of the five states of mind. The mind is capable of a sattwic flow of concentration, but this is interrupted by distractions born of rajas. The stage when the mind is fit for yoga; see Manas. विक्षिप्त

Viloma inverted, inverse, contrary, opposite; produced in the reverse order; backward, against the hair, against the grain, against the natural order of things. विलोम

Viloma Pranayama /Viloma Praanaayaama/ technique to interrupt the natural flow of inhalation or exhalation: the inhalation or exhalation is not one continuous process, but is done gradually with several pauses. विलोम प्राणायाम

Vimala full of purity, i.e. absence of duality or subject/object. विमल

Vimarsha dissatisfaction, displeasure, impatience; term for the counterpart of prakasha in Kashmir Shaivism; the aspect of prakasha by which it knows itself; the inner nature (swabhava) of

Shiva, the self-consciousness of the supreme; another name for the shakti aspect leading to the world process; see Kashmir Shaivmata. विमर्श

Vinashi /Vinaashee/ perishable. विनाशी

Vinayaka /Vinaayaka/ literally 're-mover of obstacles', another name of Ganesha. विनायक

Viniyoga application. विनियोग

Vipaka /Vipaaka/ ripening, ripe-ness, development; consequence, fruit, result, the result of actions either in this or in former births; difficulty; cooking; dressing; di-gestion. विपाक

Viparita /Vipareeta/ inverted, re-versed, contrary, opposite; false, untrue; disagreeable; inauspi-cious. विपरीत

Viparita Bhavana /Vipareeta Bhaavanaa/ wrong conception, such as conceiving the body as the self; perverted understand-ing or imagination. विपरीत भावना

Viparitakarani Mudra /Vipareetakaranee Mudraa/ in-verted psychic attitude, which changes the sexual energy into ojas shakti; acting in a contrary manner; see Mudra. विपरीतकरणी मुद्रा

Viparitata /Vipareetataa/ dissimi-larity in objects; reversion. विपरीतता

Viparyaya contrariety, reverse, inversion; change; absence or non-existence; loss of conscious-ness; complete destruction; er-ror, mistake; distraction of mind; wrong knowledge, wrong cogni-tion; one of the five modifica-tions of mind (vrittis) described by Patanjali's *Yoga Sutras*; see

Vritti. विपर्यय

Vipralayah complete destruction or dissolution, annihilation. विप्रलय:

Viprayoga disunion, separation, dissociation, especially separation of lovers. विप्रयोग

Vira /Veera/ man; hero; son; male animal; courageous. वीर

Virabhava /Veera-bhaava/ warrior personality. वीरभाव

Virachara /Veeraachaara/ tantric course of discipline for the he-roic type of devotees. वीराचार

Virya /Veerya/ heroism, prowess, valour; vigour, strength, energy, firmness, courage; power, po-tency; efficacy (of medicines); se-men, virility; splendour, lustre; the result of mastering brahm-acharya according to Patanjali's *Yoga Sutras*. वीर्य

Viryavat /Veeryavat/ strong, vigorous; efficacious. वीर्यवत्

Viraja literally 'free from rajas (pas-sion)'; renunciation; a river which has to be crossed before the world of Brahma can be reached and which only eminent and saintly people devoid of passions and desires can cross; see Sthita-prajna. विरज

Virajahoma /Virajaa-homa/ offer-ing oblations to the fire; a ritual performed during the initiation of sannyasa. विरजाहोम

Virat /Viraata/ literally 'enormous'; the sum total of the entire mani-fest universe; macrocosm; the physical world that we perceive; the Lord in the form of the mani-fest universe. विराट

Viratpurusha /Viraat-purusha/ the deity presiding over the universe; the cosmic or universal aspect of the deity; see Vaishvanara. विराटपुरुष

Virochanah sun; moon; fire; name of the demon king of Patalam, son of Prahlada and father of Bali; see Trivikrama. विरोचन:

Visarga in the Devanagri script used for Sanskrit, it is half of the 'ha' sound and is represented by ':'; emission, pouring out, flow; to donate; creation; dismissal, release; liberation, final emancipation; end, dissolution; a name of Lord Shiva. विसर्ग

Visarjana final act of worship where a murti is immersed in water. विसर्जन

Visha /Visha/ poisonous element; see Amrit; see Vishuddhi Chakra. विष

Vishad /Vishaada/ unhappiness, dejection, despair. विषाद

Vishala /Vishaala/ spacious, large; eminent. विशाल

Vishama uneven; rough, rugged; irregular, unequal; difficult, hard to understand, mysterious; dangerous, fearful. विषम

Vishama Vritti uneven or vehement movement (of thoughts in the mind, or breathing). विषम वृत्ति

Vishama Vritti Pranayama /Vishama Vritti Praanaayaama/ so called because the same length of time for inhalation, retention and exhalation is not maintained. This leads to interruption of rhythm and the difference in ratio creates difficulty and danger for the student. विषम वृत्ति प्राणायाम

Vishaya object of sense. There are five gross types corresponding to representations of the tanmatras, viz. 1. sound (shabda), 2. touch (sparsha), 3. form (rupa), 4. taste (rasa) and 5. smell (gandha). These are projected or grasped by the five organs of sense, viz. ears, skin, eyes, tongue and nose respectively; a worldly object or concern, an affair, a transaction; the pleasures of worldly or sensual enjoyments; an object, a thing, matter; topic, subject; see Tanmatra. विषय

Vaishayika relating to an object of sense, sensual, carnal. वैषयिक

Vishayabhoga sensorial enjoyment. विषयभोग

Vishayachaitanya consciousness as object; the object known; the consciousness determined by the object cognized. विषयचैतन्य

Vishayakara /Vishaya-aakaara/ the form of the objects perceived; condition of the mind in perception. विषयाकार

Vishayasamsara /Vishaya-samsaara/ objective or sensorial world, the world of the senses; see Samsara; see Viraja. विषयसंसार

Vishayavritti thought of objects of the senses; see Vritti. विषयवृत्ति

Vishayavritti Pravaha /Vishaya-vritti Pravaaha/ the continuous thought current on worldly objects; the flow of objective thinking. विषयवृत्ति प्रवाह

Vishayin sensual, carnal; man of the world; worldly thinking; the god of love; a sensualist. विषयिन्

Vishesha speciality; peculiar; characteristic difference. विशेष

Visheshaguna special quality. विशेषगुण

Visheshajnana /Vishesha-jnaana/ special knowledge of the self as opposed to the knowledge of phenomenal science; special knowledge; detailed knowledge. विशेष ज्ञान

Visheshana attribute, property; an invariable and distinguishing attribute; specification; an adjective. विशेषण

Vishishta distinguished; distinct, particular, special, peculiar; characterized by, endowed with, possessed of, having; superior, best (of all), eminent, excellent. विशिष्ट

Vishishta Advaita Ramanuja's philosophy of qualified monism which opposes Adi Shankaracharya's philosophy of Advaita Vedanta or monism; an offshoot of Advaita Vedanta; the doctrine of conditioned non-dualism held by the Vedantic school, upholding that the one actually becomes many; a doctrine of Ramanuja which regards Brahman and prakriti as identical and real identities. विशिष्ट अद्वैत

Vishishtadvaitavada /Vishishta-advaitavaada/ the doctrine of Vishishta Advaita. विशिष्टाद्वैतवाद

Vishkambha obstruction; width; interlude. विष्कम्भ

Vishnu vedic deity; preserver of the universe; supreme consciousness; the second deity of the Hindu trinity, entrusted with the preservation of the world, a duty which obliges him to appear in several incarnations; deity often associated with water; name of Agni; see Avatara; see Vaishnava; see Anantapadmanabha. विष्णु

Vishnu Granthi psychic knot or block particularly related to manipura, anahata and vishuddhi chakras, symbolizing the bondage of personal and emotional attachment; see Granthi. विष्णु ग्रन्थि

Vishnu Maya /Vishnu Maayaa/ illusion wielded by the supreme being so that the unreal seems real; the illusory form of Lord Vishnu, usually conceived of as a female deity who makes the universe appear as real. विष्णु माया

Vishnu Purana /Vishnu Puraana/ name of one of the most celebrated of the 18 Puranas; see Puranam. विष्णु पुराण

Vishnu Taila a kind of medical oil. विष्णु तैल

Vishuddha purified, cleansed; sanctified. विशुद्ध

Vishuddhatman /Vishuddha-aatman/ cleansed, purified, spotless. विशुद्धात्मन्

Vishuddhi purification, sanctification; purity, complete purity; correctness, accuracy; rectification, removal of error. विशुद्धि

Vishuddhi Chakra literally 'centre of purification', the psychic/pranic centre located at the level of the throat pit or the thyroid gland and associated with the cervical and laryngeal plexus at the base of the throat. It is the psychic centre particularly connected with purification and communication; see Chakra; see Ham; see Shuddhi. विशुद्धि चक्र

Vishuddhi Marga a Buddhist treatise about yoga. विशुद्धि मार्ग

Vishva cosmos, universe, the whole world; name of the jiva in the waking state; every, everyone; eternal; all, whole, entire; universal; see Vaishvanara. विश्व

Vishvadeva /Vishvadevaah/ gods of the universe; class of divine beings operating as mediums in funeral ceremonies between the granter and the grantee of the oblations. विश्वदेवा:

Vishvadharini /Vishvadhaarinee/ the planet Earth. विश्वधारिणी

Vishvaguru guru of the universe. विश्वगुरु

Vishvakarma, Vishvakarman name of the architect and engineer of the gods; epithet of the sun. विश्वकर्म, विश्वकर्मन्

Vishvakarma Puja /Vishva-karmaa Poojaa/ ritual worship to bless tools and machines. विश्वकर्मा पूजा

Vishvarupa /Vishva-roopa/ cosmic form; omnipresent, existing everywhere; many-coloured; various; creating all forms. विश्वरूप

Vishvarupadarshanayoga /Vishva-roopa-darshana-yoga/ 'yoga of the vision of the cosmic form', the 11th chapter of the *Bhagavad Gita*, in which Arjuna is overwhelmed by darshan (seeing the reality) of the Lord and begs to see him again in the form of his friend, Krishna avatara. विश्वरूपदर्शनयोग

Vishvataijasaprajna /Vishva-taijasa-praajna/ a being (jiva) in the waking, dreaming and deep sleep states of consciousness respectively, in the individual aspect; see Aum. विश्वतैजसप्राज्ञ

Vishvayogi epithet of Brahma or Vishnu. विश्वयोगी

Vishvamitra /Vishvaamitra/ literally 'friend of the world' or 'friend of the universe'; name of a celebrated sage or patriarch of mankind. He was a member of the warrior caste (kshatriya), who by his piety and asceticism raised himself to priestly (brahmana) status. During his arduous penance, the heavenly nymph Menaka seduced him and conceived Shakuntala, the heroine of Kalidasa's famous drama; see Nandini. विश्वामित्र

Vishvasa /Vishvaasa/ trust, confidence, faith, reliance; a secret, confidential communication. विश्वास

Vishvasin /Vishvaasin/ trustworthy. विश्वासिन्

Vismriti loss of memory, forgetfulness. विस्मृति

Vistara /Vistaara/ expansion; seat,

stool, chair; layer, bed or handful of kusha grass; seat of the presiding priest (brahma) at a sacrifice. विस्तार

Vitala second centre of the instinctive or animal body below mooladhara chakra; see Patalam. वितल

Vitarka reasoning, argument, inference; fancy, thought; guess, conjecture. वितर्क

Vitarka Samadhi /Vitarka Samaadhi/ a type of samadhi with seed (sabija samadhi) which can be experienced in two phases: savitarka (with reasoning, thoughts, mental vision and awareness of objective events), and nirvitarka (without reasoning, etc.); see Samprajnata Samadhi. वितर्क समाधि

Vitarka Vritti mental waves existing as a part of the human personality and destructive to that personality. Such waves, which comprise a person's demonic nature, give rise to all illogical and destructive thinking, but are controlled by yama and niyama. वितर्क वृत्ति

Vitteshana /Vitteshanaa/ (Vittaeshanaa); the desire for money, material possessions or security; see Eshana Traya. वित्तेषणा

Vivaha /Vivaaha/ marriage ceremony. विवाह

Vivarta illusory appearance; doctrine of the non-dualistic school of Vedanta philosophy, explaining creation as only an illusory appearance or manifestation of the absolute Brahman; apparent variation or unreal change; superimposition. विवर्त

Vivarta Srishti an explanation of creation where the original reality remains what it is and yet apparently brings about the effect (according to the Advaita Vedanta school of thought). विवर्त सृष्टि

Viveka discrimination; right knowledge or understanding; sense of discrimination between the self and the not-self, between the eternal and the transitory, between consciousness and unconsciousness, between prakriti and purusha; judgement; consideration, discussion, investigation; distinction, difference; true knowledge; see Sadhana Chatushtaya. विवेक

Viveka Buddhi discriminative intellect. विवेक बुद्धि

Viveka Chudamani /Viveka Choodaamani/ a book by Adi Shankaracharya with instructions for spiritual progress and self-realization; see Adi Shankaracharya. विवेक चूडामणि

Viveka Jnanam /Viveka Jnaanam/ the faculty of discrimination. विवेक ज्ञानम्

Vrata vow; resolution to carry out a particular vow under strict rules, e.g. in regard to food, sleep, bathing and the like. व्रत

Vratya /Vraatya/ pertaining to vows; unpurified one. व्रात्य

Vrindavana /Vrindaavana/ name of a forest near Gokula where Lord

Krishna used to play as a child; also called Brindavana. वृन्दावन

Vritra name of a demon killed by Indra, considered the personification of darkness; cloud; darkness; enemy; sound; mountain; see Indra. वृत्र

Vritti a modification arising in consciousness; circular movement of consciousness; the five mental modifications described in Patanjali's *Yoga Sutras* are 1. right knowledge (pramana), 2. wrong knowledge (viparyaya), 3. dream or fancy (vikalpa), 4. sleep (nidra) and 5. memory (smriti); being, existence; abiding, remaining; attitude, being in a particular state or condition; action, movement, function; operation of mind; thought waves; the power or force of a word by which it expresses, indicates and suggests a meaning; patterns, circles; a whirlpool; see Chitta Vritti. वृत्ति

Vritti Jnana /Vritti Jnaana/ secular science; knowledge obtained through the mind; experience of the world. वृत्ति ज्ञान

Vritti Laya dissolution of the mental modification. वृत्ति लय

Vritti Sahita associated with thought. वृत्ति सहित

Vritti Vyapti /Vritti Vyaapti/ the mind assuming the form of objects perceived; pervasion of psyche. वृत्ति व्याप्ति

Vyabhichara /Vyabhichaara/ moving from one object to another searching for pleasure; fluctuating and flirting action. व्यभिचार

Vyadhi /Vyaadhi/ disease, sickness, illness; one of the unavoidable

sufferings of life. व्याधि

Vyaghra Kriya /Vyaaghra Kriyaa/ a form of dhauti, one of the six cleansing techniques of hatha yoga. The stomach is cleansed by voluntary vomiting using warm saline water, performed on a full stomach; see Shatkarma; see Vamana Dhauti. व्याघ्र क्रिया

Vyahriti /Vyaahriti/ the sacred triads, such as 'Bhuh, Bhuvah, Swah' etc.; utterance, statement, exclamation. व्याहृति

Vyakarana /Vyaakarana/ the science of grammar, one of the sciences auxiliary to the Vedas; see Vedanga. व्याकरण

Vyakta manifest, seen; manifest universe. व्यक्त

Vyakta Prakriti manifest nature; see Prakriti. व्यक्त प्रकृति

Vyakta Prana /Vyakta Praana/ manifest life force. व्यक्त प्राण

Vyaktitva personality. व्यक्तित्व

Vyakti Upasana /Vyakti Upaasanaa/ meditation on the manifested God. व्यक्ति उपासना

Vyana Vayu /Vyaana Vaayu/ one of the five energy fields (prana), the reserve of pranic energy pervading the whole body, it circulates the energy from food and breathing; see Vayu; see Pancha Prana. व्यान वायु

Vyasa /Vyaasa/ name of a great sage who wrote the *Brahma Sutra* and the *Mahabharata* (which includes the *Bhagavad Gita*), and codified the four Vedas etc.; also called Rishi Krishnadvaipayana, Rishi Veda Vyasa and Badarayana, and considered to be an avatara of Lord Vishnu; see Puranam. व्यास

Vyavahara /Vyavahaara/ behaviour; worldly activity, relative activity as opposed to absolute being; worldly relation; phenomenal world. व्यवहार

Vyavaharasapeksha /Vyavahaara-saapeksha/ with a view to the world of appearance or relativity. व्यवहारसापेक्ष

Vyavaharika /Vyaavahaarika/ practical, phenomenal, empirical, relative (as opposed to absolute or paramarthika). व्यावहारिक

Vyavaharikasatta /Vyaavahaarika-sattaa/ empirical reality. व्यावहारिकसत्ता

Vyavasaya /Vyavasaaya/ settled concentration and perseverance; application; cultivation. व्यवसाय

Vyavasayatmika /Vyavasaayaatmika/ one with resolution and determination. व्यवसायात्मिक

Vyoma space; sky or firmament, ether; another name for akasha; see Pancha Mahabhuta. व्योम

Vyoma Panchaka five intermediate spaces; five subtle spaces (within consciousness). व्योम पञ्चक

Vyoma Panchaka Dharana /Vyoma Panchaka Dhaaranaa/ techniques of concentration on the five subtle spaces within consciousness; see Guna Rahita Akasha; see Param Akasha; see Maha Akasha; see Tattwa Akasha; see Surya Akasha. व्योम पञ्चक धारणा

Y

Yachchati /Yachchhati/ to check, curb, restrain, control, subdue, stop, suppress; offer, give, bestow. यच्छति

Yajna, Yajana sacrifice or sacrificial rite; vedic sacrifice; offering oblations to the fire; yajna consists of three syllables, ya, ja and na, which refer to the three processes involved in every act performed and which must be balanced – production (ya), distribution (ja) and assimiliation (na); yajna has three components: ritual or worship (puja), satsanga and unconditional giving (dana); see see Adhiyajna; see Antaryajna; see Baliyajna; see Chandi Yajna; see Kalpa; see Pancha Mahayajna; see Purnahuti; Rajasooya Yajna; see Samhita; see Shrauta Yajna; see Smarta Yajna; see Yajurveda. यज्ञ, यजन

Yajamana /Yajamaana/ one who performs yajna; the master of a sacrifice; person who performs a regular sacrifice and pays for its expenses or who employs a priest or priests to sacrifice on their behalf; host, patron, rich person; head of a family. यजमान

Yajati to sacrifice, worship with sacrifices; to make an oblation to; to worship, adore, honour, revere. यजति

Yajna Diksha /Yajna Deeksha/ admission or initiation to a sacrificial rite; performance of a sacrifice. यज्ञ दीक्षा

Yajnopavita /Yajnopaveeta/ (Yajna-upaveeta); sacred thread worn by a new initiate into Gayatri mantra; see Upanayanam. यज्ञोपवीत

Yaju sacrifice, sacrificial rites; act of worship, any pious or devotional act; every householder, but particularly a brahmana, has to perform five such devotional acts every day); name of Agni; name of Vishnu; see Pancha Mahayajna. यजु

Yajurveda (Yajus-veda); literally 'knowledge of sacrifice'; Veda containing all the rituals, mantras, karmas and resulting fruits or effects of karmas (karmaphala) relating to sacrifice. The second of the four principal Vedas, it is a collection of sacred texts in prose relating to sacrifices; see Veda; see Brihadaranyaka; see Vajasaneyin; see Yajna. यजुर्वेद

Yajus sacrificial prayer or formula; text of the *Yajurveda*, the body of sacred mantras in prose uttered at sacrifices; name of the *Yajurveda*. यजुस्

Yakan, Yakrit the liver. यकन्, यकृत्

Yaksha name of a certain type of demi-god described as attendants of Kubera, the god of riches. They are employed in guarding his gardens and treasures; a kind of ghost or spirit; name of the palace of Indra; name of Kubera. यक्ष

Yakshna pulmonary disease. यक्ष्ण

Yam bija mantra of the air element and therefore of anahata chakra; see Mahabhuta. यं (यम्)

Yama /Yaama/ one-eighth part of a day, a period of three hours; a watch. याम

Yama self-restraints or rules of conduct which render the emotions tranquil; the first of eight limbs or means of attaining samadhi in the ashtanga yoga of Patanjali's *Yoga Sutras*. The five mentioned by Patanjali are: 1. non-violence (ahimsa), 2. truth (satya), 3. non-stealing (asteya), 4. continence (brahmacharya) and 5. non-covetousness (aparigraha); universal moral commandments or ethical disciplines transcending creed, country, age and time; restraint, forbearance, self control; restraining, controlling, any great moral or religious duty or observance; god of death; see Ashtanga Yoga; see Maha Vrata. यम

Yamala pair or couple; sexual union; intimate union; a name of the consort of Rudra; name of the tantric scriptures (tantra shastra) said to have been revealed by Devi (Shakti) to Shiva. यमल

Yamuna /Yamunaa/ tributary of the river Ganges (Ganga) and a sacred river associated with Lord Krishna; another name for ida nadi; see Triveni. यमुना

Yantra, Yantram geometric symbol designed for concentration or meditation in order to unleash the hidden potential within the consciousness; visual form of mantra used for concentration and meditation; astronomical diagram; an amulet; any prop or support; any machine; that which restrains or fastens, a stay, fetter, band, fastening, tie, thong; surgical instrument, especially a blunt instrument. यन्त्र, यन्त्रम्

Yashas fame, reputation, glory, renown. यशस्

Yashodhana one whose wealth or valued treasure is fame, rich in fame, very renowned. यशोधन

Yashoda /Yashodaa/ name of the wife of Nanda and foster mother of Lord Krishna. यशोदा

Yata held (forth); moderated; governed. यत

Yatamana /Yatamaana/ one who attempts to keep the mind free from sensual attractions; state of non-attachment; see Vairagya. यतमान

Yati Dravidian ascetics; earliest sannyasins; to control oneself. यति

Yatna effort, exertion, attempt, endeavour; diligence, perseverance; care, watchfulness, vigilance; pains, trouble, labour, difficulty, trial. यत्न

Yathartha /Yathaartha/ in accordance with reality; real; correct; suitable. यथार्थ

Yathartha Swarupa /Yathaartha Svaroopa/ essential nature. यथार्थ स्वरूप

Yatra /Yaatraa/ going on a pilgrimage; a journey; going, motion; march of an army, expedition, invasion; kind of dramatic entertainment, festival, fair, festive or solemn occasion; course of time; common practice; livelihood;. यात्रा

Yauvana youthfulness, prime or bloom of youth, puberty; a number of young persons, especially women. यौवन

Yoga the root is yuj, meaning 'to join, to yoke, to concentrate one's attention'; a method of practice leading to conscious union of the human being (atman) with the universal existence or Brahman; practices, philosophy and lifestyle to achieve peace, power and spiritual wisdom as well as perfect health, a sound mind and a balanced personality; methods and practices leading to a state of union between two opposite poles, i.e. individual and universal awareness; union, communion; one of the six main systems of philosophy (darshanas) of India; see Shaddarshana. योग

Yogabala the power of devotion or abstract meditation; any supernatural power; the power of God in the creation of the world personified as a deity; name of Durga. योगबल

Yogabhrashta one who has fallen from the high state of yoga. योगभ्रष्ट

Yogabhyasa /Yoga-abhyaasa/ practice of yoga. योगाभ्यास

Yogachara /Yoga-aachaara/ practice or observance of yoga; a follower of the Buddhist school which maintains the eternal existence of intelligence (vijnana) alone. योगाचार

Yogacharya /Yoga-aachaarya/ teacher of yoga philosophy and practice. योगाचार्य

Yogadanda a stick placed under the arm with one end in a U-shape, used for regulating the breath. योगदण्ड

Yoga Darshana yoga philosophy, yogic vision of reality; see Yoga Shastra. योग दर्शन

Yoga Dharana /Yoga Dhaaranaa/ perseverance or steady continuance in devotion. योग धारणा

Yoga Drishti yogic vision. योग दृष्टि

Yoga Maya /Yoga Maayaa/ the power of divine illusion. योग माया

Yoga Mitra Mandala yoga fellowship circle. योग मित्र मण्डल

Yoga Mudra /Yoga Mudraa/ attitude of psychic union, a gesture which helps to channel the flow of energy or prana in the body and awaken the dormant spiritual forces. It is especially useful in awakening kundalini shakti; see Mudra. योग मुद्रा

Yoganga /Yoga-anga/ limbs, parts or aspects of yoga. योगाङ्ग

Yoga Nidra /Yoga Nidraa/ 'psychic sleep'; practice where the body sleeps while the mind remains aware although its movements are quietened, inducing deep relaxation; a state of complete bodily relaxation and magnetization in which the mind rests in a suspended state; awake yet calm and free from all distractions; sleep of Vishnu during the end of a yuga. योग निद्रा

Yogapati literally 'lord of yoga'; an epithet of Vishnu. योगपति

Yogapatta literally the 'seat' or designation given to the aspirant when initiated. योगपट्ट

Yogarudha /Yoga-aaroodha/ one who is established in yoga; one engaged in profound and abstract meditation. योगारूढ

Yoga Samadhi /Yoga Samaadhi/ spontaneous state which results in self-knowledge or liberation; absence of identification with the body; being established in the supreme state of consciousness. योग समाधि

Yoga Shakti power of yoga, power of kundalini. योग शक्ति

Yoga Shastra /Yoga Shaastra/ the yoga system of philosophy and practice where the chief aim is to teach the means for the human soul to unite completely with the supreme spirit; elaborate rules for the proper practice of concentration of mind; deep and abstract meditation; contemplation of the absolute reality. योग शास्त्र

Yoga Sutra ancient authoritative text on raja yoga by sage Patanjali, it consists of 105 aphorisms on yoga and is divided into four parts dealing respectively with samadhi, the means by which yoga is attained, the powers the seeker comes across in the quest and the final state of liberation (kaivalya); see Raja Yoga; see Ashtanga Yoga; see Samadhi Pada; see Sadhana Pada; see Vibhooti Pada; see Kaivalya Pada. योग सूत्र

Yogavasishtha /Yogavaasishtha/ a monumental work on Vedanta in the form of a dialogue between Shri Rama and his guru Vasishtha. योगवाशिष्ठ

Yogavid, Yogavit literally 'knower of yoga'. This is equated to knowledge of Brahman in *Gherand Samhita*; see Brahmavit. योगविद्, योगवित्

Yogayukta one who is established in yoga or linked through yoga. योगयुक्त

Yogendra, Yogesha, Yogeshvara (Yoga-indra, Yoga-eesha, Yoga-eeshvara) yoga adept; master of yoga; one who has obtained superhuman faculties; Lord of yoga, a name of Lord Krishna; a name of Lord Shiva. योगेन्द्र, योगेश, योगेश्वर

Yogi, Yogin /Yogee, Yogin/ an adept in yoga; follower of the yoga system of philosophy and practice; one connected or endowed with yoga; one possessed of magical powers. योगी, योगिन्

Yogini /Yoginee/ female yogi. योगिनी

Yojanam joining, uniting, yoking; applying, fixing; preparation, arrangement; grammatical construction, construing the sense of a passage; concentration of the mind; abstraction; a measure of distance. योजनम्

Yogya fit, proper, suitable, appropriate, qualified; capable of, able

to; useful; fit for yoga. व्योग्य

Yogyata /Yogyataa/ fitness; qualification; ability, capability. योग्यता

Yoni womb, uterus, vulva, the female organ of generation; any place of birth; source, origin; generating cause; spring, fountain. योनि

Yoni Mudra /Yoni Mudraa/ attitude by which the primal energy inherent in the womb or source of creation is invoked by a hand mudra; see Shanmukhi Mudra; see Mudra. योनि मुद्रा

Yuddha war, battle, fight, engagement, contest, struggle; the opposition or conflict of planets. युद्ध
  Yudhishthira literally 'firm in battle'; name of the first Pandava who was the son of Kunti by the grace of Yama, also known as the king of dharma (Dharmaraja) or the epitome of dharma. युधिष्ठिर
  Yudhyate to fight, struggle, contend with; to wage a war. युध्यते

Yuga /Yugaa/ aeon, age; according to yogic understanding advanced civilizations have risen and fallen many times as the universe pulsates through phases of evolution and manifestion (a day of Brahma) and phases of involution or dissolution where there is no manifestation (a night of Brahma). There are four aeons of the world, viz. 1. Krita or Satya yuga, 2. Treta yuga, 3. Dwapara yuga, 4. Kali yuga. It is possible to know general qualities of a specific yuga. These four yugas combined make one mahayuga, while 1000 mahayugas make a day of Brahma and 1000 more make a night. युग

Yugam yoke, team, pair, couple; generation; a mundane period. युगम्

Yuj to join, yoke, unite; to concentrate one's attention. युज्

Yukti skill, cleverness; device; union of yoga. युक्ति
  Yukta one who has attained communion with the supreme spirit pervading the universe. युक्त